Communications
in Computer and Information Science　2542

Series Editors

Gang Li , *School of Information Technology, Deakin University, Burwood, VIC, Australia*
Joaquim Filipe , *Polytechnic Institute of Setúbal, Setúbal, Portugal*
Zhiwei Xu, *Chinese Academy of Sciences, Beijing, China*

Rationale

The CCIS series is devoted to the publication of proceedings of computer science conferences. Its aim is to efficiently disseminate original research results in informatics in printed and electronic form. While the focus is on publication of peer-reviewed full papers presenting mature work, inclusion of reviewed short papers reporting on work in progress is welcome, too. Besides globally relevant meetings with internationally representative program committees guaranteeing a strict peer-reviewing and paper selection process, conferences run by societies or of high regional or national relevance are also considered for publication.

Topics

The topical scope of CCIS spans the entire spectrum of informatics ranging from foundational topics in the theory of computing to information and communications science and technology and a broad variety of interdisciplinary application fields.

Information for Volume Editors and Authors

Publication in CCIS is free of charge. No royalties are paid, however, we offer registered conference participants temporary free access to the online version of the conference proceedings on SpringerLink (http://link.springer.com) by means of an http referrer from the conference website and/or a number of complimentary printed copies, as specified in the official acceptance email of the event.

CCIS proceedings can be published in time for distribution at conferences or as post-proceedings, and delivered in the form of printed books and/or electronically as USBs and/or e-content licenses for accessing proceedings at SpringerLink. Furthermore, CCIS proceedings are included in the CCIS electronic book series hosted in the SpringerLink digital library at http://link.springer.com/bookseries/7899. Conferences publishing in CCIS are allowed to use Online Conference Service (OCS) for managing the whole proceedings lifecycle (from submission and reviewing to preparing for publication) free of charge.

Publication process

The language of publication is exclusively English. Authors publishing in CCIS have to sign the Springer CCIS copyright transfer form, however, they are free to use their material published in CCIS for substantially changed, more elaborate subsequent publications elsewhere. For the preparation of the camera-ready papers/files, authors have to strictly adhere to the Springer CCIS Authors' Instructions and are strongly encouraged to use the CCIS LaTeX style files or templates.

Abstracting/Indexing

CCIS is abstracted/indexed in DBLP, Google Scholar, EI-Compendex, Mathematical Reviews, SCImago, Scopus. CCIS volumes are also submitted for the inclusion in ISI Proceedings.

How to start

To start the evaluation of your proposal for inclusion in the CCIS series, please send an e-mail to ccis@springer.com.

Isaac Wiafe · Areej Babiker · Jaap Ham ·
Kiemute Oyibo · Elena Vlahu-Gjorgievska
Editors

Persuasive Technology

PERSUASIVE 2025 Satellite Events

Limassol, Cyprus, May 5–7, 2025
Proceedings

 Springer

Editors
Isaac Wiafe 🄳
University of Ghana
Accra, Ghana

Areej Babiker 🄳
Hamad Bin Khalifa University
Doha, Qatar

Jaap Ham 🄳
Eindhoven University of Technology
Eindhoven, The Netherlands

Kiemute Oyibo 🄳
York University
North York, ON, Canada

Elena Vlahu-Gjorgievska 🄳
University of Wollongong
Wollongong, NSW, Australia

ISSN 1865-0929   ISSN 1865-0937 (electronic)
Communications in Computer and Information Science
ISBN 978-3-031-97176-1   ISBN 978-3-031-97177-8 (eBook)
https://doi.org/10.1007/978-3-031-97177-8

This Springer imprint is published by the registered company Springer Nature Switzerland AG
The registered company address is: Gewerbestrasse 11, 6330 Cham, Switzerland

If disposing of this product, please recycle the paper.

Preface

The concept of persuasive technology (PT) and the idea that technology influences human behavior and thinking have permeated and spread throughout our societies, with researchers and practitioners worldwide conducting innovative research aimed at promoting behavior change in various domains. The PT conference is the flagship platform for the distribution of such research outcomes and findings. After the 19th International Conference on Persuasive Technology (PERSUASIVE 2024) in Wollongong, Australia, the conference returned to Cyprus this year. Like the 14th International Conference on Persuasive Technology (PERSUASIVE 2019), the 20th edition of the conference (PERSUASIVE 2025) took place in Limassol, Cyprus on May 5–7, 2025.

This volume focuses on the proceedings of the satellite events of the conference. While the accepted full papers have been published in Lecture Notes in Computer Science by Springer, these proceedings cover the accepted papers in the Late Breaking Results track, Posters, Demonstrations and Artefacts, and Doctoral Consortium papers.

Six (6) papers were accepted and presented in the Late Breaking Results track. Other presentations included three (3) posters, two (2) demonstration and artifacts papers, and four (4) doctoral consortium papers. There were 19 submissions in total in these categories. All papers underwent a double-blind review process conducted in EasyChair, with each paper receiving at least 2 reviews by the program committee members. The final acceptance of the papers was decided after thorough consideration of the reviews.

We would like to thank the program committee members and organizers of the PERSUASIVE 2025 conference, track chairs, and all those who contributed towards the successful publication of the satellite proceedings. We would also like to thank EasyChair for enabling the submission and review process, and Springer for making these proceedings available to the public.

Isaac Wiafe
Areej Babiker
Jaap Ham
Kiemute Oyibo
Elena Vlahu-Gjorgievska

Organizing Committee

General Chairs

Evangelos Karapanos   Cyprus University of Technology, Cyprus
George A. Papadopoulos   University of Cyprus, Cyprus

Program Chairs

Raian Ali   Hamad Bin Khalifa University, Qatar
Khin Than Win   University of Wollongong, Australia

Workshops and Tutorial Chairs

Rhodora Abadia   University of South Australia, Australia
Kaoru Sumi   Future University of Hakodate, Japan
Wenzhen Xu   Hitotsubashi University, Japan

Doctoral Consortium Chairs

Jaap Ham   Eindhoven University of Technology, Netherlands
Sriram Iyengar   University of Arizona, USA
Roberto Legaspi   KDDI Research, Inc., Japan
Shahla Meedya   Australian Catholic University, Australia

Demo, Poster and Artefacts Track Chairs

Rúben Gouveia   Universidade de Lisboa, Portugal
Hanne Spelt   Philips, Netherlands

Late Breaking Results Chairs

Areej B. Babiker   Hamad Bin Khalifa University, Qatar
Jaap Ham   Eindhoven University of Technology, Netherlands

Isaac Wiafe   University of Ghana, Ghana

Proceedings Chairs

Kiemute Oyibo   York University, Canada
Elena Vlahu-Gjorgievska   University of Wollongong, Australia

Publicity Chair

Ifeoma Adaji   University of British Columbia, Canada

Program Committee Members

Rhodora Abadia   University of South Australia, Australia
Ifeoma Adaji   University of British Columbia, Canada
Syed Ishtiaque Ahmed   University of Toronto, Canada
Dena Al-Thani   Hamad Bin Khalifa University, Qatar
Aftab Alam   Hamad Bin Khalifa University, Qatar
Mona Alhasani   Dalhousie University, Canada
Raian Ali   Hamad Bin Khalifa University, Qatar
Alaa Ali S. Almohanna   University of Wollongong, Australia
Nawaf Almutairi   University of Hail, Saudi Arabia
Sameha Alshakhsi   Hamad Bin Khalifa University, Qatar
Alaa Alslaity   Dalhousie University, Canada
Saleh Altuwayrib   University of Hail, Saudi Arabia
Yutaka Arakawa   Kyushu University, Japan
Emily Arden-Close   Bournemouth University, UK
Areej Babiker   Hamad Bin Khalifa University, Qatar
Shlomo Berkovsky   Macquarie University, Australia
Barbara Caci   University of Palermo, Italy
Luca Chittaro   University of Udine, Italy
Nelly Condori Fernández   Universidad Santiago de Compostela, Spain
Peter De Vries   University of Twente, Netherlands
Huseyin Dogan   Bournemouth University, UK
Dimitra Dritsa   Eindhoven University of Technology, Netherlands
Alia El Bolock   American University of Cairo, Egypt
Alexander Felfernig   TU Graz, Austria
Mark Freeman   University of Sydney, Australia
Nanami Furue   Hitotsubashi University, Japan

Yann Glémarec	Inria Rennes, Université de Rennes, France
Ruben Gouveia	University of Lisbon, Portugal
Luke Haliburton	LMU Munich, Germany
Jaap Ham	Eindhoven University of Technology, Netherlands
Sanaul Haque	LUT University, Finland
Sriram Iyengar	University of Arizona, USA
Evangelos Karapanos	Cyprus University of Technology, Cyprus
Roberto Legaspi	KDDI Research Inc., Japan
Magnus Liebherr	University of Duisburg-Essen, Germany
Uwe Matzat	Eindhoven University of Technology, Netherlands
Alexander Meschtscherjakov	University of Salzburg, Austria
Christos Mettouris	University of Cyprus, Cyprus
Cees Midden	Eindhoven University of Technology, Netherlands
George Mikros	University of Athens, Greece
Niko Männikkö	Oulu University of Applied Sciences, Finland
Iolie Nicolaidou	Cyprus University of Technology, Cyprus
Harri Oinas-Kukkonen	University of Oulu, Finland
Rita Orji	Dalhousie University, Canada
Oladapo Oyebode	Dalhousie University, Canada
Kiemute Oyibo	York University, Canada
Constantina Panourgia	Bournemouth University, UK
George Angelos Papadopoulos	University of Cyprus, Cyprus
Daniel Playne	Massey University, New Zealand
Deborah Richards	Macquarie University, Australia
John Rooksby	Northumbria University, UK
Akihiro Sasaki	KDDI Research, Inc., Japan
Stefan Schiffer	iTec|RWTH Aachen University, Germany
Marta Serafini	University of Udine, Italy
Zubair Shah	Hamad Bin Khalifa University, Qatar
Hanne Spelt	Philips Research, Netherlands
Kaoru Sumi	Future University Hakodate, Japan
Franci Suni-Lopez	Universidad de Lima, Peru
Tuğba Taşkaya Temizel	Middle East Technical University, Turkey
Christos Themistocleous	Cyprus University of Technology, Cyprus
Evangelia Vanezi	University of Cyprus, Cyprus
Julita Vassileva	University of Saskatchewan, Canada
Elena Vlahu-Gjorgievska	University of Wollongong, Australia
Maria Voutsa	Cyprus University of Technology, Cyprus
Isaac Wiafe	University of Ghana, Ghana
Khin Than Win	University of Wollongong, Australia
Burkhard Wuensche	University of Auckland, New Zealand
Wenzhen Xu	Hitotsubashi University, Japan

Ala Yankouskaya   Bournemouth University, UK
Affan Yasin   Tsinghua University, China
Donghuo Zeng   KDDI Research, Japan

Sponsoring Organizations

Contents

Demonstrations and Artefacts

Doctoral Consortium Papers

Late Breaking Results

Immersive Virtual Reality to Support Hand Exercises for Stroke Rehabilitation: A Design Science Research Approach

Md. Sanaul Haque[1]([✉]), Isak Zhang[1], Bruce Ferwerda[2], Jari Porras[1],
S. M. Musfequr Rahman[3], A. M. Meshkatur Rahman[1], Sheikh Rupu Rayhan[4],
Akib Ahmed[1], and Micael Sousa[5]

[1] LUT University, Lappeenranta, Finland
{sanaul.haque,isak.zhang,jari.porras}@lut.fi
[2] Jönköping University, Jönköping, Sweden
bruce.ferwerda@ju.se
[3] Tampere University, Tampere, Finland
smmusfequr.rahman@tuni.fi
[4] Nottingham Trent University, Nottingham, UK
[5] Lusófona University, Lisbon, Portugal

Abstract. A variety of therapies are used in stroke rehabilitation to help patients regain abilities that they may have lost following a stroke. Virtual hand exercises present a low-cost approach to enabling stroke patients to embark on immersive journeys to do hand movement via immersive virtual reality (IVR). With technological advancements, ongoing evaluation and integration of the latest IVR innovations will be crucial to maximizing their potential in enhancing the quality of life for individuals with mobility disorders and stroke survivors. A total of 68 participants took part in our study, followed by a design thinking process. Using Unity software, we developed a VR gamified system that allows users to enter a museum and feel, enjoy, track, and explore a VR-based painting (Mona Lisa Frame and The Art Basel Banana) as game elements. These lead to moving or holding the VR-based painting as a hand exercise. We tested the VR gamified system on relevant stakeholders (patients and their relatives and physiotherapists), where they filled out a qualitative survey and a quantitative SUS (System Usability Scale) questionnaire. The result of the study showed that the usability effect of the game elements was positive in the context of user satisfaction in supporting virtual hand exercises.

Keywords: IVR · Stroke Rehabilitation · Game Elements · DSR

1 Introduction

Virtual Reality (VR) now provides citizens with an engaging and valuable educational experience [1]. VR has recently overcome technical challenges that previously limited its widespread use and recognition, as noted by [2, 3]. Virtual Reality (VR) technology has

I. Wiafe et al. (Eds.): PERSUASIVE 2025, CCIS 2542, pp. 3–17, 2026.
https://doi.org/10.1007/978-3-031-97177-8_1

emerged as a promising tool for rehabilitating individuals with mobility disorders and those recovering from strokes. The immersive nature of VR environments offers a unique platform for developing rehabilitation protocols that simulate real-life scenarios, which enhances patient engagement and motivation [4]. VR simulations can replicate various terrains and environments, enabling patients to practice and improve their walking and balance skills in a controlled yet realistic setting [4]. Furthermore, personalized VR rehabilitation can be utilized to tailor exercises that address specific impairments and promote neuroplasticity in stroke patients. VR represents a promising approach for integration into medical solutions for stroke patients.

VR's immersive nature encourages educators to transition from traditional online learning environments to innovative VR settings [5]. Meanwhile, software developers embrace gamification as a promising strategy to enhance engagement and improve user experience [6]. Game elements are the fundamental building blocks of gamification techniques, a concept thoroughly examined in scholarly works such as those by [7] and the insights provided by [8]. The widespread adoption of affordable VR games and gamified systems among citizens is experiencing significant growth. These VR gamified systems simplify educational modules or subjects, making them more accessible and engaging for the public. As this trend continues to expand, it is anticipated that in the future, a variety of VR games and gamified systems will be readily available to users, tailored to their specific areas of interest, such as promoting virtual hand exercises. Although, in theory, VR could replace physical travel, people still value the authentic physical experience of engaging in activities themselves (first person), with all their senses gathering more information [9, 10]. This individual physical experience is reflected in a renewed interest in analog activities and a reluctance towards digital technologies [11]. It can also be viewed as part of the post-digital movement, where interacting with things in a non-digital way gains new significance [12].

There are rehabilitation therapies for post-stroke balance impairment, but their effectiveness remains unclear [13]. VR and conventional physiotherapy have significantly improved stroke patients' balance, gait, trunk control, and overall functional mobility. To enhance at-home rehabilitation, future research should explore solutions that are more affordable, safe, and easily accessible [4]. Therefore, incorporating VR and game elements can offer a cost-effective and socially engaging way for stroke patients to participate in physical activities, such as hand exercises at home. However, it is essential to maintain a balanced perspective on using VR technology in rehabilitation. Establishing standardized protocols, validating long-term effectiveness, and considering individual responses to VR interventions are crucial [14]. Given the rapid technological advancements, ongoing evaluation and integration of the latest VR innovations will be vital for maximizing their potential to improve the quality of life for individuals with mobility disorders and stroke survivors. Thus, this study aims to identify the following research questions:

RQ1) How do we design and develop an Immersive VR (IVR) gamified system to support stroke patients with hand exercises?
RQ2) What is the usability of the Immersive VR (IVR) gamified system to support stroke patients with hand exercises?

To answer the research question, we designed and developed an IVR gamified system enabling users to enter a virtual museum, explore paintings as a game element, and move their body parts virtually for hand exercise. This system was crafted using an iterative design thinking process, where users tested the prototype, followed by a qualitative survey and a SUS 5-Likert scale quantitative questionnaire. Sixty-eight participants (9 in the empathy and 59 in the test stage) participated in our study.

2 Background

2.1 Immersive Virtual Reality (IVR) and Stroke Rehabilitation

The concept of immersive Virtual Reality (IVR) is understood as lifelike simulations presented through head-mounted displays (HMDs), allowing users to engage in purposeful actions within a virtual environment [15, 16]. Immersive VR is distinctive because of its ability to evoke "presence," the feeling of being in the simulated environment, and "agency," the ability to interact independently [17]. Moreover, immersive VR promotes learning through experiential engagement, involving physical movements to control and interact with the virtual space [18]. Meta-analyses indicate that educational content delivered via Immersive VR outperforms traditional methods in terms of effectiveness [19, 20]. The efficacy of immersive VR is evident across various academic levels, including primary [21], secondary, and tertiary education [22]. Immersive VR is especially beneficial for facilitating the acquisition of conceptual and procedural knowledge [23, 24], enhancing knowledge transfer to real-world situations [25], and providing experiences that are otherwise unattainable, dangerous, or economically impractical [26, 27]. A unique advantage of immersive VR is its ability to allow users to manipulate three-dimensional objects in ways that other media cannot [22], thus aiding in the understanding of complex concepts [28] and helping to develop initial mental models [29] and utilizing immersive VR as a promising tool for educating individuals about eco-friendly practices [27, 30], such as cost-effective virtual hand exercises for stroke rehabilitation. VR-based rehabilitation programs effectively improve various outcomes for patients with mobility disorders and those recovering from strokes. Researchers have found that telerehabilitation is an effective alternative for stroke patients [31], while virtual reality training enhances upper limb function and balance in this population [32]. IVR-based training motivates patients and accelerates their recovery [33]. IVR serves as a versatile, accessible, and affordable tool that can complement traditional rehabilitation therapies or function as a standalone method. Overall, IVR is a promising new resource for rehabilitating mobility disorder and stroke patients. It is safe, effective, and engaging and can be tailored to meet patient's rehabilitation needs.

2.2 Game Elements in IVR

Researchers [34] have contributed to developing a taxonomy encompassing common game elements, extending their applicability beyond traditional gaming and into gamification. This scholarly pursuit has resulted in the identification of 15 pivotal components, including avatars, points, badges, leaderboards, and teams, meticulously cataloged by

[8]. Among this comprehensive array, specific game elements have been seamlessly integrated into games or gamified systems. The empirical assessment of the impact of selected game elements, including but not limited to points, badges, progress bars, and graphs, has been executed through a dual-method approach, combining both quantitative and qualitative analyses, as elucidated by [35]. Within the scope of this investigation, our scholarly undertaking is focused on a detailed examination of the consequences associated with a particular game element. For example, IVR gaming could be dedicated to stroke patients to give them the experience of virtually traveling to a museum, allowing them to feel connected, share virtual experiences, and engage in physical activities such as hand exercises. A game element could be utilized to monitor the virtual hand exercises of stroke patients, featuring a virtual Mona Lisa painting on the wall alongside The Art Basel Banana. On the other hand, avatars serve as the pictographic symbols of art in a gamified setting [8]. Users' identification—such as stroke patients who wish to travel using body movement virtually—is the primary recognized characteristic of an avatar, which can be distinguished from other avatars controlled by either computer machines or humans [36]. Avatars enable users to create an alternative identity as part of a community through cooperative games [37]. For example, an IVR gamified system is designed for stroke patients to virtually travel through a museum, allowing them to explore and interact with objects, such as artwork and paintings (for instance, a virtual Mona Lisa and The Art Basel Banana). This game element was selected because it represents experiencing an avatar-focused wall painting (a virtual Mona Lisa portrait painting and the Art Basel Banana). In this way, users in the VR environment cannot know what will happen when they grab or move the virtual Mona Lisa portrait painting. VR is a promising approach to improve outcomes in stroke rehabilitation [38]. Facilitating a game element in the VR game may increase users' engagement to explore body physical activities in the virtual environment and experience virtual objects such as grabbing and moving wall paint (a virtual Mona Lisa portrait painting and The Art Basel Banana) with their hands periodically in the virtual environment.

3 Methodology

We applied the Design Science Research (DSR) method from June 2023 to May 2024 to conduct the study. Design science research is an approach to qualitative research in which the target area of focus is the design process. It generates information about the method used to develop a system and the design or the artifact itself [39]. Therefore, we adopted the Peffers' DSR method [40] due to its simple system development steps. Following the Peffers', the DSR research process consists of six phases: 1. Problem identification and motivation; 2. Objectives of the solution; 3. Design and development, 4. Demonstration; 5. Evaluation; and 6. Communication (Fig. 1).

3.1 Problem Identification and Motivation

There are rehabilitation therapies for poststroke balance impairment, and the effectiveness of these rehabilitation therapies is still unclear [13]. Using VR alongside a conventional physiotherapy technique, stroke patients' balance, gait, trunk control, and

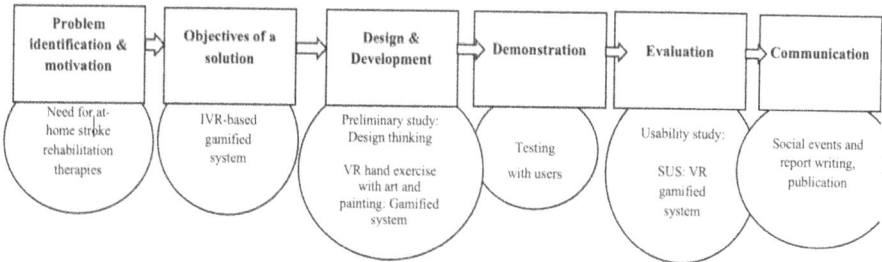

Fig. 1. Design Science Research (DSR) through the lens of Peffers' model.

functional level of gait were significantly improved. To facilitate and enhance at-home rehabilitation, future research may look at more affordable, secure, and easily accessible gadgets [4]. Using VR and game elements can be an inexpensive and socially engaging way to do physical activities, such as hand exercises for stroke patients at home.

3.2 Objectives of a Solution

The objectives of an IVR-gamified system are to support stroke rehabilitation for patients by helping them develop their body movements, specifically through hand exercises. This can be achieved by conducting hand exercises in a virtual environment that incorporates enjoyable experiences through gamification techniques.

3.3 Design and Development

We have employed the Design Thinking iterative process as a guiding framework for designing and developing our immersive VR gamified system. Design Thinking represents a structured and iterative approach to application design, characterized by active user involvement throughout its various stages. The Design Thinking methodology consists of five distinct phases: empathize, define, ideate, prototype, and test [41]. This methodology has created games by engaging users in all design and development phases [32, 41]. Sixty-eight participants (nine in the empathy stage and fifty-nine in the test stage) participated in our study. We have utilized the design thinking process to create and construct games that cost-effectively support stroke patients with virtual hand exercises. From a game design perspective, analog game prototypes can implement design thinking approaches by building manual game systems [42] or by playtesting the ideas for further development through face-to-face play [43].

3.4 Demonstration

An initial pilot investigation was conducted on the prototype. Users tested the program, and their writing skills were assessed. Semi-structured individual interviews highlighted the effectiveness of a low-cost virtual reality intervention. The results indicated that the gamified intervention could enhance art manipulation and digital painting. They later expressed interest in using virtual murals, such as the Mona Lisa and The Art Basel Banana—elements of games. The feedback from the pilot and interviews was utilized to refine the prototype further.

3.5 Evaluation

The SUS (System Usability Scale) [44] was implemented using a set of standardized questions that evaluate the usability of software services.

3.6 Communication

The study results were successfully reported at local events, such as the gaming showcase in Lahti and Lappeenranta campus, LUT University, Finland, in October 2024, which was attended by high school students and their parents.

4 Iterative Prototyping and Evaluation in the Design Process

4.1 Empathize

We started with the empathizing step, focusing on observing and understanding the users and their perspectives on the VR gamified system. Our goal was to monitor the behavior of relevant stakeholders in the Lappeenranta region by engaging them through interviews and closely observing and listening to them. In-person empathizing sessions were conducted with nine local stakeholders (five males and four females, aged 21 to 37) residing in Sweden and Finland from May 15 to 25, 2023. The number of participants in the empathy study was sufficient, resulting in a balanced gender ratio of 5:4. They were asked to describe their ability to perform hand exercises and suggest what technological tools could assist them in doing hand exercises virtually if they could not visit physical locations. Eight participants (89%) expressed a desire for more opportunities for hand exercises as part of their physical activities. The reasons cited included the need for enjoyable activities among stroke patients, as typical rehabilitation exercises tend to be monotonous, and they preferred to exercise from home. All nine participants (100%) strongly recommended an affordable, personalized VR gamified system to explore the museum, engage with art and paintings, and learn more, such as virtually manipulating painting objects with their hands. Consequently, they showed interest in incorporating game elements like virtual wall paintings. They believed this system could significantly enhance stroke rehabilitation through hand exercises.

4.2 Define

The results of the interviews from the empathy phase have led us to the following point-of-view (POV): *"Stroke patients experience a lack of opportunities to engage in activities using modern technologies due to low social engagement, community-based platforms, and physical limitations. An IVR gamified system that incorporates game elements can assist them in learning and experiencing different artifacts, interacting with the paintings, and performing hand exercises by placing the VR object."*

4.3 Ideate

Based on the point-of-view from the Define step, we aimed to design the Immersive VR gamified system prototype. We observed users' responses and how they responded using a VR-gamified system. The prototype of the VR game was developed by adding game elements (Mona Lisa wall paint and The Art Basel Banana) (Fig. 2).

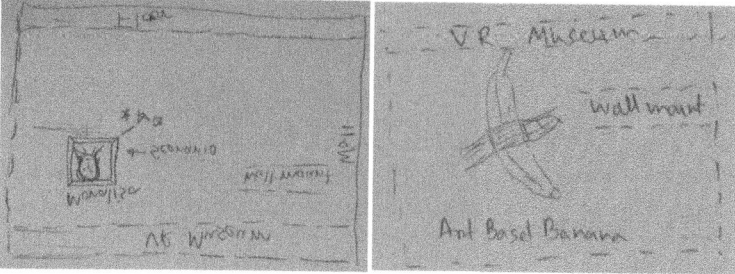

Fig. 2. Ideation on utilizing a game element (Mona Lisa wall paint and the Art Basel Banana).

4.4 Prototype

The aim of constructing the prototype was to validate whether users can run a VR-gamified system and how they react to it. Firstly, we developed a low-fidelity prototype (see Fig. 3). An example of an immersive VR gamified prototype is shown in Fig. 4. Central to the experimental paradigm is the binding of the tracker to the physical framework. Upon initiating the virtual reality program, participants can tangibly perceive their interactions within the virtual environment. This heightened tactile engagement amplifies the experience, encouraging further interactive behaviors. Notably, the synchronization of real-world manual actions with their virtual counterparts arises from the intrinsic action capture functionality of the Leap Motion system.

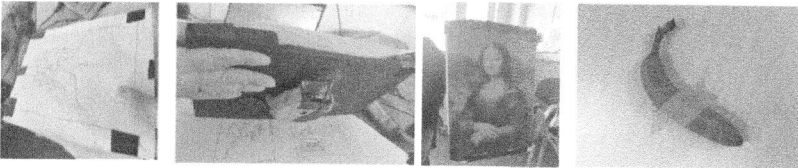

Fig. 3. Low-fidelity (paper) prototype of the game element (virtual Mona Lisa wall painting) and a mid-fidelity prototype (Banana on the wall) of the game element (The Art Basel Banana).

4.5 Test

In this study for the testing event, participants completed a set of qualitative open-ended questions (developed by two researchers) and a SUS quantitative questionnaire [44]. The System Usability Scale (SUS) measures individuals' subjective perceptions regarding the usability of a system and is notable for its ease of use and simplicity [45–47]. We selected SUS because it effectively evaluates user satisfaction, is relatively inexpensive, has a fast-processing time, and can be leveraged to improve system performance. The study occurred between October 2023 and March 2024.

Participants. An invitation email with a Google link to complete a survey questionnaire was sent out mainly to the students. We instructed on how the users play the VR gamified system to experience virtual hand exercises via traveling in the museum environment, such as grabbing famous paintings, like the Mona Lisa and The Art Basel Banana, in their hands and virtually feeling them as if they were not applicable in the physical world. However, forty-four (44; 18 female, 23 male, two prefer not to say, and 1 Genderflux) participants agreed to take the test and filled out the questionnaire. Another fifteen (15 females and seven males) participants filled out the SUS questionnaire. All those participants were residing in Finland. They were originally from Finland, the UK, Bangladesh, the USA, Canada, Denmark, Italy, Serbia, and Slovenia by birth. Ethical clearance protocol was followed according to the Finnish National Board on Research Integrity (TENK), and oral consent was obtained from participants.

Materials. We have chosen HTC Vive equipment. The HTC Vive equipment encompasses head-mounted display units, base stations, and tracking devices. The hardware configuration is centered around a sophisticated computing system, incorporating high-performance components such as the Intel Core i9-9900K CPU, accompanied by 32 GB of RAM and an Nvidia GeForce GTX 1080 Ti 11 GB GPU. The development ecosystem is seamlessly orchestrated on the software front by integrating SteamVR, a software client, and utilizing the versatile 3D modeling tool Blender. Real-time 3D development is founded in Unity.

Procedure. At first, participants were provided with a Google link in their email and WhatsApp, and they were instructed to follow the procedure to play the IVR gamified system. Participants were given a lecture about stroke patients' situation. They were asked to use the VR-gamified system. They visualized and experienced the virtual hand exercise in a VR museum environment. They can enter the VR environment (Fig. 6). While wearing the VR headset, they can see their virtual hand, which can move and grab objects like virtual wall paint hanging onto the museum wall. While holding it, they think about making decisions that affect the outcome, e.g., grabbing and shifting to different places, what they will do when seeing the virtual Mona Lisa painting and the Art Basel Banana from nearby, or what to do next with the art painting (Fig. 4).

Fig. 4. The user is trying to grab the virtual Mona Lisa painting from the wall mount (top left), holding it (middle), and thinking of what to do with it (top right).

Measures. After the testing phase, a follow-up questionnaire was sent to all the participants to know their feelings about the game element and other features they would like to see, the ease of using the VR environment to keep their virtual hand exercise running, etc. Participants also completed another SUS questionnaire [45] with a 5-Likert scale and an adjective rating scale [46] to determine the game elements' usability features.

Data Analysis. Sample sizes of at least 12–14 people are sufficient to provide realistically reliable SUS analysis findings [48]. On the contrary, 44 participants in this research completed the SUS questionnaire, and their responses were evaluated using an Excel data sheet. The formula for calculating the *SUS score is (X0 + Y0) x 2.5. Here, X0 = X (sum of odd number points)—5, and Y0 = 25–Y (sum of even number points).*

Interview with Stakeholders. Following the guidelines in [49], a 20-min semi-structured interview was conducted with each participant (15), including relevant stakeholders such as relatives of patients, patients, and physiotherapists. The participants were asked about their feelings and thoughts regarding using the IVR gamified system prototype. The paper's first author performed content analysis using Microsoft Excel to examine the responses. Three stages of analysis were executed: (1) familiarity was assessed by reading the data repeatedly; (2) words or phrases aligning with the main themes were highlighted and categorized; and (3) the frequency and context of sentences related to the themes were noted.

5   Results

5.1   How Do We Design and Develop an Immersive VR (IVR) Gamified System to Support Stroke Patients with Hand Exercises? (RQ 1)

The design thinking technique resulted in an immersive IVR gamified system by incorporating art-based game elements such as the Mona Lisa art-based painting and the Art Basel Banana. Working with the virtual game elements is essential to reaching the research goal. Further development is carried out by testing the users. Using an iterative design and incorporating both participants' qualitative feedback and needs via observational study was beneficial in developing the system.

5.2   What is the Usability of the Immersive VR (IVR) Gamified System to Support Stroke Patients with Hand Exercises? (RQ 2)

System Usability Scale (SUS). The measured SUS score of the IVR gaming environment surpassed 85. This score was higher than the SUS score range of 80.3 and received a scoring grade of "A". According to SUS, ratings of more than 80.3 suggest a well-designed system, with minor adjustments not required. This is an excellent technique for developing an IVR gamified system that incorporates intrinsic motivation in users to improve their hand exercise, hence supporting RQ2.

Open Questions. Table 1 describes the open questions and the acquired result.

Table 1. Qualitative results based on users' interview data.

Question	Description
Q1) How does this game element (Moving Virtual Mona Lisa Painting, The Art Basel Banana) make you feel?	Of 44 participants, most (n = 35; 78%) reported that the VR gamified prototype is motivating and user-friendly, answering the first question. Participants stated as "Playing with a VR gamified system where I can move a virtual Mona Lisa painting can excite and excite me. It's like being inside the art, which is interesting. I can learn about it and uniquely enjoy its beauty."; "It makes me happier. I feel like it improves my resilience and is a mode of expressing emotions for me."; "I feel like it's a great game to play…."
Q2) Is there anything that you want to change about this VR gamified system or anything you would like to add to this VR gamified system?	Most participants reported some changes or additions within the system but did not explicitly highlight anything subversive to the game element. Participants reported for the "Improvement of graphics,"; "Touch sensitivity…"'; "The movements could have been smoother,"; "Take a virtual picture." Another insightful comment from a participant: "Since this is only a demo of the actual game, I don't see the actual concept or the end goal. Displacing an object only to return it to its original position wastes time. The whole experience would have been better if there was an endpoint or motivation behind the task. More details in the game would make a nice addition, e.g., the painting holder."
Q3) How easy or difficult is this process?	Most participants found the Immersive VR gamified system easy to play. Although, n = 7 participants (16%) did not find it user-friendly or did not make any comments about it. Participants stated, "The ease or difficulty of enhancing the game depends on the specific features…" which is the game element. Regarding the fourth and final question, most participants (n = 31; 70.5%) like to use and play with this type of game element within the VR gamified system
Q4) Would you like to play this VR gamified system to keep your virtual hand exercise running?	Most participants showed interest in playing the system twice a week, from 20 min to one hour, while only a few reported playing in natural fields. Some highlighted the design as this is not a game but something else, while others considered it as a game, such as, "With a game like this, it would be best if it had the option to pause and save the game at any point. I would feel better if the tasks were easier. I would play this game for 10–20 min in one go."

6   Discussion

The main findings of the study are described in Table 2.

6.1   Design Process

Engaging stakeholders, such as stroke patients and their relatives, during the design process and highlighting their needs and preferences can promote the sustainable development of software systems [50]. In our study, local citizens whose relatives are stroke patients co-designed the IVR gamified system. The users were evaluated separately throughout the iterative design phase, and they expressed a desire to frequently utilize

Table 2. Main Findings.

Theory applied	Findings
Gamification	Positive impact in doing virtual hand exercise
IVR	IVR gaming was satisfactory in motivating the users to do virtual hand exercise

the system for enjoyable activities and hand exercises in the IVR environment. The IVR gamified system benefited the participants, who emphasized the game elements, motivating them to engage in hand exercises by interacting with the virtual wall. This influence is evident throughout these activities, as gamification impacts people's engagement behaviors and motivational affordances [51]. We designed the IVR gamified system based on local citizens' viewpoints, thoughts, and feedback. However, using the IVR gamified system may yield different effects by encouraging stroke patients to perform hand movements that align with rehabilitation requirements. During the pre-evaluation study of the IVR gamified system, users reported that the IVR environment facilitated hand movement by allowing them to grab the virtual painting of the Mona Lisa and the Art Basel Banana, providing them with a unique experience of exploring art that they could not have in a real-life context. The IVR gamified system was customized based on their needs and recommendations, followed by a usability study.

6.2 Theoretical Implication

The theoretical outcome of this study marks a significant advancement in integrating stroke patients into an iterative design process for developing applications that employ gamification. For instance, human-computer interaction (HCI) users exhibit distinct cognitive approaches, as illustrated by participatory design research [52]. The study applied the DSR and successfully implemented every step to create a novel gamified system. By incorporating a game-design element, such as hand exercises, and deepening our understanding of how to integrate the portrait of the Mona Lisa into the design and development of an IVR gamified system, this work enriches the field of HCI. This study explores how consumers interact with VR-based art and paintings (the Mona Lisa Frame and the Art Basel Banana) as a gaming feature absent when visiting a museum.

6.3 Practical Implication

Our study utilized the free version of Unity software, allowing us to develop the VR gaming environment at no extra cost. The VR environment is tailored for patients facing challenges traveling to the clinic and thirty other centers. This VR setup can be installed on their laptops, enabling them to perform hand exercises at home. This approach offers a sustainable method for creating an IVR gamified system. It lacks any specific goals or finishing points. We will enhance the IVR environment by introducing additional features, such as more opportunities for grabbing and holding art and paintings, assigning tasks while carrying the art, and implementing negative points for any paintings that fall due to hand imbalances. Further enhancements can be made to the IVR gamified system.

Discussing gamification techniques, such as awarding points and badges, may negatively impact participants in the gamified system [53]. Earning points or badges could lead to adverse effects in the context of gamification [54]. While accruing points might motivate high performers, it's essential to recognize the potential demotivating effect of ranking lower than one's peers. Exploring alternative methods that consider the overall context, users' personal preferences, and game progression for different audiences to define the game's interconnected narratives and mechanical dimensions is crucial for future research [55, 56]. The design of the Immersive VR gamified system is still in early development and requires further refinement through iterative Design Thinking processes involving stroke patients. It's important to note that participants in this study only interacted with prototypes and not the actual functioning system, which may lead to different insights. Gamification positively affects certain users, but these effects are often short-lived [57]. In this research, participants engaged with an IVR gamified system. The insights gained from literature reviews, suggestions, and participant feedback will guide the development of a fully functional IVR gamified system. VR holds great promise for neurorehabilitation, providing patients with a stimulating and reliable platform to enhance their motor and cognitive skills [58].

6.4   Limitations and Future Research

This paper is still in development. Subsequent research will concisely explain how psychological theory can be integrated into the system. In the following study, we will conduct a study on the implementation stage of the design thinking process. Our future work will contribute to additional considerations for future work, such as the implications for stroke patients, i.e., making the game more accessible. Future research should compare VR training with and without gamification elements to assess the effects. When testing with other game elements, we initially only focused on one. In the next phase, we will add more game elements such as "Girls Love of Balloon by Banksy". The VR game environment should have some end goal, such as diving into multiple episodes from start to game over. Points will be taken out if the objects in the VR environment as game elements fall from hand and double points to keep and move. A longer-duration experimental study will be conducted and statistically analyzed to determine the effect of game elements once they are removed from the system.

Acknowledgements. We want to thank all the participants, including the audiologists and speech-language pathologists Mustafizul Alam (Incredible Ltd) and Asiqur Islam Anik (PISER-BUP), for providing us with patient data from Bangladesh. EULiST funded this project.

References

1. Marougkas, A., Troussas, C., Krouska, A., Sgouropoulou, C.: How personalized and effective is immersive virtual reality in education? A systematic literature review for the last decade. Multimed. Tools Appl. (2023)

2. Lanier, J.: Dawn of the New Everything: A Journey Through Virtual Reality. Random House (2017)
3. Slater, M.: Immersion and the illusion of presence in virtual reality. Br. J. Psychol. **109**, 431–433 (2018)
4. Peláez-Vélez, F.J., Eckert, M., Gacto-Sánchez, M., Martínez-Carrasco, Á.: Use of virtual reality and videogames in the physiotherapy treatment of stroke patients: a pilot randomized controlled trial. Int. J. Environ. Res. Public Health **20**(6), 4747 (2023)
5. Bisht, B., Hope, A., Paul, M.K.: From papyrus leaves to bioprinting and virtual reality: history and innovation in anatomy. Anat. Cell Biol. **52**, 226–235 (2019)
6. Hofacker, C.F., de Ruyter, K., Lurie, N.H., Manchanda, P., Donaldson, J.: Gamification and mobile marketing effectiveness. J. Interact. Mark. **34**, 25–36 (2016)
7. Deterding, S., Khaled, R., Nacke, L., Dixon, D.: Gamification: toward a definition. CHI 2011 gamification workshop proceedings. In: 2011 Annual Conference on Human Factors in Computing Systems (CHI 2011) (2011)
8. Werbach, K., Hunter, D., Dixon, W.: For the win: How Game Thinking can Revolutionize Your Business. Wharton Digital Press Philadelphia (2012)
9. Spiers, H.J., Maguire, E.A.: A 'landmark' study on the neural basis of navigation. Nat. Neurosci. **7**, 572–574 (2004)
10. Suma, E., Finkelstein, S., Reid, M., Babu, S., Ulinski, A., Hodges, L.F.: Evaluation of the cognitive effects of travel technique in complex real and virtual environments. IEEE Trans. Vis. Comput. Graph. **16**, 690–702 (2009)
11. Sax, D.: The Revenge of Analog: Real things and why they Matter. Public Affairs (2016)
12. Cramer, F.: What is 'post-digital'? In: Postdigital Aesthetics: Art, Computation, and Design (2015)
13. Li, J., et al.: Rehabilitation for balance impairment in patients after stroke: a protocol of a systematic review and network meta-analysis. BMJ Open. **9**(7), e026844 (2019)
14. Baniasadi, T., Ayyoubzadeh, S.M., Mohammadzadeh, N.: Challenges and practical considerations in applying virtual reality in medical education and treatment. Oman Med J. (2020)
15. Slater, M.: Place illusion and plausibility can lead to realistic behavior in immersive virtual environments. Philos. Trans. R. Soc. B Biol. Sci. **364**, 3549–3557 (2009)
16. Slater, M., Sanchez-Vives, M.V.: Enhancing our lives with immersive virtual reality. Front. Robot. AI. **3**, 74 (2016)
17. Makransky, G., Petersen, L.: Beyond visual and auditory immersion in VR: examining perceptual stimuli for inducing presence and agency. Educ. Tech. Res. Dev. **69**(1), 141–158 (2021)
18. Lindgren, R., Johnson-Glenberg, M.: Emboldened by embodiment: six precepts for research on embodied learning and mixed reality. Educ. Res. **42**, 445–452 (2013)
19. Wu, H.-K., Lee, S.W.-Y., Chang, H.-Y., Liang, J.-C.: Current status, opportunities and challenges of augmented reality in education. Comput. Educ. **62**, 41–49 (2013)
20. Coban, M., Bolat, Y.I., Goksu, I.: The potential of immersive virtual reality to enhance learning: a meta-analysis. Educ. Res. Rev. **36** (2022)
21. Villena-Taranilla, R.M., Botturi, L., Inversini, A., Gozzi, M.: Can virtual reality enhance constructivist practices in primary education? Less. Case Study. Educ. Tech. Res. Dev. **70**(1), 311–335
22. Pellas, N., Mystakidis, S., Kazanidis, I.: Immersive virtual reality in k-12 and higher education: a systematic review of the last decade scientific literature. Virt. Real. **25** (2021)
23. Makransky, G., Sørensen, A.M., Havmose, P.: Disentangling the effects of virtual reality and real estate: in situ comparison of embodied presence and real estate validity. Interact. Learn. Environ. **27**(1), 51–67 (2019)

24. Andreasen, N.K., Baceviciute, S., Pande, P., Makransky, G.: Virtual reality instruction followed by enactment can increase procedural knowledge in a science lesson. In: 2019 IEEE Conference on Virtual Reality and 3D User Interfaces (VR), pp. 840–841. IEEE (2019)
25. Araiza-Alba, P., Neumann, S., Müller, D.M., Helbing, J.: Virtual reality in the classroom: effects on students' learning outcomes and conceptual understanding. Educ. Tech. Res. Dev. **69**(6), 3333–3356 (2021)
26. Bailenson, J.: Experience on Demand: what Virtual Reality is, How it Works, and What it Can Do. WW Norton & Company (2018)
27. Markowitz, D.M., Bailenson, J.N.: Immersive virtual reality and pro-environmental behavior: an exploratory study. J. Appl. Res. Mem. Cogn. **10**(1), 59–67 (2021)
28. Azhar, M.S., Tang, W.H., Latip, N.A.A.: An analysis of student performance using immersive virtual reality in architectural education. Autom. Constr. **94** (2018)
29. Vogt, K., Bipp, T., Davidovic, N., Boll, S.: Effects of an immersive virtual reality learning environment on cognitive processing and the development of transferable mental models in teacher education. Front. Virt. Reality **2**, 24 (2021)
30. Taufik, D., Sasono, M., Asy'ari, M. The effectiveness of virtual reality media in shaping the behavior of waste management among students. J. Phys. Conf. Ser. **1811**(1), 012025 (2021)
31. Hao, J., Pu, Y., Chen, Z., Siu, K.: Effects of virtual reality-based telerehabilitation for stroke patients: a systematic review and meta-analysis of randomized controlled trials. J. Stroke Cerebrovasc. Dis. **32**(3), 106960 (2023)
32. Wu, J., et al.: Effects of virtual reality training on upper limb function and balance in stroke patients: systematic review and meta-meta-analysis. J. Med. Internet Res. **23**, e31051 (2021)
33. Sevcenko, K., Lindgren, I.: The effects of virtual reality training in stroke and Parkinson's disease rehabilitation: a systematic review and a perspective on usability. Eur. Rev. Aging Phys. Act **19**, 4 (2022)
34. Werbach, K., Hunter, D.: The Gamification Toolkit: Dynamics, Mechanics, and Components for the Win. University of Pennsylvania Press (2015)
35. Haque, S., O'Broin, D., Kehoe, J.: Using game elements to guide postgraduate research students to promote progression and social connectedness. In: Proceedings of the 11th European Conference on Games Based Learning, pp. 881–889 (2017)
36. Robinson, D., Belloti, V.: A preliminary Taxonomy of Gamification Elements for Varying Anticipated Commitment. CHI 2013. Paris, France (2013)
37. Annetta, L.A.: The "I's" have it: a framework for serious educational game design. Rev. General Psychol. **14**(2) (2010)
38. Khokale, R., et al.: Virtual and augmented reality in post-stroke rehabilitation: a narrative review. Cureus **15**(4), e37559 (2023)
39. Peffers, K., et al.: The design science research process: a model for producing and presenting information systems research. In: 1st International Conference, DESRIST 2006 Proceedings, pp. 83–106. Claremont Graduate University (2006)
40. Carstensen, A.K., Bernhard, J.: Design science research – a powerful tool for improving methods in engineering education research. Eur. J. Eng. Educ. **44**(1–2), 85–102 (2018)
41. Experience, W.L. in R.-B.U.: Design thinking 101, https://www.nngroup.com/articles/design-thinking/, Accessed 10 Sep 2024
42. Haque, M. S., Lanzilotti, R., Jämsä, T.: Do nudges work? Using personal normative message in mHealth intervention to dissuade from physical inactivity. In: First International Workshop on Digital Nudging and Digital Persuasion, DNDP (2022)
43. Ham, E.: Tabletop Game Design for Video Game Designers. CRC Press (2015)
44. Sousa, M.: Gamifying serious games: modding modern board games to teach game potentials. In: International Simulation and Gaming Association Conference. Springer (2021)
45. Brooke, J.: SUS: a 'quick and dirty' usability scale. In: Jordan, P.W., Thomas, B., Weerdmeester, B.A., McClelland, I.L. (eds.) Usability Evaluation in Industry (1996)

46. Bangor, A., Kortum, P., Miller, J.: Determining what individual SUS scores mean: adding an adjective rating scale. J. Usability Stud. **4**, 114–123 (2009)
47. Brooke, J.: SUS: a retrospective. J. Usability Stud. **8**(2), 29–40 (2013)
48. Tullis, T., Stetson, J.: A comparison of questionnaires for assessing website usability. Usability Prof. Assoc. Conf. **1**, 1–12 (2004)
49. Kallio, H., Pietilä, A.M., Johnson, M., Kangasniemi, M.: Systematic methodological review: developing a framework for a qualitative semi-structured interview guide. J. Adv. Nurs. **72**(12), 2954–2965 (2016)
50. Nipa N.S, Alam, M., Haque, M.S.: Identifying relevant stakeholders in digital healthcare. In: Mahmud, M., Kaiser, M.S., Kasabov, N., Iftekharuddin, K., Zhong, N. (eds.) Applied Intelligence and Informatics. AII 2021. Communications in Computer and Information Science, vol. 1435. Springer, Cham, pp. 349–357 (2021)
51. Lavoué, E., Ju, Q., Hallifax, S., Serna, A.: Analyzing the relationships between learners' motivation and observable engaged behaviors in a gamified learning environment. Int. J. Hum.-Comput. Stud. **154**(2021), 102670 (2021)
52. Olesen, J.F., Kannabiran, G., Hansen, N.B.: What do hackathons do? Understanding participation in hackathons through program theory analysis. In: Proceedings of the 2021 CHI Conference on Human Factors in Computing Systems (2021)
53. Thom, J., Millen, D., DiMicco, J.: Removing gamification from an enterprise SNS. In: Proceedings of the ACM 2012 Conference on Computer-Supported Cooperative Work (2012)
54. Hamari, J.: Perspectives from behavioral economics to analyzing game design patterns: Loss aversion in social games. In: CHI (2011), Vancouver, Canada, 7–12 May 2011
55. Chou, Y.: Actionable Gamification: Beyond Points, Badges, and Leaderboards. Packt Publishing Ltd (2019)
56. Farzan, R., DiMicco, J.M., Millen, D.R., Dugan, C., Geyer, W., Brownholtz, E.A.: Results from deploying a participation incentive mechanism within the enterprise. In: Proceedings of the SIGCHI Conference on Human Factors in Computing Systems, pp. 563–572 (2008)
57. Robaina-Calderín, L., Martín-Santana, J.D., Muñoz-Leiva, F.: Immersive experiences as a resource for promoting museum tourism in the Z and millennials generations. J. Destin. Mark. Manag. **29**, 100795 (2023)
58. Holden, M.K., Dyar, T.A., Dayan-Cimadoro, L.: Telerehabilitation using a virtual environment improves upper extremity function in patients with stroke. IEEE Trans. Neural Syst. Rehabil. Eng. **15**, 36–42 (2007)

Training for Defense: The Influence of Knowledge About Influencing Strategies on Phishing Email Recognition Accuracy

Asal Hojjati[1] and Jaap Ham[2]($\boxtimes$)

[1] Industrial and Systems Engineering Department, North Carolina State University, Raleigh, NC, USA

[2] Human-Technology Interaction, Eindhoven University of Technology, PO Box 513, 5600 MB Eindhoven, The Netherlands
j.r.c.ham@tue.nl

Abstract. Phishing can cause severe security breaches and its frequency and diversity has rapidly increased. Current countermeasures consist mostly of training users in identifying phishing emails by their appearance. However, we argue that in the long run the effect of such trainings will be limited because phishers rapidly evolve their email design and this makes phishing attacks unrecognizable.

Still, phishing emails have a universal characteristic: They attempt to influence the users to perform certain behaviors using influencing strategies. Thus, we argue that training users in recognizing the influencing strategies used by technology helps them to defend themselves against (even very advanced, visually unrecognizable) phishing emails. In this study, we randomly assigned 151 participants to two groups (trained on influencing strategies vs. trained on the history of emails). Our learning material was a six-minute training video. After watching the video, participants were presented with a series of emails that contained influencing strategies. These emails were followed by questions about recognition of influencing strategies and the user's behavioral intentions towards the email.

Results provided no evidence that a participant's intension of clicking on links was influenced by the influencing strategy training video. Importantly, results did show that participants who had watched the influencing strategy training video, correctly recognized more influencing strategies in emails. Also, participants who recognized the use of manipulation techniques in emails, intended to click on less links. These results open a new line of defense against persuasive technology: harnessing users by training them in influencing strategy recognition.

Keywords: Influencing Strategies · Phishing · Persuasive Technology · Compliance Behavior · Recognition of Manipulation · Video Training

1 Introduction

Phishing is a form of socially engineered cyber threat in which a message, typically an email, with a malicious attachment or link is sent to a victim with the intent of tricking the recipient to click on the link or open the attachment [1].

© The Author(s), under exclusive license to Springer Nature Switzerland AG 2026
I. Wiafe et al. (Eds.): PERSUASIVE 2025, CCIS 2542, pp. 18–31, 2026.
https://doi.org/10.1007/978-3-031-97177-8_2

Phishing attacks have led to numerous security breaches in recent years, occurring more frequently [2], diversifying in appearance [3], and leading to large costs [4]. Despite the development of countermeasures, phishing attacks continue to rise, necessitating more proactive measures.

Various technical solutions have been proposed to address phishing threats, as for example machine learning based techniques for identifying phishing emails and websites [5]. While these automated solutions provide a strong defense, phishing attacks remain a significant threat. Moreover, cybercriminals continuously adapt their tactics to evade automatic detection [6].

Recognizing that automated measures alone are insufficient, recent research has focused on training users to identify phishing emails. Most of these trainings are based on the visual and textual characteristics of phishing emails. For instance, Volkamer et al. developed phishing awareness videos that educated users on common phishing tactics [7]. Similarly, Tschakert and Ngamsuriyaroj created a training video that provided an overview of phishing tactics, potential impacts, and key indicators of fraudulent emails and URLs [8].

Although these training programs have attempted to raise awareness, their long-term effectiveness remains uncertain. Phishers rapidly evolve their email designs, reducing the effectiveness of traditional training methods focused on email appearance and structure. Advanced phishing techniques, such as link manipulation and website forgery, further limit the usefulness of conventional training approaches.

Importantly, phishing emails share a common characteristic: They leverage persuasion principles to manipulate victims into compliance. Phishers employ various psychological influencing strategies in their phishing emails, preying on users' susceptibility to certain persuasion tactics [9]. Indeed, phishing emails make massive use of influencing strategies [9–11].

Therefore, in this study we aim to answer the following research question, *does training on influencing strategies affect compliance behavior and recognition of manipulation?*

We argue that helping people recognize and become aware of the influencing strategies commonly used in phishing attempts can empower them to better defend themselves, even against authentic-looking phishing emails. Indeed, earlier research presents evidence that training users on identifying persuasion principles (albeit in scammer phone calls) increases user's susceptibility to recognize such strategies and influencing attempts. That is, recent research by Hashmi and colleagues attempted to measure the impact of training people to identify the persuasion principles used by scammers in telephone calls [12]. Their intervention was implemented via a WhatsApp chatbot that provided example audio recordings and exercises of scam calls for users. Results showed that training users on persuasion principles using an automated chatbot, and in particular incorporating example voice recordings was a promising direction.

Drawing on prior literature, the tendency of people comply with another's request can be explained using six principles of influence: reciprocation, scarcity, consistency, authority, social proof or validation, and liking [10]. Phishers often embed these strategies into their messages to increase the likelihood of compliance [9].

In the domain of persuasive technology, earlier research has focused on the design, development, and evaluation of interactive technologies intended to influence users' attitudes and behaviors [13–16]. The current study bridges persuasive technology and cybersecurity by investigating whether user training based on established principles of influence can enhance phishing detection and reduce compliance with deceptive requests.

As of this writing the evidence of effective training on influencing strategies for countering phishing emails is yet to be shown. Earlier research, to the best of our knowledge, has not investigated how to assist people to recognize phishing attacks that use these influencing strategies.

In this study our main focus was on training users on Cialdini's principles of liking, reciprocity, consistency, scarcity, social proof, and authority [10]. These influencing strategies are known to be the most frequently used in phishing emails [9]. Thus, learning how to identify the use of these strategies could be a very effective way of recognizing phishing threats.

To study the current research question, we trained participants either on influencing strategies or on the history of email (as a control group) by watching one of two training videos. Afterward, all participants were shown a set of phishing emails (some employing multiple influence strategies, others relying solely on one influencing strategy), and answered five questions to measure behavior toward these emails (whether they would click on them or not) and to measure participants' recognition of influencing strategies.

We expected that, for emails that included many influencing strategies, participants who had watched the influencing strategy training video would intend less to click on links than participants who watched the control training video. (H1).

Also, we expected that, for emails that included many influencing strategies, participants who had watched the influencing strategy training video would perceive to be manipulated (by the email) more than participants who watched the control training video, while for emails that included one influencing strategy, we expected the participants who had watched the influencing strategy training video would perceive to be manipulated (by the email) as much as participants who watched the control training video. (H2a).

Moreover, we expected that, for emails that included many influencing strategies, participants who had watched the influencing strategy training video would correctly recognize more influencing strategies in emails than participants in the control group. (H2b).

Finally, we expected that participants who expressed a higher certainty of recognizing manipulation (by emails) would express a lower level of certainty of intending to click on links in emails with influencing strategies included. (H3).

2   Method

2.1   Participants and Design

Overall, 151 individuals participated in this study, with 64 of them being Dutch and 87 being Iranian. Six participants were excluded from the analyses because they failed to answer a control question about the training video correctly, indicating that they had not paid sufficient attention. Of the remaining 145 participants, 71 (48.96%) were males, 73 (50.34%) of them were females, and one (0.7%) participant specified other as gender. Participants had a mean age of 25.68 (SD = 9.6; range = 16 to 70 years old).

Participants' demographic information was collected, including age, gender, nationality, education level, and prior knowledge of phishing or influencing strategies. These variables were considered in exploratory analyses to examine their influence on the main outcomes.

Participants were recruited from two sources. The first one was a participant database of the Human Technology Interaction group at Eindhoven University of Technology. Around 2500 people received an invitation and 63 of them accepted. The second one was the Industrial Engineering telegram channel of the students in Sharif University of Technology. This method of selection may have introduced a degree of selection bias toward more tech-savvy individuals. To address this, we collected and report participants' demographic and background information.

Participants' educational backgrounds ranged widely, from no schooling completed to a doctorate degree. To estimate participants' level of technology use and familiarity with email we asked how many emails they received per day. Responses were as follows: 23% reported receiving fewer than 3 emails per day, 35% selected 3 to 5 emails, 19% selected 5 to 7 emails, 6% selected 7 to 9 emails, and 17% reported more than 9 emails per day.

Additionally, participants were asked whether they had any former knowledge of influencing strategies. 44% responded "yes," while 56% responded "no." We also asked if they had prior experience with phishing attacks, with 46% reporting such experiences.

These background variables were included to assess baseline familiarity with email use and phishing-related content. Where relevant, we conducted additional analyses controlling for education level, age, and prior knowledge of influencing strategies, to account for potential confounding effects.

To test our hypotheses, we used a 2 (training: identifying influencing strategies vs. not aimed at identifying influencing strategies) x 2 (influencing strategies in email: many vs. one) mixed experimental design, in which training was manipulated between participants, and influencing strategies in email was manipulated within participants. In the "many" condition, emails combined three to five distinct influence strategies (e.g., authority, scarcity, social proof), while the "one" condition included only the authority strategy.

An individual participant needed approximately 20 min to complete the study. For all participants, we used a raffle system for payment. Each participant had a twenty percent chance of winning twenty euros for participating in our research.

Prior to the main study, we conducted a pilot test with 10 participants to ensure the clarity and realism of the phishing emails and the comprehensibility of the training videos. Feedback from the pilot was used to make minor revisions to wording and email formatting.

To determine the sample size for this study, we used a 2×2 F-test power analysis. The power of the study was set to be 0.90, with an effect size of 0.25 and $\alpha = 0.05$. Since earlier studies had not investigated the current research question, there was no earlier effect size available, but we aimed at being able to find evidence for at least a medium to small effect size. For this, according to our power analysis, the total number of participants needed should be 130 or more [17].

2.2 Materials

In the study, all participants viewed an educational video. Participants in the influencing strategy training condition were presented with a video that was designed to train them on influencing strategies. Participants in the control condition were presented with a control video that was designed with the aim of presenting comparable information in a video of the same length, toughing on comparable topics, but refraining from any training or information about influencing strategies.

The Influencing Strategy Training Video. This video was aimed to train participants in the influencing strategy training condition about "the influencing strategies used in the world around us". For this, we created a video of 6 minutes. A link to this video can be found in Appendix. In the video, using graphical representations, a female voice-over (actor was not visible on screen) presented a training on influencing strategies. More specifically the video training started with a brief introduction about the importance of knowing about influencing strategies in our everyday life. This introduction was followed by detailed explanations about the use of six main influencing strategies [10]: liking, reciprocity, social proof, consistency, authority, and scarcity. After explaining each of these principles, the female voice-over provided one or two examples to clarify their use in daily live, using mainly examples related to technology. For example, the liking principle was described with the following sentences:

"According to the liking principle, we are more likely to be persuaded by people we know and like. We like people who are similar to us, who pay us compliments, and who cooperate with us towards mutual goals. So, a person may attempt to earn liking through devices such as compliments, flattery, humor, or an emphasis on similarities. Persuaders try to gain receivers' liking in order to generate compliance with their requests."

Then the following example was explained by the female vice-over:

"Microsoft accounts team might send you the following message after a password reset request:

Your safety is our highest goal and we are honored to have great customers like you who also care about that. Please update your privacy settings to the latest version."

For a detailed breakdown of how each of Cialdini's six principles was operationalized in the training video, please refer to the Appendix. The table titled *Operationalization of Influence Principles* outlines how each principle was explained and which example was used to illustrate its application in a phishing email. The descriptions were carefully developed to align with Cialdini's original definitions of the principles [10]. This table not only clarifies the content of the training but also demonstrates that each principle was represented in a way that is consistent with established theoretical understandings.

At the end of the video, the video showed an unrelated item (i.e., a carrot) and the voice-over asked the participant to remember what it was. The goal of presenting this item was to include a manipulation check question in the questionnaire at the end of the study, probing participants' memory for that item, to check whether they had indeed watched the video until the end.

The Control Training Video. The control video presented a description of the evolution of emails. The link of this video can be found in Appendix. This topic was selected to match the experimental video in terms of length, format, and contextual relevance. Both were approximately six minutes long, professionally narrated, and email-related, while deliberately avoiding any mention of phishing or influencing strategies. The videos were designed to look and feel similar in style and tone to control for visual and auditory presentation effects. The primary difference between them was the content focus, with the experimental video targeting persuasion awareness and the control video offering neutral, factual information about emails.

The Emails

The topics of the phishing emails were: Microsoft account password change, Microsoft office update, Spotify premium account, new features on google chrome, new IOS update, and job offers on LinkedIn. For each topic, we created two versions of a phishing email: one containing multiple distinct influencing strategies (ranging from three to five), and another that included only one strategy (authority).

The multiple-strategy emails combined various principles from Cialdini's framework: liking, reciprocity, social proof, consistency, scarcity, and authority. Importantly, authority was included in all emails, to maintain a consistent core manipulation while varying the presence of additional influencing strategies. Each email presented a scenario with a clickable link and a call-to-action relevant to the topic (e.g., updating an account, reviewing job offers). You can view these emails in Appendix.

The strategies were implemented as distinct and non-overlapping tactics within each email. For example, in the Microsoft password email with many strategies, the message appealed to liking through flattery, to social proof by referencing other users, and to scarcity by warning of limited time to act, alongside authority cues. In contrast, the single-strategy version of that same topic relied solely on an authoritative tone and identity.

Participants were randomly shown a set of six emails, three that included multiple influence strategies and three that included only authority, with email topics and versions counterbalanced across participants to avoid order effects. The full mapping of strategies used in each email is provided in Appendix.

2.3 Measures

This survey consisted of six different topics, which were: Microsoft account password change, Microsoft office update, Spotify premium account, new features on google chrome, new IOS update, and job offers on LinkedIn. Each participant was asked to take a look at the text of each email and answer the five questions which followed it. So, we presented participants with five questions about each email.

The first two questions served to test our first hypothesis (H1) by measuring participants' certainty of intending to click on the link in emails by asking them two questions. The first one was a yes/no question which was: "If you had seen this email in your inbox, would you click on the link?". In the next question, we assessed the certainty level of participants by asking "How certain are you that you would/would not click on the link?" Participants could answer on a scale from 1 (anchored with "I was not certain at all that I would/would not click on the link") to 7 (anchored with "I was so certain that I would/would not click on the link"). Then, we combined these two questions by multiplying the answers of the second question by 1 (for participants who declared they would click on the link) or -1 (for participants who declared they would not click on the link). This way we created a measure of participant's certainty of intending to click on the links in emails which ranged from -7 (meaning the participant was so certain to not click) to 7 (meaning the participant was so certain to click).

For our second hypothesis (H2) we measured participants' certainty of recognizing manipulation with the same approach. First, we proposed the following question: "Did you feel that this email was trying to manipulate you?", to which they could answer with yes/no, and then we presented this question: "How certain are you that this email was/wasn't trying to manipulate you?". Again, participants could answer on a scale of 1 (anchored by "I was not certain at all that this email was/ was not trying to manipulate me") to 7 (anchored by "I was so certain that this email was/ was not trying to manipulate me"). Then by multiplying the answers of the second question by 1 (for participants who declared that the email was trying to manipulate them) or -1 (for participants who declared the email was not trying to manipulate them). Therefore, we had a range of -7 (anchored by "I was so certain that this email was not trying to manipulate me") to 7 (anchored by "I was so certain that this email was trying to manipulate me").

Furthermore, when participants declared that they felt the email was trying to manipulate them, the following question would be presented in order to evaluate which influencing strategies they could recognize: "In which way did you feel this email was trying to manipulate you?" Participants could answer this question by typing in a description of the manipulation that they recognized in the email. By counting the correctly identified influencing strategies included in the email, we were able to construct for each participant, for each email that they evaluated, a manipulation recognition correctness score.

Finally, participants were asked to answer general questions about age, gender, level of education, number of emails they opened per day, former experience of phishing attacks, and former knowledge about influencing strategies.

2.4 Procedure

Participants were invited to participate in our study via an invitation email. Participants who responded positively to our invitation email, were randomly assigned to one of the two experimental conditions (training: identifying influencing strategies vs. not aimed at identifying influencing strategies) and send a confirmation email. The confirmation email contained the link to the lime survey. After clicking on that link, participants were taken to the lime survey, where they were first asked to read and indicate whether they agreed with the informed consent form. Next, participants were presented with the educational video (dependent on condition) and presented with the email and the sets of questions one after the other. Next, we thanked participants and informed them that payment for their participation was the twenty percent chance to win twenty euros in a raffle, and that they would be informed about the raffle outcome within several weeks. After the experiment was over, we performed the raffle, contacted the winners and then transferred the money to them. Finally, at the end of this study, participants were given the opportunity to withdraw from the study which would result in removal of all their data. However, none of the participants requested withdrawal. All collected data was processed anonymously. This study was approved by the Ethics Committee of Eindhoven University of Technology.

3 Results

3.1 Certainty of Intending to Click on Links

Results did not support our first hypothesis (H1). That is, there was no significant interaction between email type (including many vs. one influencing strategy) and training condition (trained vs. control) on participants' certainty of intending to click on the link, $F(1, 433) = 1.69$, $p = .194$, $\eta2 = .004$.

A follow-up analysis examining only emails with many influencing strategies showed that trained participants ($M = -1.88$, $SD = 0.36$) did not differ significantly from control participants ($M = -2.40$, $SD = 0.36$), $F(1, 433) = 3.69$, $p = .056$, $\eta2 = .008$. This suggests that the training had no clear effect on participants' intention to click on links, even in emails designed to be more persuasive.

3.2 Certainty of Manipulation

Results supported our second hypothesis (H2a). A significant interaction was found between email type (many vs. one influencing strategy) and training condition (trained vs. control) on participants' certainty of recognizing manipulation, $F(1, 433) = 23.25$, $p < .001$, $\eta2 = .051$.

Follow-up analyses showed that for emails including many influencing strategies, trained participants reported higher certainty in recognizing manipulation ($M = 2.47$, $SD = 0.34$) compared to control participants ($M = 1.21$, $SD = 0.34$), $F(1, 866) = 6.68$, $p = .010$.

In contrast, for emails that included only one influencing strategy, there was no difference between trained ($M = -0.04$, $SD = 0.35$) and control participants ($M = -0.01$, $SD = 0.35$), $F(1, 866) = 0.003$, $p = .954$. This indicates that training increased recognition only when multiple strategies were used in the email (Fig. 1).

3.3 The Number of Correctly Recognized Influencing Strategies

Results supported our second hypothesis (H2b). For emails that included many influencing strategies, participants who received the influencing strategy training correctly recognized more strategies ($M = 1.04$, $SD = 0.87$) than those in the control group ($M = 0.36$, $SD = 0.58$), $t(209) = 6.48$, $p < .001$. Levene's test indicated unequal variances, so the Welch's t-test was used. The effect size, calculated using Cohen's d, was 0.89, indicating a large effect.

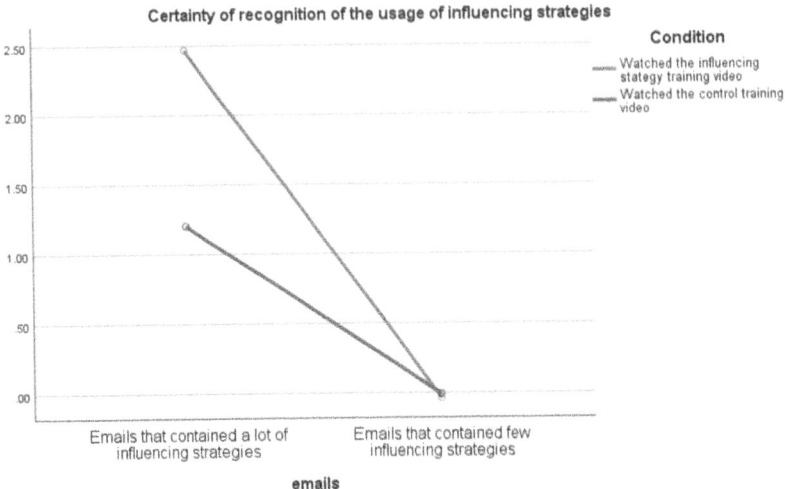

Fig. 1. This figure shows the intension of clicking on the links in emails with many influencing strategies (vs. one influencing strategy) in participants who have watched the influencing strategy training video (vs. participants in the control group)

3.4   Recognition of Influencing Strategies and Intension of Clicking on Links

Finally, results supported hypothesis H3. A moderate negative correlation was found between participants' certainty of recognizing manipulation and their certainty of intending to click on links in emails containing influencing strategies, $r = -.47, p < .001$. This Pearson correlation suggests that greater confidence in recognizing manipulation was associated with a lower intention to click on potentially deceptive links.

3.5   Exploratory Analyses

In addition to our main analyses, we conducted a series of exploratory analyses to examine the potential role of demographic and behavioral variables. These analyses were not pre-registered and should be interpreted with caution due to the increased risk of Type I errors resulting from multiple comparisons.

We first examined the effect of gender on phishing-related outcomes. Independent samples t-tests revealed no significant differences between male and female participants in terms of certainty to intend to click on links, certainty to recognize manipulation, or the number of correctly recognized influencing strategies.

A Pearson correlation showed a weak positive correlation between age and certainty of recognizing manipulation ($r = .10, p = .038$), and a weak negative correlation between age and certainty of intending to click on links ($r = -.16, p < .001$). These results suggest that older participants tended to feel slightly more confident in recognizing manipulation and were slightly less inclined to click on potentially deceptive emails.

An independent samples t-test revealed that participants with former knowledge of influencing strategies reported a statistically significant but small increase in certainty when recognizing manipulation ($M = 2.51$) compared to those without such knowledge

($M = 1.27$), $t = 2.57$, $p = .011$, $d = 0.25$. However, there was no significant difference between the two groups in their certainty to click on links ($M = -2.28$ vs. -2.06), $t = -0.43$, $p = .666$, with a negligible effect size ($d = -0.04$).

A Pearson correlation revealed no significant relationship between the number of emails participants reported receiving daily and their certainty to click on links ($r = -.08$, $p = .088$). However, there was a weak but statistically significant positive correlation between email frequency and certainty of recognizing manipulation ($r = .10$, $p = .037$), suggesting that more frequent email users may feel slightly more confident in detecting manipulation.

These findings provide initial insights into potential individual differences that may influence susceptibility to phishing emails. However, they were exploratory in nature and should be interpreted cautiously.

4 Discussion and Conclusion

The countless security breaches caused by phishing attacks during the past years urge effective countermeasures [18]. In this study, we approached a new technique of countering these attacks by training people on recognizing influencing strategies (through a video training). After that, we measured the effect of such trainings on users' certainty to intend to click on links, certainty of recognizing influencing strategies and the number of correctly recognized influencing strategies in phishing emails. Thereby, we answered the research question: *Does training on influencing strategies affect compliance behavior and recognition of manipulation?*

First of all, the current results provided no evidence that participants who had watched our influencing strategy training video expressed less certainty to intend to click on links than participants in the control group. While this might initially seem counterintuitive, several post-hoc explanations may account for this outcome. Notably, 43 participants in the control group self-reported prior knowledge of influencing strategies, gained through fields such as psychology, marketing, or advertising. This suggests that a substantial portion of the control group may have already been familiar with the types of persuasive tactics targeted by our training. Although we did not formally assess the depth or accuracy of this prior knowledge, its presence may have reduced the contrast between groups. This limits our ability to assume that the control group lacked relevant background knowledge and should be considered a constraint in interpreting the training effect.

Secondly and importantly, results showed that participants who had watched the influencing strategy training video could correctly recognize more influencing strategies in phishing emails and their level of certainty of recognizing influencing strategies was higher than the participants in the control group. This finding showed that our method was effective in raising awareness about influencing strategies. So, video trainings that explain influencing strategies and provide examples of them from real-life can be used for training people to identify manipulation and we believe this could be an initial step of helping people to make informed decisions when facing manipulation and lower their compliance with phishers.

Moreover, results showed a negative correlation between a participant's certainty of recognizing influencing strategies and their certainty of intending to click on phishing links. This suggests that participants who recognized manipulative intent were more likely to avoid engaging with the email, potentially reducing their susceptibility to phishing attacks. One possible explanation is that recognizing manipulation may trigger heightened skepticism or critical thinking, prompting individuals to reevaluate the legitimacy of the message. Awareness of persuasive tactics could also increase the perceived risk or sense of threat, leading to more cautious behavior [19]. In this way, the ability to identify influence strategies may act as a cognitive defense mechanism that discourages impulsive or compliant responses to deceptive content.

The findings suggest that age may play a modest but meaningful role in phishing susceptibility. Older participants appeared more confident in their ability to recognize manipulation and were also less inclined to click on potentially deceptive links. Our findings are somewhat contrary to previous work that has shown older adults to be less accurate in their detection of phishing emails [20, 21]. This could reflect greater caution developed through years of online experience, or perhaps a more skeptical attitude toward unsolicited digital communication [22]. These patterns highlight the potential benefit of tailoring training content to different age groups, possibly offering more detailed or experiential learning for younger users who may be more vulnerable [23]. In contrast, gender did not appear to influence phishing-related outcomes. Participants from different genders showed similar levels of certainty in recognizing manipulation, intention to click, and ability to identify influencing strategies. This suggests that phishing vulnerability and training effectiveness may not need to be differentiated based on gender, at least within the context of this study.

Also, participants who reported receiving a high volume of daily emails were also more confident in spotting manipulation. This may reflect a form of exposure-based learning, where repeated encounters with spam or suspicious emails help users develop a better "radar" for manipulative content [24].

This study has several limitations that should be acknowledged. First, we relied on self-reported intentions rather than actual behavior. While intentions are a strong predictor of behavior, they are not perfect substitutes, and actual behavior is influenced by situational factors, perceived control, and context. Thus the results may be subject to biases such as overconfidence or social desirability [25]. The study was also conducted in an artificial setting, which may not reflect real-world urgency or distraction [26]. Relatedly, the brief training duration (six-minute video) may not support long-term learning or behavioral change. Also, the control video, while matched in length and topic context, may not have controlled for differences in engagement or relevance, potentially introducing placebo effects or demand characteristics such as the John Henry effect [27].

Another important limitation of this study is that it used participants from two distinct cultural backgrounds (Dutch and Iranian). Cultural norms can influence how individuals respond to cues like authority, reciprocity, or social proof [28], which may have introduced unmeasured variability into our results. While our study was not designed to test cultural differences, future research should consider exploring how cultural context shapes the effectiveness of influence-based phishing defenses. Additionally, the emails were presented in English, which was not the native language of most participants, possibly affecting comprehension or engagement.

We also observed low internal consistency across email items, suggesting variability in how persuasive or manipulative different emails were perceived. Cronbach's alpha for both the certainty to click and certainty of recognizing manipulation measures fell below the commonly accepted threshold of .60, suggesting that participants' responses varied notably across different emails. This variability may indicate that the emails differed in how persuasive or manipulative they were perceived to be. As a result, combining responses into a single composite score should be interpreted with caution. Future research may benefit from increasing the number of items, standardizing the persuasive strength across emails, or analyzing responses individually rather than as a unified scale.

Finally, because participants self-selected into the study, there may have been a recruitment bias, with those more interested in phishing, persuasion, or cybersecurity being more likely to participate [29]. This could limit the generalizability of the findings to broader populations.

Still, the results of the current research suggest that enhancing users' ability to recognize manipulation is effective for improving their avoidance behavior. Therefore, training people on identifying influencing strategies seems a practical solution for lowering the chances of successful phishing attacks, even when the methods for such training might differ from our intervention. Other studies have suggested that different training methods including the use of chatbots [12] can be useful in this context. Future research could explore different training methods and their effectiveness to influence users' ability to recognize influencing strategies being used.

The results of this study open up a new domain of research questions in the field of persuasion and phishing research. There are many studies aiming to assess the power of influencing strategies used by phishers on users' susceptibility to phishing [30–32]. However, very few studies have used this knowledge to counter phishing attacks.

In sum, our study suggests a potential avenue for countering phishing attacks by training users to recognize the persuasive strategies commonly embedded in deceptive emails. While the training did not significantly reduce participants' self-reported intention to click on phishing links, it did improve their ability to detect manipulation and correctly identify influence techniques. These results point to the promise of persuasion-awareness training as a complementary tool in phishing prevention, particularly in enhancing users' cognitive defenses. Future research should continue to explore how this form of training can be strengthened and combined with other approaches to produce measurable changes in behavior.

Acknowledgments. Many people contributed to this article. First, we express our appreciation for the financial support of Eindhoven University of Technology. Second, we are grateful to our participants. Also, we would also like to thank the organizers of the Persuasive 2023 conference for giving us an opportunity to present parts of our work as a poster presentation helping us to improve our work.

Disclosure of Interests. The authors have no competing interests to declare that are relevant to the content of this article.

Appendix

All study materials, including the dataset, stimulus emails, survey structure, and training content, are available on the Open Science Framework (OSF) at:
   https://osf.io/jctqs/files/osfstorage?view_only=3b1e931c4c2a411f9928fe8b7ae 7f24c

References

1. Alkhalil, Z., Hewage, C., Nawaf, L., Khan, I.: Phishing attacks: a recent comprehensive study and a new anatomy. Front Comput. Sci. **3** (2021). https://doi.org/10.3389/fcomp.2021.563060
2. APWG | Phishing activity trends reports (2023). https://apwg.org/trendsreports/. Accessed 15 Feb 2025
3. Robila, S.A., Ragucci, J.W.: Don't be a phish: steps in user education. SIGCSE Bull **38**, 237–241 (2006). https://doi.org/10.1145/1140123.1140187
4. Konradt, C., Schilling, A., Werners, B.: Phishing: an economic analysis of cybercrime perpetrators. Comput. Secur. **58**, 39–46 (2016). https://doi.org/10.1016/j.cose.2015.12.001
5. Hamid, I.R.A., Abawajy, J.H.: An approach for profiling phishing activities. Comput. Secur. **45**, 27–41 (2014)
6. Wash, R., Cooper, M.M.: Who provides phishing training?: Facts, stories, and people like me. In: Proceedings of the 2018 CHI Conference on Human Factors in Computing Systems, ACM, Montreal QC Canada, pp 1–12 (2018)
7. Volkamer, M., Renaud, K., Reinheimer, B., et al.: Developing and evaluating a five minute phishing awareness video. In: Furnell, S., Mouratidis, H., Pernul, G. (eds.) Trust, Privacy and Security in Digital Business. Springer, Cham, pp 119–134 (2018)
8. Tschakert, K.F., Ngamsuriyaroj, S.: Effectiveness of and user preferences for security awareness training methodologies. Heliyon **5** (2019)
9. Zielinska, O.A., Welk, A.K., Mayhorn, C.B., Murphy-Hill, E.: A temporal analysis of persuasion principles in phishing emails. Proc. Hum. Factors Ergon. Soc. Annu. Meet. **60**, 765–769 (2016). https://doi.org/10.1177/1541931213601175
10. Cialdini, R.B., Cialdini, R.B.: Influence: The Psychology of Persuasion. Collins New York (2007)
11. Ferreira, A., Coventry, L., Lenzini, G.: Principles of persuasion in social engineering and their use in phishing. In: Tryfonas, T., Askoxylakis, I. (eds.) Human Aspects of Information Security, Privacy, and Trust. Springer, Cham, pp. 36–47 (2015)
12. Hashmi, S.I., George, N., Saqib, E., et al.: Training users to recognize persuasion techniques in vishing calls. In: Extended Abstracts of the 2023 CHI Conference on Human Factors in Computing Systems. ACM, Hamburg Germany, pp. 1–8 (2023)
13. Fogg, B.J.: Persuasive technology: using computers to change what we think and do. Ubiquity **2002**(5), 2 (2002). https://doi.org/10.1145/764008.763957
14. Hamari, J., Koivisto, J., Pakkanen, T.: Do persuasive technologies persuade? - A review of empirical studies. In: Spagnolli, A., Chittaro, L., Gamberini, L. (eds.) Persuasive Technology. Springer, Cham, pp 118–136 (2014)
15. Oinas-Kukkonen, H., Harjumaa, M.: Persuasive systems design: key issues, process model, and system features. Commun. Assoc. Inf. Syst. **24**, 28 (2009)
16. Wang, Y.D., Emurian, H.H.: An overview of online trust: concepts, elements, and implications. Comput. Hum. Behav. **21**, 105–125 (2005)
17. Faul, F., Erdfelder, E., Lang, A.-G., Buchner, A.: G*Power 3: a flexible statistical power analysis program for the social, behavioral, and biomedical sciences. Behav. Res. Methods **39**, 175–191 (2007). https://doi.org/10.3758/BF03193146

18. The Latest Phishing Statistics (updated January 2025) | AAG IT Support. https://aag-it.com/the-latest-phishing-statistics/. Accessed 26 Mar 2025

19. Friestad, M., Wright, P.: The persuasion knowledge model: how people cope with persuasion attempts. J. Consum. Res. **21**, 1–31 (1994)

20. Grimes, G.A., Hough, M.G., Signorella, M.L.: Email end users and spam: relations of gender and age group to attitudes and actions. Comput. Hum. Behav. **23**, 318–332 (2007). https://doi.org/10.1016/j.chb.2004.10.015

21. Kircanski, K., Notthoff, N., DeLiema, M., et al.: Emotional arousal may increase susceptibility to fraud in older and younger adults. Psychol. Aging **33**, 325–337 (2018). https://doi.org/10.1037/pag0000228

22. A review of Internet use among older adults - Amanda Hunsaker, Eszter Hargittai, 2018. https://doi.org/10.1177/1461444818787348. Accessed 26 Mar 2025

23. Sheng, S., Holbrook, M., Kumaraguru, P., et al.: Who falls for phish? A demographic analysis of phishing susceptibility and effectiveness of interventions. In: Proceedings of the SIGCHI Conference on Human Factors in Computing Systems. Association for Computing Machinery, New York, NY, USA, pp. 373–382 (2010)

24. (PDF) Training to Detect Phishing Emails: Effects of the Frequency of Experienced Phishing Emails. ResearchGate (2024). https://doi.org/10.1177/1071181319631355

25. Ajzen, I.: The theory of planned behavior. Organ. Behav. Hum. Decis. Process. **50**, 179–211 (1991). https://doi.org/10.1016/0749-5978(91)90020-T

26. Kumaraguru, P., Sheng, S., Acquisti, A., et al.: Lessons from a real world evaluation of anti-phishing training. In: 2008 eCrime Researchers Summit, pp. 1–12 (2008)

27. Cook, T.D., Campbell, D.T.: Day A Quasi-experimentation: Design & Analysis Issues for Field Settings. Houghton Mifflin Boston (1979)

28. The Impact of Cultural Differences on the Persuasiveness of Influence Strategies. In: ResearchGate. https://www.researchgate.net/publication/308905740_The_Impact_of_Cultural_Differences_on_the_Persuasiveness_of_Influence_Strategies. Accessed 27 Mar 2025

29. Das, S., Kim, A., Tingle, Z., Nippert-Eng, C.: All about phishing: exploring user research through a systematic literature review (2019)

30. Butavicius, M., Parsons, K., Pattinson, M., McCormac, A.: Breaching the Human Firewall: Social engineering in Phishing and Spear-Phishing Emails (2016)

31. Williams, E.J., Hinds, J., Joinson, A.N.: Exploring susceptibility to phishing in the workplace. Int. J. Hum-Comput. Stud. **120**, 1–13 (2018)

32. Wright, R.T., Jensen, M.L., Thatcher, J.B., et al.: **Research note** —influence techniques in phishing attacks: an examination of vulnerability and resistance. Inf. Syst. Res. **25**, 385–400 (2014). https://doi.org/10.1287/isre.2014.0522

The Effect of the Timing of Emotional Expression on Robot Persuasiveness

Matouš Jelínek$^{(\boxtimes)}$ (ID), Caroline Willum Bech (ID), and Kerstin Fischer$^{(\boxtimes)}$ (ID)

University of Southern Denmark, Kolding, Denmark
{matous,kerstin}@sdu.dk

Abstract. This paper presents an analysis of the effects of the timing of emotional expression in human-robot interaction, exploring the hypothesis that emotional expression in human conversation is largely a matter of social practice and hence conventionally required at specific places in dialog. To identify when and how humans express emotions while speaking, a pre-study was carried out in which participants produced the robot's utterances in dialog with another human interaction partner. Two coders analyzed participants' non-verbal behaviors in these dialogs and translated these into non-verbal behaviors of the robot. A between-subject experiment was then carried out in which participants evaluated a social robot that provided emotional expression either after its utterances or based on the timing of emotional expression by human speakers. Participants evaluated the robot's competence, warmth and their discomfort in the interaction, and responded to two behavioral variables that provide evidence of the robot's persuasiveness. The results show that participants consistently produce emotional expression at similar places in dialog, confirming the conventional nature of emotional expression, but reveal only subtle effects on human-robot interaction.

Keywords: Human-robot interaction · Emotional expression · Persuasiveness

1 Introduction

Robots are increasingly being developed to take over roles such as advice giving [10,17], motivating [5,23] or behavior change coaching [13]. The social roles of caregivers, service workers and coaches inherently involve persuasive communication, i.e., a caregiver convinces a patient to take his medicine, a service worker influences a customer to purchase a service or product, and a coach motivating a subject to follow a plan. In such situations, robots have to be credible communication partners, which may include human-like emotional expression [6,14].

In human interaction, there are many situations in which the expression of emotion is conventionally required; for instance, when a story is told, listeners are expected to produce emotional expressions that match the emotional expressions

I. Wiafe et al. (Eds.): PERSUASIVE 2025, CCIS 2542, pp. 32–43, 2026.
https://doi.org/10.1007/978-3-031-97177-8_3

the speaker is producing when approaching the story climax [24]. This kind of requirement also holds for artificial agents; for example, when delivering bad news, robots, like people, are expected to show empathy concerning the negative effects the bad news may have on their interaction partners [7]. Thus, emotional expression can be expected at very specific places in interaction.

Beyond these few specific communicative activities, not much is known about what exactly these expectations are in discourse in general, and even less is known about the interactional consequences of failure to produce those emotional signals at the right time, especially not about the effects on the persuasiveness of the respective speaker. The current paper thus presents two studies, where the first seeks to identify the regularities in emotional expression by human speakers, while the second investigates what effects the timing of these signals has on the persuasiveness of a (simulated) robot.

2 Study I: Emotional Expression in Interaction

Very little work on affect in conversation has provided data on emotional expression in interaction; beyond storytelling [24], the delivery of bad news [7] and apologies [2,12], emotional expression has been described only in very specific social practices, like in tasting [19]. In human-robot interaction, robots are generally assigned certain emotional states, such as joy, anger or fear, depending on the situation the robot is in (e.g. [3]). However, as Jung [16] shows, emotions in interaction are not static, but change dynamically and based on the conversational context.

In order to determine when and how people produce emotional signals in interaction, we elicited dialogical interactions in the target scenario behavior change coaching, which corresponds to the role the robot is supposed to fulfill in the future [15].

2.1 Methodology

A convenience sample of ten participants aged 22 to 30 years (M = 26.5), 3 females and 7 males, were recruited to interact with each other based on the conversational script developed for a robotic behavior change coach described in Jelínek et al. [15]. Participants were part of the 2nd author's personal network and participated voluntarily and without compensation; data elicitation in this project was approved by the university's internal review board. Most of the participants were of Danish nationality and nine out of ten spoke Danish as their native language. Only three participants were female, however two of these were assigned the role of the behavior change coach, resulting in an equal gender distribution for this role in the dialogue. Each of the five pairs of participants were acquainted prior to the experiment, ranging from classmates, via friends, to boyfriend and girlfriend.

The dialog introduces the *tiny habits* method [9], which is based on Fogg's Behavioral Model [8]; it views behavior as a combination of motivation, ability, and prompt. For a behavior to occur, a person must be (i) sufficiently motivated, (ii) have the ability to carry the behavior change out, and (iii) have an appropriate trigger present. The Tiny Habits method seeks to address these elements by anchoring new, small habits to existing routines, breaking aspirations into manageable actions, and rewarding completion with positive emotions to ensure longer-term adoption.

In the study, half of the participants assumed the role of the robot behavior change coach and the other the role of a potential coachee. Data elicitation proceeded based on the recommendations by Niebuhr & Michaud [22], according to which high quality speech data can be elicited experimentally if participants a) are given the opportunity to practice before, b) are allowed to change the one word or other if that makes them feel more comfortable with the text, and c) have real interaction partners. Niebuhr & Michaud demonstrate that spoken language data elicited in this way are of similar quality as naturally occurring data.

For the video recording of participants' multimodal behaviors, i.e. to capture their speech, mimics and gesture, participants, who knew each other well, were allowed to practice and to get acquainted with the recording situation. They were placed in front of each other at a comfortable distance they chose themselves, and cameras were placed at a slightly tilted angle so that they were not directly in participants' view, but still recording each participant's non-verbal behaviors. The length of the five recordings of the participants performing the robot part were between 3 min 20 s and 4 min.

The video recordings were marked up word-wise for nonverbal signals produced by the participants. The code book was iteratively developed based on the whole data set; the final set of codes consists of 10 nonverbal behaviors, including raising eyebrows, moving the head forward and backward, and blinking, as well as one code for prosodic prominence. A second coder coded the first 30 s of two dialogs; intercoder reliability was calculated by comparing the codings for each word (plus a context of one word to the left and to the right to account for the occasional difficulty to specify the timing of the nonverbal behaviors). The calculation reveals (perfect) agreement ratings from 72.9% agreement (gaze), via 84.3% (head movement), 92.9% (eyebrows), 93.3% (prosodic prominence), 97.1% (blinking) to 100% agreement (smile) (Fig. 1).

In a next step, the occurrence of similar nonverbal behaviors at similar places in the dialogs was determined; if three out of five participants produced a nonverbal signal in the same place, we took an emotional expression to be socially expectable in this position.

2.2   Results

The analysis of the contributions of the behavior change coaches yielded 568 mark-ups of 595 data units in total; of these, 363, i.e. 64%, were used by three or more speakers in the same place (see Table 1). For instance, in the utterance "I know change can be hard. But what if I told you there's a method that makes big changes easier, more manageable, and fun.", three speakers were found to use

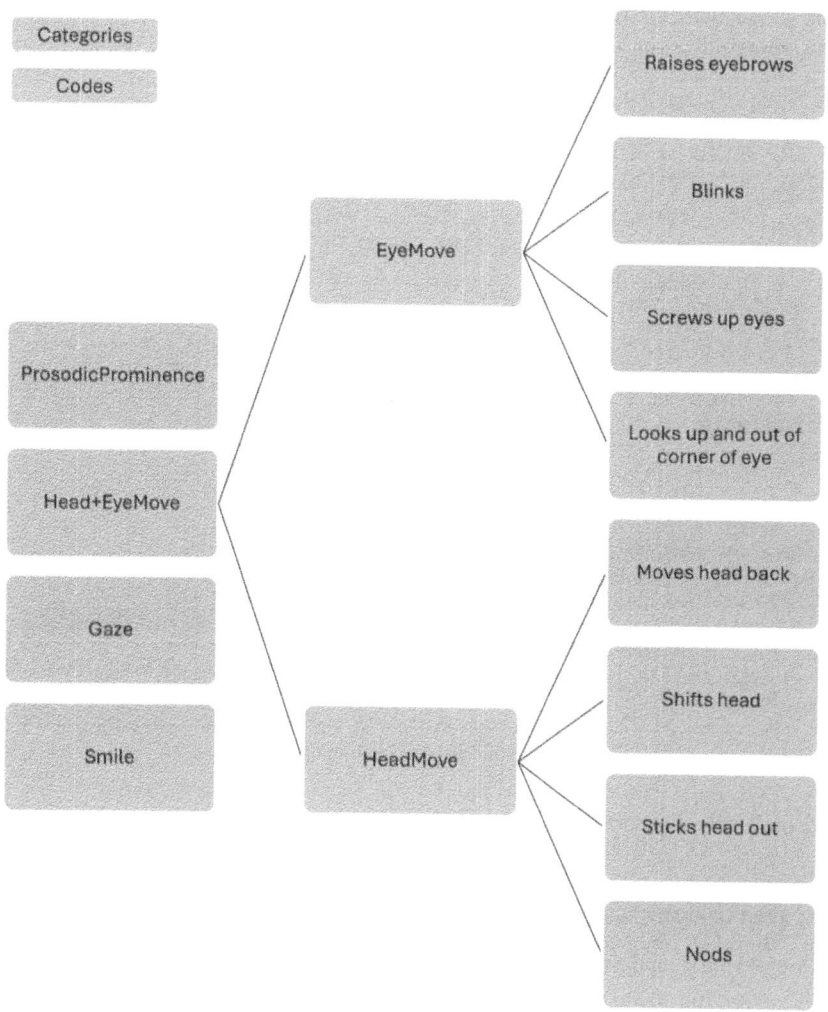

Fig. 1. The coding scheme developed for the coding of participants' emotional expression

either head movements or raised eyebrows on "big changes easier". The emotional expressions used were thus subtle, yet remarkably homogeneous with respect to their timing with respect to the dialog utterances.

The positions at which emotional expressions are expected to occur based on the results of the analysis are highlighted in the script in Fig. 2. Gaze is omitted as an emotional expression since participants continuously kept eye contact during the first part of the dialogue when the utterances of the script were easier to memorize. This is also reflected in the high percentage of positions where three or more participants gaze concurrently.

Table 1. Number of coded emotional expressions, number of expressions used by three or more (out of five) participants, and percentage of those shared emotional expressions

	coded expressions	expressions used by >3	percent expressions used by >3
voice	144	109	76%
head+eye	121	38	31%
gaze	233	183	79%
smile	70	33	47%
total	568	363	64%

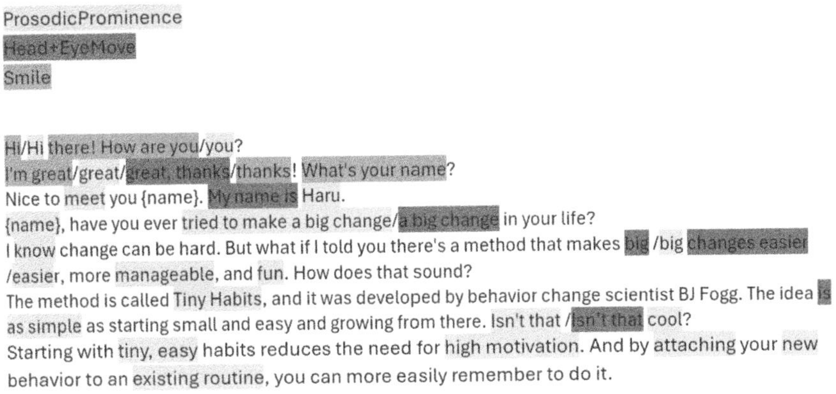

ProsodicProminence
Head+EyeMove
Smile

Hi/Hi there! How are you/you?
I'm great/great/great, thanks/thanks! What's your name?
Nice to meet you {name}. My name is Haru.
{name}, have you ever tried to make a big change/a big change in your life?
I know change can be hard. But what if I told you there's a method that makes big /big changes easier /easier, more manageable, and fun. How does that sound?
The method is called Tiny Habits, and it was developed by behavior change scientist BJ Fogg. The idea is as simple as starting small and easy and growing from there. Isn't that /Isn't that cool?
Starting with tiny, easy habits reduces the need for high motivation. And by attaching your new behavior to an existing routine, you can more easily remember to do it.

Fig. 2. The dialog script marked up with the common emotional expressions

2.3 Discussion

While the dialogs elicited are based on a script and are hence not authentic, naturally occurring data, the precautions taken based on the results from Niebuhr & Michaud [22] enable the controlled and comparable collection of multimodal dialogs comprising speech, mimics and gesture that are likely to exhibit similar characteristics as naturally occurring data. These data were characterized by considerable consistencies of emotional expressions of similar types and at similar sequential positions in the dialogs. Future work will have to verify the positions identified in naturally occurring data comprising of a larger and more diverse participant pool. Our results on gaze have also shown that the elicitation method influenced our findings for this communicative channel, since participants' gaze behavior turned out to be more dependent on their memory capacity concerning what to say next than a communicative signal. Thus, while the approach chosen was suitable for the analysis of multimodal signaling in general, it does not do justice to gaze to the same extent.

Nevertheless, the information about the sequential positions in which emotional expression are used by the majority of the participants can be assumed to be appropriate to inform the design of the behavior of the robotic behavior change coach for Study II.

3 Study II: The Effects of the Timing of Emotional Expression

The purpose of Study II is to assess the effects of the timing of emotional expression in robot utterances.

3.1 Methodology

To design an introduction to behavior change coaching by a robotic coach, utterances were selected from the dialog tested in Study I to compose a monological text for the robot. Furthermore, two behavioral variables were added: Participants were asked whether they would be willing to fill out a longer rather than a shorter questionnaire and whether they would like to receive more information on the tiny habits method introduced by the robot.

Next, the video stimuli for the experiment were created on the basis of a lip-synchronized video of the robot producing the speech to which pre-recorded emotional routines were added. The nonverbal behaviors used by the human interlocutors in Study I were translated as closely as possible to the robot behaviors in this study, while taking the specific robot morphology into account [18]. For instance, when participants in Study 1 threw their heads backwards, we used an expressive routine of the robot in which the robot moved its two screens on which its eyes are depicted backwards.

The experiment uses a between-subject design: For the control condition, emotional expressions were played at the end of the respective utterance; for the experimental condition, the same emotional expressions were played at the places identified in Study I. Thus, both the audio and the emotional expressions used are identical in both conditions, and the two versions of the video differ only in the timing of the emotional behaviors used by the robot. This ensures that participants see an equally engaging, fun robot.

An online questionnaire was created with two conditions, where half of the participants saw the video in the control condition while the other half saw the video in the experimental condition. In line with prior online studies in HRI (e.g. [26]), a total of 80 participants were recruited via the platform Prolific and paid .49GBP for their time (approximately 4 min on average). Two participants did not finish the survey and had to be discarded, leaving 78 valid participants. The sample consists of 41 males, 34 females, and 3 participants who preferred not to disclose their gender. Their ages range from 18 to 71 years (M = 35.8, SD = 13.1). To ensure that they all understood the robot well, only native speakers of English were recruited.

To measure the effect of the timing of emotional expression on participants' perception of the robot, the RoSAS was used [4], which consists of measures for perceived robot competence, warmth and participant discomfort. Participants

 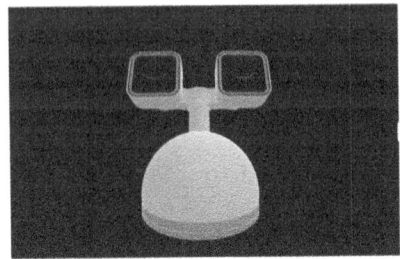

(a) Example: "I know change can be hard." (Haru tilts its head slightly forward.)

(b) Example: "... big changes easier, more manageable, and fun!" (Haru moves its head back.)

Fig. 3. Examples of the Haru robot used in the experiment mimicking human-like nonverbal behaviors, based on the results from Study 1.

rated how closely a set of adjectives was associated with the robot they observed in the video on a 9-point Likert scale (1 = "definitely not associated" to 9 = "definitely associated").

Compliance with the robot's suggestions was measured by recording how many participants chose to fill out the allegedly longer questionnaire, and how many participants chose to reveal their e-mail address to receive further information on the behavior change coaching method.

The robot used is Haru [11], a tabletop robot (see Fig. 3). The robot has two eyes consisting of LCD screens and an LED matrix mouth. It has seven degrees of freedom, including eye tilt, rotation, inner eye movement, base rotation, and body leaning, which provide opportunity for dynamic emotional expression. For the experiment, we used the default voice [20] and a set of pre-recorded expressive routines from Haru's behavior library [21], such as blinking, nodding and other head movements and smiling.

3.2   Results

Participants' engagement with the robot was measured through their willingness to request additional information about the behavior change method. In total, 33.3% of the participants asked for additional information about the tiny habits method, which suggests that the robot was overall an effective communicator in terms of raising interest in the behavior change method. Furthermore, 43.6% of the participants were willing to fill out the long questionnaire because the robot had asked them to.

The behavioral variables *Willingness to download additional information* and *Choice of long versus short questionnaire* were analyzed using a Chi-square test, but no significant effects of condition could be identified.

For the analysis of the RoSAS questionnaire, independent samples t-tests were carried out. The statistical analysis of the subjective evaluation reveals a significant difference regarding robot responsiveness ($F(1,78)=7.176$; $p=.009$), such that the robot that used the appropriately timed emotional expression was perceived to be more responsive; the other differences do not reach significance, though Fig. 4 shows that the robot in Condition 2, in which the emotional expression was timed based on the results of Study 1, are overall more positive. To investigate whether demographic factors influenced participants' responses, we conducted additional analyses including gender as an independent variable. A chi-square analysis revealed no significant interaction effects between gender and participants' choices regarding questionnaire length or willingness to download additional materials.

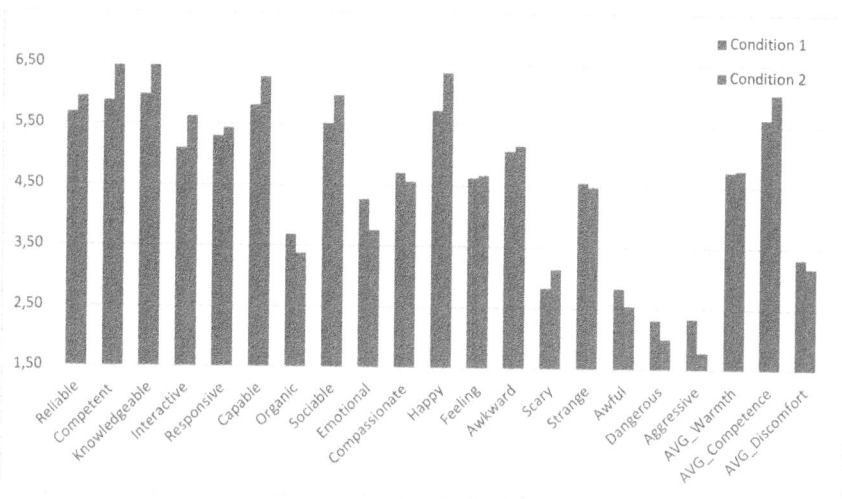

Fig. 4. The perceptive rating of the robot by condition: Condition 1: baseline; Condition 2: appropriately placed emotional expression

3.3   Discussion of the Results

The study shows that the effects of the timing of the emotional expression of Haru are very subtle; most probably a much larger participant pool would be necessary to prove an effect of the timing of emotional expression. The fact that the evaluation of the robot's *responsivity* is significantly affected by the differences in timing of emotional expressions suggests that the main effects of those differences may lie in the interactional domain and thus go by unnoticed in this monological situation, in which participants merely watched a short video of the robot. Still, based on the results of Study 1, we had expected the timing differences to have a significant effect on the credibility of the robot and therefore on its persuasiveness.

4   General Discussion

Study 1 has shown that emotional expression in dialogs in which one participant informs the other about the tiny habits behavior change coaching method is subtle, but surprisingly consistent, such that 64% of the emotional signs are used in the same places by the majority of the participants. While Study I revealed a high amount of consistency between speakers' use of nonverbal signals in inter-action, the study was carried out on 10 subjects only, which is appropriate for a qualitative study and appropriate given the aim to provide an empirical basis for the design of the stimuli for Study II, but a larger database with more diverse participants and possibly automatic data coding would be preferable to confirm the findings. Furthermore, the finding that participants' gaze behavior is influenced by the experimental situation constitutes a limitation of the methodology for the elicitation of multimodal information.

Study 2 showed that the robot was overall quite effective as a persuasive agent, by getting one third of the participants interested in the behavior change method the robot introduced and by getting almost half of the participants to fill out the allegedly longer questionnaire, even though they are not paid for the extra time. Given the demographic data from a recent survey of crowd workers [1], depending on the platform, between 50% and 90% have an income of less that 25.000 dollars per year and create daily earning goals of, for instance 20 dollars, for themselves. From this perspective, that so many followed the robot's suggestion can be counted as successful communication.

However, the expected significant effect of the timing of emotional expression and the evaluation of the robot could not be demonstrated. Transferring the observed human emotional expressions into robot behavior and comparing their naturalistic placement with a baseline condition in which the same emotional routines are played after the utterance has ended was not as effective as expected; one reason may be that participants in Study II only saw a video of a robot and were not actually interacting with it, and prior work has shown that watching videos of robots and interacting with them are different activities and have been shown to lead to different evaluations [25]. Furthermore, the timing of emotional expression after the utterance, as in the baseline condition, can lead to uncertainties regarding turn-taking [15], which just does not become apparent to people observing a video of a robot presenting a monologue.

It is also possible that people simply perceive the robot in both conditions as novel and thus did not compare it with human interaction, or at least did not consider what it would be like to interact with the robot itself. It is possible that the effect of the timing of emotional expression would be evaluated differently when people interacted with the robot directly, since the timing of the emotional expressions also impacts the efficiency of the interaction. The fact that the only significant difference between the conditions concerns the perceived responsiveness of the robot makes this suggestion plausible.

Future work will therefore have to investigate whether the timing of emotional expression has significant effects on robots' credibility and persuasiveness when people are interacting with them directly. To address this, we plan to conduct follow-up studies where participants engage in real-time dialogue with the robot rather than passively watching videos. These studies will allow for a more ecologically valid assessment of interaction dynamics, including turn-taking and responsiveness. Additionally, we consider including a condition in which participants receive the same persuasive content without emotional routines, allowing us to better assess the robot's communicative effectiveness.

Finally, the study of long term effects of emotional expression in robotic behavior change coaching would also be desirable, but this would presuppose that such robots can be robustly deployed in people's homes over longer periods of time, which will have to be left for future work in the more distant future.

5 Conclusion

While our investigation of the timing of human emotional expression has revealed considerable consistency regarding the kind and places of emotional signals in a short dialog introducing a behavior change method, transferring these signals into nonverbal robot behaviors and presenting them either at the places identified or at the ends of the respective utterances had no impact on participants' evaluation of the robot or its persuasiveness. The most plausible explanation for this lack of finding seems to be that the timing differences really only take effect when directly interacting with the robot, not in the monological situation used in this experimental set-up. Future work will have to shed further light on the effects of emotional timing on robot persuasiveness.

Acknowledgments. This study was funded by the Honda Research Institute.

References

1. Abbas, T., Gadiraju, U.: Goal-setting behavior of workers on crowdsourcing platforms: an exploratory study on MTurk and prolific. In: Proceedings of the AAAI Conference on Human Computation and Crowdsourcing. vol. 10, pp. 2–13 (2022)
2. ten Brinke, L., Adams, G.S.: Saving face? When emotion displays during public apologies mitigate damage to organizational performance. Organ. Behav. Hum. Decis. Process. **130**, 1–12 (2015)
3. Bucci, P.H., Cang, X.L., Mah, H., Rodgers, L., MacLean, K.E.: Real emotions don't stand still: toward ecologically viable representation of affective interaction. In: 8th International Conference on Affective Computing and Intelligent Interaction, pp. 1–7. IEEE (2019)
4. Carpinella, C.M., Wyman, A.B., Perez, M.A., Stroessner, S.J.: The robotic social attributes scale (RoSAS) development and validation. In: International Conference on Human-Robot Interaction, pp. 254–262 (2017)
5. Esterwood, C., Robert, L.P.: A systematic review of human and robot personality in health care human-robot interaction. Front. Robot. AI **8**, 748246 (2021)

6. Fischer, K.: Why collaborative robots must be social (and even emotional) actors. Techne: Res. Philos. Technol. **23**(3) (2019)
7. Fischer, K., Jung, M., Jensen, L.C., aus der Wieschen, M.V.: Emotion expression in HRI–when and why. In: 14th ACM/IEEE International Conference on Human-Robot Interaction, pp. 29–38. IEEE (2019)
8. Fogg, B.: A behavior model for persuasive design. In: Proceedings of the 4th International Conference on Persuasive Technology, pp. 1–7. ACM (2009). https://doi.org/10.1145/1541948.1541999
9. Fogg, B.J.: Tiny habits: The small changes that change everything. Harvest (2020)
10. Giorgi, I., et al.: I am robot, your health adviser for older adults: do you trust my advice? International Journal of Social Robotics, pp. 1–20 (2023)
11. Gomez, R., et al.: Design of embodied mediator Haru for remote cross cultural communication. In: International Conference on Robotics and Automation (ICRA), pp. 5505–5511. IEEE (2024)
12. Hornsey, M.J., Wohl, M.J., Harris, E.A., Okimoto, T.G., Thai, M., Wenzel, M.: Embodied remorse: physical displays of remorse increase positive responses to public apologies, but have negligible effects on forgiveness. J. Pers. Soc. Psychol. **119**(2), 367 (2020)
13. Jelínek, M., Fischer, K.: The role of a social robot in behavior change coaching. In: Companion of the 2021 ACM/IEEE International Conference on Human-Robot Interaction, pp. 434–438 (2021)
14. Jelínek, M., Fischer, K.: The role of emotional expression in behavior change coaching by a social robot. In: International Conference on Persuasive Technology, pp. 193–199. Springer (2021)
15. Jelínek, M., Nichols, E., Gomez, R.: Developing autonomous robot-mediated behavior coaching sessions with Haru. In: International Conference on Human-Robot Interaction, pp. 573–577 (2024)
16. Jung, M.F.: Affective grounding in human-robot interaction. In: ACM/IEEE International Conference on Human-Robot Interaction, pp. 263–273 (2017)
17. Kim, J., Merrill, K., Jr., Xu, K., Collins, C.: My health advisor is a robot: understanding intentions to adopt a robotic health advisor. Int. J. Hum. Comput. Interact. **40**(19), 5697–5706 (2024)
18. Löffler, D., Schmidt, N., Tscharn, R.: Multimodal expression of artificial emotion in social robots using color, motion and sound. In: Proceedings of the 2018 ACM/IEEE International Conference on Human-Robot Interaction, pp. 334–343 (2018)
19. Mondada, L.: The multimodal interactional organization of tasting: practices of tasting cheese in gourmet shops. Discourse Stud. **20**(6), 743–769 (2018)
20. Nichols, E., Siskind, S.R., Kamino, W., Šabanović, S., Gomez, R.: Iterative design of an emotive voice for the tabletop robot Haru. In: Li, H., et al. (eds.) Social Robotics, pp. 362–374. Springer International Publishing, Cham (2021)
21. Nichols, E., Szapiro, D., Vasylkiv, Y., Gomez, R.: I can't believe that happened!: Exploring expressivity in collaborative storytelling with the tabletop robot Haru, pp. 59–59 (2022). https://doi.org/10.1109/RO-MAN53752.2022.9900606
22. Niebuhr, O., Michaud, A.: Speech data acquisition: the underestimated challenge. KALIPHO-Kieler Arbeiten zur Linguistik und Phonetik **3**, 1–42 (2015)
23. Ros, R., et al.: A motivational approach to support healthy habits in long-term child-robot interaction. Int. J. Soc. Robot. **8**, 599–617 (2016)
24. Selting, M.: Affectivity in conversational storytelling: an analysis of displays of anger or indignation in complaint stories. Pragmatics **20**(2), 229–277 (2010)

25. Strait, M., Canning, C., Scheutz, M.: Let me tell you! Investigating the effects of robot communication strategies in advice-giving situations based on robot appearance, interaction modality and distance. In: International Conference on Human-Robot Interaction, pp. 479–486 (2014)
26. Xu, H., Ray, L.: Cohesiveness of robots in groups affects the perception of social rejection by human observers. In: 2022 17th ACM/IEEE International Conference on Human-Robot Interaction (HRI), pp. 1100–1104. IEEE (2022)

Empathy-Driven Persuasion: A Serious Game for Anti-bullying Education via First-Person Perpetrator Experience

Kaoru Sumi(✉) 📵 and Ryoma Tanabe

Future University Hakodate, Hakodate, Hokkaido, Japan
kaoru.sumi@acm.org

Abstract. This study introduces a serious game that leverages Persuasive Technology to promote anti-bullying awareness by placing players in the role of a bully from a first-person perspective. While traditional anti-bullying educational tools often focus on the victim's perspective or aim to convey preventive knowledge, limited attention has been given to help individuals reflect on their own potential behaviors as perpetrators. By integrating persuasive elements such as narrative branching, gender-specific scenarios, and mini-games simulating bullying actions, the game subtly guides players through decision-making processes and enables them to witness the consequences of their actions, including simulated arrest and guilt-inducing outcomes. An evaluation involving 21 fifth-grade students demonstrated the game's effectiveness in enhancing understanding of bullying as a serious issue with legal and moral implications. Questionnaire results revealed increased empathy, fear, and sadness in response to the scenarios, with 90% of participants acknowledging the game's impact on their awareness of guilt and the severity of bullying. Notably, the system was shown to evoke emotional engagement and moral reflection through first-person experiential learning and persuasive design techniques. However, potential risks—such as players experiencing amusement during bullying scenes—were also identified, indicating the need for further investigation and refinement.

Keywords: Serious Games · Game-Based Learning · Anti-Bullying Education · Persuasive Technology · Moral Reflection · Behavior Change

1 Introduction

The OECD's Programme for International Student Assessment (PISA), an international survey of academic performance, categorizes various forms of bullying behavior across countries [1]. These behaviors include "Any type of bullying act," "Other students left me out of things on purpose," "Other students made fun of me," "I was threatened by other students," "Other students took away or destroyed things that belong to me," "I got hit or pushed around by other students," and "Other students spread nasty rumors about me." This classification highlights how bullying manifests differently depending on regional and cultural contexts [2, 3]. For example, in Japan, "Other students made

© The Author(s), under exclusive license to Springer Nature Switzerland AG 2026
I. Wiafe et al. (Eds.): PERSUASIVE 2025, CCIS 2542, pp. 44–58, 2026.
https://doi.org/10.1007/978-3-031-97177-8_4

fun of me" and "I got hit or pushed around by other students" are prevalent, whereas in the United Kingdom, the United States, France, Sweden, and Germany, "Other students made fun of me" and "Other students spread nasty rumors about me" are more common.

Bullying and discrimination are significant social problems with profound psychological and societal consequences [4, 5, 24]. The Ministry of Education, Culture, Sports, Science and Technology in Japan identifies schools and classrooms as environments where group dynamics often lead to exclusion. These dynamics, coupled with stress and dissatisfaction, can result in maladjustment and distorted relationships. The Ministry emphasizes that fostering inclusion and reducing exclusion tendencies can be achieved through targeted educational interventions.

Recent research on virtual embodiment suggests that taking on a role in an immersive environment can significantly influence users' emotions and behaviors. The concept of the sense of embodiment in virtual reality has been introduced, highlighting how bodily ownership, agency, and self-location contribute to immersive experiences [6]. This framework is particularly relevant to this study, as players embody a perpetrator's role, potentially affecting their moral cognition and empathy. Furthermore, research has shown that embodying a historical genius in VR can enhance creative performance, reinforcing the idea that role-playing in virtual environments can shape cognitive and behavioral outcomes [7]. These insights support the hypothesis that taking on the role of a bully in a virtual setting can promote self-reflection and prosocial behavior by evoking guilt and moral awareness.

Building on this, our study employs Persuasive Technology [8–11] to further reinforce behavioral change through interactive storytelling and role-playing mechanics. Specifically, we propose a serious game [12–14] that leverages Persuasive Technology to discourage children from engaging in bullying. Unlike conventional anti-bullying interventions that focus on victims or bystanders, our approach allows players to experience the role of a perpetrator, encouraging them to reflect on the moral, social, and legal consequences of their actions. This unique perspective aims to foster empathy and accountability among players.

Existing research highlights the potential of Persuasive Technology in educational contexts [14]. Many anti-bullying games primarily focus on providing knowledge about bullying prevention [15–20], while others support educators in addressing bullying situations effectively [21–23]. However, few games incorporate Persuasive Technology explicitly or allow players to experience bullying from the perpetrator's perspective. Narrative-driven games, for example, have been utilized to help teachers develop strategies for preventing mobbing [25] and to promote inclusivity for LGBTQ students [26].

Persuasion is a powerful mechanism for behavioral change, making it integral to our approach. Prior studies demonstrate that games employing persuasive elements—such as role-playing and interactive storytelling—can foster empathy and reduce harmful behaviors [25, 26]. While many games have focused on victim perspectives, our study explores how allowing players to embody a perpetrator can deepen moral reflection and understanding of bullying behaviors.

In this study, we developed a serious game that integrates key principles of Persuasive Technology to address bullying. The game enables players to simulate bullying actions through mini-games—such as hitting, swearing, and ignoring others—from a first-person perspective. These experiences are embedded within a structured narrative that connects player choices with real-world consequences, including guilt and simulated legal repercussions. Persuasive strategies such as personalized feedback, point-based incentives, and reinforcement for abstaining from bullying are implemented to guide players toward prosocial behavior.

Our objective is to demonstrate how Persuasive Technology can create immersive educational experiences that encourage children to reject bullying behaviors while fostering empathy and moral responsibility. This paper introduces the game's design and evaluates its effectiveness in promoting anti-bullying attitudes through a combination of persuasive gameplay mechanics and immersive storytelling.

2   Anti-bullying Serious Game by Experiencing Bullying

This system introduces an anti-bullying serious game where players experience the perspective of a perpetrator of bullying. Unlike traditional educational tools that focus on victims, this game provides a first-person perspective, encouraging players to critically reflect on their actions. The game unfolds through a predefined narrative with branching scenarios based on the player's gender, offering a personalized and immersive experience.

2.1   Game Structure and Flow

The story begins with the player, a new student at school, being introduced to their classroom by a peer of the same gender. Players are presented with interactive choices that influence the progression of the story. The narrative includes several bullying scenarios, each framed as a mini-game, such as Exclusion, Verbal Attack, and Ignoring, depending on the player's gender.

Figure 1 illustrates the game's overall flow, showing how player decisions lead to different story branches and outcomes. Players may face consequences such as arrest for bullying actions or praise for abstaining, reinforcing the moral weight of their decisions.

2.2   Mini-game Design

Each mini-game is designed to simulate common bullying behaviors while subtly encouraging players to reflect on their choices. For instance:

Exclusion
This mini-game involves using keyboard input to push a boy character out of the classroom. The game is cleared once the character is fully excluded from the room. To achieve this, the player must press the key five times, gradually moving the boy toward the exit. Figure 2(a) shows an example of this mini-game.

Ignoring
Players must avoid incoming text, symbolizing attempts by the bullied character to interact. The game ends when all text is avoided. Figure 2(b) depicts the interaction mechanics, highlighting the subtlety of ignoring as a form of bullying.

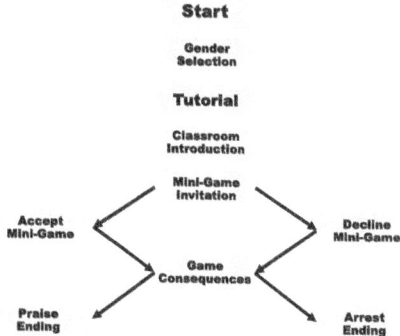

Fig. 1. Game flowchart depicting the narrative structure, including key decision-making points and branching paths that lead to different outcomes. The diagram shows a representative example of a Mini-Game Invitation, where the player chooses to Accept or Decline participation. Although only one instance is displayed for space considerations, this invitation process occurs four times throughout the gameplay. These repeated decisions allow players to reflect on their actions in multiple bullying scenarios, reinforcing the connection between choices and consequences.

2.3 Gender-Specific Scenarios

The system tailors scenarios based on gender differences in bullying behaviors, ensuring that experiences are realistic and contextually appropriate. Based on OECD PISA research, boys encounter direct forms of bullying, such as physical aggression, while girls face indirect forms, such as backbiting.

Figure 3 contrasts the gameplay of two mini-games:

- Direct swearing for boys, representing verbal aggression.
- Backbiting for girls, illustrating relational bullying.

These differences align with real-world bullying tendencies observed in educational research.

2.4 Decision-Making and Consensus

Players are faced with a moral choice: to participate in bullying mini-games or abstain. Each choice significantly affects the narrative and eventual outcome. If the player engages in bullying, a police officer appears at the end of the game to explain the criminal severity of their actions. In contrast, abstaining leads to praise, reinforcing prosocial decision-making. Figure 4 shows the divergent endings based on player actions.

2.5 Persuasion

The game implements several persuasive strategies based on B.J. Fogg's principles of social influence in Persuasive Technology [9]. Specifically, it applies the principle of Praise by reinforcing prosocial choices through verbal encouragement and in-game rewards. When players choose to abstain from bullying, they are praised by characters or earn points, which positively reinforce their moral decisions.

Fig. 2. Examples of gameplay in bullying mini-games: (a) Exclusion (left), where players use repeated key inputs to simulate physically pushing a classmate out of the classroom, illustrating the coercive nature of physical exclusion; (b) Ignoring (right), where players avoid incoming messages such as "Hey!" and "What's your name?" to symbolize social neglect, emphasizing the emotional effects of being deliberately ignored.

Fig. 3. Gender-specific mini-games illustrating different expressions of bullying behavior: (a) Verbal Attack (left): Designed for male players, this scene features direct verbal aggression with phrases such as "You're so annoying," "Piss off," and "Die already," simulating the harsh language used in bullying. (b) Backbiting (right): Tailored for female players, this interaction depicts relational aggression through indirect criticism—for example, the line "Eri thinks she's so cute," spoken behind the victim's back. These scenarios highlight gender-based variations in how bullying is expressed and experienced in social contexts.

The Similarity principle is reflected in the design of same-gender peer characters who introduce the player to the classroom environment. By aligning the helper character's gender and demeanor with that of the player, the game increases relatability and trust, thereby enhancing the effectiveness of persuasive elements.

The Liking principle is utilized in the initial interaction, where a friendly classmate greets the player as a transfer student. This early positive encounter creates emotional affinity and encourages the player to value social acceptance—making the choice to engage in bullying more emotionally difficult later in the narrative. Moreover, as players form social bonds with these characters, they may experience subtle peer pressure, making it harder to resist participation in bullying when invited, for fear of disrupting group harmony or losing friendship.

Incorporating the Authority principle, the game concludes with the appearance of a police officer if the player engages in bullying behaviors. This authoritative figure

Fig. 4. Divergent game endings based on player choices: (a) Arrest (left), where a police officer declares "You are under arrest," representing the consequences of engaging in bullying mini-games and emphasizing the legal seriousness of such behavior; (b) Praise (right), where players are told "You made the right choice," reinforcing prosocial decision-making by acknowledging their choice to abstain from bullying.

explains the legal and social consequences of bullying, reinforcing the seriousness of the player's actions and anchoring them in real-world implications.

These persuasive strategies are embedded within the game's character dialogues, branching storylines, and interactive mini-games. Together, they create an immersive and emotionally resonant learning experience. By aligning gameplay with Fogg's social influence framework, the system effectively fosters empathy, self-reflection, and behavioral change in young learners.

3 Experiment

This experiment aimed to evaluate the effectiveness of the serious game in promoting understanding of bullying and eliciting feelings of guilt and empathy among fifth-grade students. A total of 21 students (11 boys and 10 girls) participated in the study. The experiment combined questionnaire-based feedback, heart rate monitoring, and video recordings to analyze psychological responses and decision-making behavior.

3.1 Procedure

The students participated in the experiment as part of their class activities, where they individually played the game. The procedure was as follows:

Introduction
Participants were informed that the game simulates daily school life and is designed to teach about bullying and its consequences.

Game Play
Each student played the serious game individually. The gameplay was recorded to observe their reactions and decision-making processes.

Questionnaire
After completing the game, participants answered a structured questionnaire on a 5-point Likert scale and provided open-ended feedback.

Heart Rate Monitoring
Heart rate data were collected throughout the gameplay session using the "NAOS QG" mouse to analyze physiological responses during key game events.

3.2 Questionnaire Design

The questionnaire used in this study was divided into two main sections: one focusing on bullying issues and the other on the game experience itself.

The first section assessed participants' understanding of bullying and their attitudes toward it. Questions were designed to evaluate how much the participants learned from the game and how they perceived the seriousness of bullying. Sample items included statements such as, "You were able to learn about the bullying problem," "You think bullying is absolutely wrong," and "You have learned about the seriousness of the crime of bullying.

The second section focused on the design and emotional impact of the game, as well as its usability. Participants were asked to reflect on how the game made them feel and whether they found it understandable and engaging. Examples of questions included, "You found the game's story easy to understand," "You felt fear when you played the game," and "What was your impression of the bully and the bullied character in the game?".

3.3 Results

The results of this study provide a comprehensive evaluation of the serious game's effectiveness in fostering anti-bullying awareness and empathy among participants. By combining quantitative data from structured questionnaires, physiological metrics, and qualitative insights from video recordings and open-ended feedback, the study captures a holistic picture of the system's impact.

The results are organized into key categories: participants' understanding of bullying, emotional engagement, and behavioral tendencies during gameplay. These categories reflect the system's ability to evoke emotional responses, motivate prosocial behavior, and provide an immersive learning experience.

The following subsections present detailed findings, highlighting how participants interacted with the game, their emotional reactions, and their perceptions of its educational value.

Feedback on Bullying Issues
Participants demonstrated a strong understanding of the bullying problem. All participants (100%) strongly agreed that they had learned about the issue and its seriousness. Additionally, 81% of the students strongly agreed that there is a fine line between bullying and criminal behavior.

Moreover, participants expressed a heightened motivation to prevent bullying. Specifically, 71% strongly agreed that they would take action to stop bullying if they witnessed it, and 76% indicated that they would reflect on and reconsider their own potentially careless behavior.

Game Design and Emotional Impact

In terms of engagement, 52% of the participants reported that they found the game "very interesting," while an additional 29% considered it "somewhat interesting," indicating a generally positive reception.

Regarding emotional responses, 43% of the students reported feeling "very fearful" in certain situations, particularly during scenes that involved bullying or when they were prompted to engage in such behaviors. Furthermore, 71% of participants stated that they felt "very sad" when witnessing bullying scenarios within the game. These findings suggest that the game effectively elicited emotional engagement from players. Figure 5 presents a detailed breakdown of these emotional responses.

Heart Rate Analysis

Heart rate data revealed clear physiological changes among participants, particularly during emotionally intense moments in the game. The highest peaks were observed during bullying scenes, especially during scenes involving Violence or Verbal Attack, which simulate physical aggression and verbal abuse respectively. Notably, 74% of participants exhibited a marked increase in heart rate when prompted to engage in bullying behavior, indicating psychological conflict and stress. These trends are visually summarized in Fig. 6, which shows the timeline of average heart rate changes across all participants.

The connection between physiological arousal and emotional states is well established in psychological research. For example, Carroll, Izard, and Plutchik (1970) demonstrated that sharp increases in heart rate are strongly associated with heightened emotions such as fear, anger, and sadness. These prior findings support the interpretation that the physiological responses observed in this study reflect participants' emotional engagement and moral discomfort in response to bullying scenarios [31].

3.4 Observations from Video Recording

Video recordings highlighted notable differences in decision-making behaviors between male and female participants. Boys were more likely to choose bullying-related mini-games, with 81.8% (9 out of 11) selecting Violence, and 54.5% (6 out of 11) choosing Verbal Attack or Exclusion. Additionally, 45.5% (5 out of 11) selected Hiding Belongings.

In contrast, girls displayed more hesitation. Backbiting was the most selected mini-game among girls, with 40% (4 out of 10) choosing it, followed by Ignoring and Teasing, each selected by 30% (3 out of 10). Notably, Hiding Belongings was not selected by any female participants. These patterns suggest gender-based differences in how participants engaged with the bullying scenarios. Table 1 provides a summary of these gender-based mini-game selections, reflecting the differing tendencies in bullying scenario engagement between boys and girls.

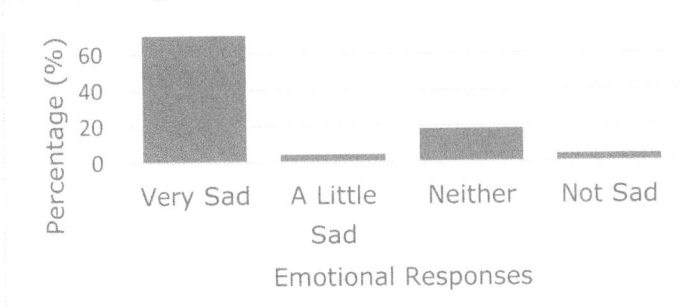

Fig. 5. Participants' emotional responses to bullying scenarios, with "Very Sad" being the most frequent choice. While the chart emphasizes sadness, open-ended responses also revealed feelings of fear and guilt, indicating a broad range of emotional engagement elicited by the game, which supports its role as an effective anti-bullying learning tool.

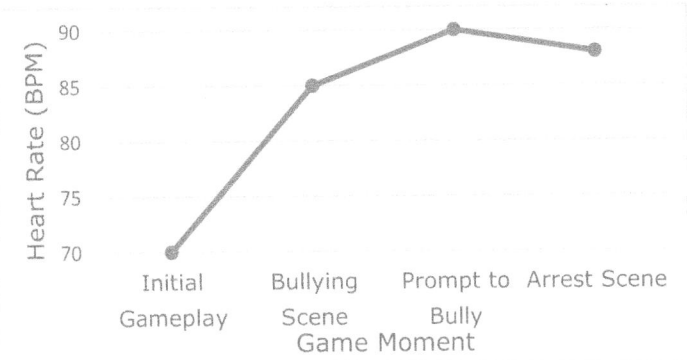

Fig. 6. Timeline of participants' average heart rate changes during gameplay, highlighting peaks during bullying scenarios such as Violence and Verbal Attack. The data reflects increased physiological arousal in response to emotionally and morally charged events, especially when players were prompted to engage in bullying.

Table 1. Frequency of mini-game selections by gender, showing distinct decision-making patterns in response to different bullying scenarios

Boy's Mini-Game	Boys (n=11)	Girl's Mini-Game	Girls (n = 10)
Exclusion	6	Ignoring	3
Violence	9	Backbiting	4
Verbal Attack	6	Hiding Belongings	0
Hiding Belongings	5	Teasing	3

3.5 Open-Ended Feedback

Participants' free-text responses offered additional qualitative insights into the game's impact. Several students provided positive feedback regarding the educational value of the game, with one participant stating, "It made me realize bullying is absolutely wrong." Emotional reactions were also evident, as exemplified by the comment, "I felt very sad for the bullied character." In terms of suggested improvements, some students requested clearer instructions for the game controls, indicating a need for greater usability.

This section builds upon earlier findings by incorporating emotional engagement, physiological data, and participant reflections to further validate the game's effectiveness. These insights reinforce the role of the system in raising emotional awareness and influencing attitudes toward prevention of bullying.

4 Discussion

The questionnaire results suggest that this system effectively served as a tool for learning about bullying. Responses indicated that students' understanding of bullying and their motivation to address it increased through the use of this system. Many participants perceived the act of bullying within the system as being as serious as a criminal offense. Additionally, some respondents emphasized that "bullying is absolutely wrong" and expressed intentions to take preventive measures, such as "stopping bullying as soon as I see it," reflecting an increased awareness of the issue. Notably, several students described severe consequences of bullying, such as "suicide" or "people who bully become criminals," which were not explicitly included in the system. These findings suggest that some students in this experiment are deeply concerned about the bullying problem.

As for the evaluation of the game, the questionnaire results indicate that this system was highly effective in maintaining motivation for learning in serious games. Students reported that they found the system highly useful. However, some participants answered "neither" or "a little disagree" regarding the comprehensibility of the narrative structure, suggesting that the narrative should be improved for deeper understanding.

We hypothesized that anti-bullying learning would be possible by experiencing the perpetrator's perspective and evoking feelings of guilt. Therefore, it was necessary to make the subjects feel fear and sadness. The questionnaire results showed that this system effectively generated fear. The game incorporated fear-inducing elements, such as the staged arrest, to emphasize the consequences of bullying. The open-ended responses revealed that half of the participants (7 out of 14) experienced fear during the staged arrest, indicating the system's effectiveness. Additionally, some participants expressed fear of bullying itself, showing that the game successfully conveyed the psychological impact of bullying.

From the answers to the open-ended questions, it can be seen that the point system was effective in motivating students to select a bullying mini-game. In addition to descriptions related to game mechanics such as points, responses included statements such as "I am angry" and "I don't want to be left out," suggesting that some students perceived the system as a real bullying situation. This behavior aligns with studies exploring the role of anonymity and group dynamics in fostering behaviors such as cyberbullying [28].

Regarding the motivation behind mini-game selection, many respondents indicated that they made their choice due to concern about the game's progression. These findings align with Self-Determination Theory (SDT), which explains how individuals' motivation is shaped by intrinsic and extrinsic factors. According to Deci & Ryan (1985), people are more likely to engage in behaviors that satisfy their psychological needs for autonomy, competence, and relatedness. In this study, some participants may have chosen mini-games due to external pressures, such as group dynamics or game progression, rather than an intrinsic desire to engage in bullying [30]. Therefore, mini-games should not be interpreted purely as acts of bullying. One common reason for selecting mini-games was the desire to avoid exclusion from the group. This aligns with research on self-efficacy and self-regulation, which highlights the role of modeling in influencing motivation and understanding in educational contexts [29, 30]. This suggests that some respondents were deeply immersed in the story and identified with the characters.

In this system, the user was given simple interactions with the characters, such as "praising the user" and "giving them something in common." To enhance effectiveness, a longer conversation process that strengthens the user's relationship with the characters before showing bullying scenes could be developed. This would allow for deeper emotional engagement and a stronger connection with the characters..

4.1 Ethical Considerations

This study was conducted with the approval of the school principal, and parental consent was obtained before the experiment. To ensure ethical compliance and participant well-being, the system included a skip function, allowing students to bypass bullying scenarios if they felt uncomfortable. Notably, several participants chose to skip certain mini-games, particularly those involving mini-games such as Violence or Verbal Attack.

Additionally, students were informed before participation that the game addressed sensitive topics, and they were encouraged to discuss any distressing feelings with their teachers. The research team monitored students' emotional responses during gameplay, and no adverse effects were reported after the experiment. These measures ensured compliance with ethical standards for research involving minors, including psychological safety and voluntary participation.

Furthermore, this study was not subject to university-level ethics review, as it did not meet the criteria for mandatory review set by the university's ethical guidelines. Specifically, the study did not include any interventions likely to cause physical or psychological harm, nor did it pose risks related to human rights violations or data privacy.

4.2 Limitations and Future Work

This study provides valuable insights into the use of a serious game to foster anti-bullying attitudes among elementary school students. However, several limitations should be acknowledged:

- The study involved a single cohort from one elementary school, which limits the generalizability of the results.

- The intervention was implemented only once, making it difficult to assess long-term behavioral effects.
- No control group was used, so direct causal effects of the game cannot be determined.
- The study relied on self-reported data, which may be subject to biases such as social desirability or inaccurate recall.

To address these limitations, future research should expand the sample to include students from multiple schools and diverse backgrounds. Longitudinal studies could help assess whether the observed educational effects are sustained over time. Additionally, integrating the game into a blended learning environment—combining gameplay with traditional moral education—may further enhance its effectiveness.

From a development perspective, future versions of the system could incorporate personalized feedback, adaptive storytelling, and scenarios covering a broader spectrum of bullying behaviors. Facilitated classroom discussions or teacher-led debriefing sessions after gameplay may also reinforce moral reflection and support deeper learning.

By building on these findings and addressing current limitations, this study lays the groundwork for advancing serious games as a powerful tool in anti-bullying education.

5 Conclusion

This study presents the development and evaluation of a anti-bullying learning system that leverages persuasive technology and first-person experiential learning by placing players in the role of a perpetrator. Unlike traditional anti-bullying tools, which often emphasize victim perspectives or abstract knowledge, this system uniquely incorporates the perpetrator's perspective to evoke empathy and promote a sense of accountability. By allowing users to embody this role, the system aims to foster moral reflection through the induction of guilt, fear, and sadness. Our findings indicate that the system effectively enhanced participants' understanding of bullying and increased their motivation to take preventive action.

The evaluation results revealed several key insights. First, the system demonstrated strong emotional engagement by using immersive gameplay mechanics and persuasive elements to elicit emotional responses—including guilt, fear, and sadness—which were critical in reinforcing the moral consequences of bullying. Second, many participants exhibited behavioral reflection, showing greater awareness of the ethical and social implications of their in-game actions. This suggests that the system encouraged meaningful introspection and potential behavior change. Third, gender-based differences were observed in decision-making patterns and emotional responses, highlighting the need for educational interventions that are responsive to gender-specific experiences.

Although the system proved to be a promising tool for anti-bullying education, several limitations were identified. Design aspects, such as narrative clarity and the user interface, require refinement to enhance the overall experience. Moreover, there is a potential risk that some students might misinterpret bullying scenarios as entertaining or humorous. To mitigate this, it is essential to implement ethical safeguards—such as clearer in-game framing and structured post-game debriefing—to ensure that the intended moral lessons are understood.

Future Directions

This study opens several avenues for future research and development. One important direction is the implementation of longitudinal studies to investigate the long-term impact of repeated exposure to the system on students' attitudes and behaviors. Such studies could help determine whether the effects observed in this research are sustainable over time.

Another potential direction involves comparative analysis, in which the system is evaluated against other anti-bullying interventions to assess its relative effectiveness. This approach could clarify the unique contributions and limitations of the proposed serious game.

Expanding the application of the system to address related issues—such as cyberbullying, discrimination, or group dynamics in schools—also represents a promising area for further development. Broadening the scope of the system may enhance its relevance and impact across diverse educational settings.

Finally, incorporating more advanced persuasive techniques, such as adaptive feedback tailored to user responses, could further individualize the learning experience and improve engagement. These enhancements may strengthen the system's ability to foster empathy, reflection, and behavioral change.

Contribution and Significance

This study introduces a pioneering use of serious games to shift the focus from victim-centric approaches to perpetrator-focused learning, a novel perspective in anti-bullying education. The unique integration of first-person perspective and persuasive technology makes this system a groundbreaking approach in moral and social education. By connecting in-game actions to real-world consequences, it offers a compelling and impactful way to address bullying behaviors. This study contributes not only to the field of serious games but also to broader discussions on the role of technology in fostering empathy and prosocial behavior.

In conclusion, this study highlights the potential of guilt-driven educational systems to effectively combat bullying by encouraging students to reflect on their actions and embrace moral responsibility. By situating students within realistic and emotionally charged scenarios, this system offers an innovative pathway for addressing complex social issues through experiential learning. With further refinement and broader application, this approach could serve as a cornerstone for future educational initiatives aimed at creating inclusive and empathetic learning environments.

Acknowledgments. This paper is based on results obtained from a project, JPNP23025, commissioned by the New Energy and Industrial Technology Development Organization (NEDO). The authors would like to express their sincere gratitude to the elementary school students in Hakodate who participated in the evaluation experiments for this study. Their cooperation and feedback were invaluable in advancing this research.

Disclosure of Interests. The authors, S and T, have no competing interests to declare that are relevant to the content of this article.

References

1. OECD. (n.d.). PISA: Programme for International Student Assessment. Retrieved from https://www.oecd.org/pisa/
2. Zych, I., Ortega-Ruiz, R., Del Rey, R.: Scientific research on bullying and cyberbullying: where have we been and where are we going. Aggress. Violent Behav. **24**, 188–198 (2015). https://doi.org/10.1016/j.avb.2015.05.015
3. Wang, C., Berry, B., Swearer, S.M.: The critical role of school climate in effective bullying prevention. Theory Into Pract. **52**(4), 296–302 (2013). https://doi.org/10.1080/00405841.2013.829735
4. Arseneault, L.: The long-term impact of bullying victimization on mental health. World Psychiatry **17**(1), 27–28 (2017)
5. Rigby, K.: New Perspectives on Bullying. Jessica Kingsley Publishers (2002)
6. Kilteni, K., Groten, R., Slater, M.: The sense of embodiment in virtual reality. Presence: Teleoper. Virtual Environ. **21**(4), 373–387 (2012). https://doi.org/10.1162/PRES_a_00124
7. Gorisse, G., Wellenreiter, S., Fleury, S., Lécuyer, A., Richir, S., Christmann, O.: I am a genius! Influence of virtually embodying Leonardo da Vinci on creative performance. IEEE Trans. Visual Comput. Graph. **29**(11), 4328–4338 (2023)
8. Fogg, B.J.: Persuasive Technology: Using Computers to Change What We Think and Do. Morgan Kaufmann (2003)
9. de Vries, P.W., Oinas-Kukkonen, H. (eds.): Persuasive Technology: Development and Implementation of Personalized Technologies to Change Attitudes and Behaviors. Lecture Notes in Computer Science, vol. 10171. Springer (2017). https://doi.org/10.1007/978-3-319-55134-0
10. MacTavish, T., Winschiers-Theophilus, H. (eds.): Persuasive Technology: Designing for Future Change. Lecture Notes in Computer Science, vol. 12064. Springer (2020). https://doi.org/10.1007/978-3-030-45712-9
11. Burtell, M., Woodside, T.: Artificial influence: an analysis of AI-driven persuasion. arXiv (2023). https://arxiv.org/abs/2303.08721
12. Abt, C.C.: Serious Games. Viking Compass (1970)
13. Gee, J.P.: What Video Games Have to Teach Us about Learning and Literacy. Palgrave Macmillan (2003)
14. Ud Din, S., Baig, M.Z., Khan, M.K.: Serious games: an updated systematic literature review. arXiv (2023). arXiv:2306.03098
15. McGonigal, J.: Reality is Broken: Why Games Make Us Better and How They Can Change the World. Penguin Books (2011)
16. Oinas-Kukkonen, H., Harjumaa, M.: Persuasive systems design: key issues, process model, and system features. Commun. Assoc. Inf. Syst. **24**(1), 485–500 (2009). https://aisel.aisnet.org/cais/vol24/iss1/28/
17. Kowalski, R.M., Limber, S.P., Agatston, P.W.: Cyberbullying: Bullying in the Digital Age. Wiley-Blackwell (2012)
18. Li, Q.: New bottle but old wine: a research of cyberbullying in schools. Comput. Hum. Behav. **23**(4), 1777–1791 (2007). https://doi.org/10.1016/j.chb.2005.10.005
19. Lepe-Salazar, F., Mejía-Romero, F., Benicio-Rodríguez, D., Hernández-Reyes, A., Nakajima, T., Salgado-Torres, S.: Game-based promotion of assertiveness to mitigate the effects of bullying in high school students: development and evaluation study. JMIR Serious Games **12**, e58452 (2024). https://doi.org/10.2196/5845
20. Wang, Y., Chai, S., Zhao, X., Ma, Y., Hu, F., Yao, C.: Hidden scars: anti-bullying serious game design for rural children. In: Figueroa, P., Di Iorio, A., Guzman del Rio, D., Clua, E.W.G., Rodriguez, L.C. (eds.) Entertainment Computing – ICEC 2024. LNCS, vol. 431–442, pp. 431–442. Springer, Cham (2024). https://doi.org/10.1007/978-3-031-74353-5_37

21. Martel-Santana, A., Martín-del-Pozo, M.: Design, development, and evaluation of a serious game aimed at addressing bullying and cyberbullying with primary school students. In: Mikropoulos, A., Chen, L.-C., Sampson, D. (eds.) Lecture Notes in Educational Technology: Innovations in Educational Gaming, pp. 203–219. Springer, Cham (2023). https://doi.org/10.1007/978-981-99-0942-1_131

22. Willems, R.A., et al.: Encouraging positive bystander responses to bias-based bullying in primary schools through a serious game approach: a non-randomized controlled evaluation of the GATE-BULL program. Int. J. Bull. Preven. (2024). https://doi.org/10.1007/s42380-024-00243-8

23. Sanoubari, E., Muñoz, J.E., Houston, A., Young, J., Dautenhahn, K.: Designing an anti bullying serious game: Insights from interviews with teachers. In: Serious Games: Joint International Conference on Serious Games (JCSG 2022). Lecture Notes in Computer Science, vol. 13476, pp. 102–121. Springer, Cham (2022). https://doi.org/10.1007/978-3-031-15325-9_9

24. Salmivalli, C.: Bullying and the peer group: a review. Aggress. Violent. Beh. 15(2), 112–120 (2010). https://doi.org/10.1016/j.avb.2009.08.007

25. Green, M.C., Brock, T.C.: The role of transportation in the persuasiveness of public narratives. J. Pers. Soc. Psychol. 79(5), 701–721 (2000). https://doi.org/10.1037/0022-3514.79.5.701

26. Calvo Morata, A., Alonso Fernández, C., Freire, M., Martínez Ortiz, I., Fernández Manjón, B.: Creating awareness on bullying and cyberbullying among young people: validating the effectiveness and design of the serious game "Conectado." Telematics Inform. 60, 101568 (2021). https://doi.org/10.1016/j.tele.2021.101568

27. Lucassen, M.F.G., Merry, S.N., Hatcher, S., Frampton, C.: Rainbow SPARX: a novel approach to addressing depression in sexual minority youth. Cogn. Behav. Pract. 22(2), 203–216 (2015). https://doi.org/10.1016/j.cbpra.2013.12.008

28. Barlett, C.P., Gentile, D.A., Chew, C.: Predicting cyberbullying from anonymity. Psychol. Popular Media Cult. 5(2), 171–180 (2016). https://doi.org/10.1037/ppm0000055

29. Schunk, D.H., Zimmerman, B.J.: Influencing children's self-efficacy and self-regulation of reading and writing through modeling. Read. Writ. Q. 23*(1), 7–25 (2007). https://doi.org/10.1080/10573560600837578

30. Deci, E.L., Ryan, R.M.: Intrinsic Motivation and Self-Determination in Human Behavior. Plenum Press (1985). https://doi.org/10.1007/978-1-4899-2271-7

31. Carroll, E.M., Izard, C.E., Plutchik, R.: Emotions in the practice of psychothera-py. Am. J. Psychother. 24(3), 403–412 (1970)

When Nudges Backfire: A Distinction Between Spillovers and Misfires

Christos Themistocleous[(✉)] [iD] and Evangelos Karapanos[(✉)] [iD]

Persuasive Tech Lab, Cyprus University of Technology, Limassol, Cyprus
{c.themistocleous,evangelos.karapanos}@cut.ac.cy

Abstract. The concept of nudging (libertarian paternalism) has been eagerly adopted in the design of digital behavioural interventions, yet discussion on adverse effects of nudges has been limited. In an attempt to enhance resolution, this theoretical paper conceptually differentiates two types of adverse effects, namely, *spillovers* and *misfires*. We propose that contrary to behavioural spillovers that occur as a consequence of a targeted behaviour, the causality of misfires is primarily attributed to the nudge type. In doing so, we employ visual representations of the behavioural trajectories that demonstrate intended and unintended effects of nudges to support choice architects in blueprinting intervention processes. We differentiate between spillovers and misfires by summarizing key empirical research that seeks to explain the causes of each and the contextual nature that distinguishes them. We conclude by drawing implications for the design of technology-mediated nudges as well as the role of its *timing*.

Keywords: Nudge Theory · Behavioural Spillover · Nudge Misfire · Behavioural Pathway · Libertarian Paternalism

1 Introduction

Behavioural sciences propose a series of intervention tools that aim to alter courses of human action to more beneficial alternatives. Such tools are wide in range and their nature is dependent on the discipline from which they emerged. The use of incentives or taxes are widely accepted propositions that stem from economics [1]; Boosting and the enhancement of human competencies in decision-making serves as a viable proposition by developmental psychologists [2], while Nudging and the use of interventions that primarily make use of human biases, originate from behavioural economics [3].

Focusing on the latter, Nudge theory, founded on Tversky's and Kahneman's [4] heuristics and biases program, is only seemingly reaching its maturity stage via a series of meta-analyses employed to assess the tool's competency [5–7] in a variety of contextual applications [8, 9]. Counterintuitive results, nevertheless, make the nudge's effectiveness inconclusive at best. For example, in a meta-analysis by Mertens et al. [10], nudges were found to be effective across a range of contextual applications, yet follow-up examinations by Maier et al. [11] refuted these findings on the basis that publication bias was not accounted for. As such, when results were adjusted using RoBMA (Robust Bayesian Meta-Analysis), favourable nudge effects eclipsed. These examples demonstrate a growing pattern in the literature that focuses on the tool's effectiveness (positive utility) and ineffectiveness (neutral utility), yet there are fewer examinations on the unintended adverse effects (negative utility) caused by failed nudges.

© The Author(s), under exclusive license to Springer Nature Switzerland AG 2026
I. Wiafe et al. (Eds.): PERSUASIVE 2025, CCIS 2542, pp. 59–70, 2026.
https://doi.org/10.1007/978-3-031-97177-8_5

Sunstein's [12] acknowledgment of failed nudges led to distinguishing between ineffective and counterproductive nudges, yet other than reactance, little is offered on the causality of the latter type and by extension on ways to mitigate it. In addressing counterproductive interventions, research on negative behavioural spillovers serves as the primary source for insights. Dolan and Galizzi [13] categorized factors like moral licensing and ego depletion, as possible predictors of spillovers. Their conceptualisation was based on how a targeted behaviour 1 can lead to an unintended behaviour 2, with the main focus fixed on behaviour 2. The premise of such conceptualisations is that spillovers occur after an individual has entered into the intended behavioural trajectory. For example, a social comparison nudge, that provides data to the user comparative to the performance of other similar users, can push an individual to start exercising (behaviour 1) yet at the end of the exercise cycle, lead the user to consume a cake (behaviour 2) demonstrating a negative spillover.

We argue that adverse effects can also occur prior to entering into behaviour 1 and as a consequence of a rejected nudge. This signifies a difference to adverse effects attributable to spillovers. For example, an individual might reject a social comparison nudge to exercise in the form of "Out of 1000 similar users you are ranked 990th for your calorie-burning performance". Due to this negative social comparison that reminds the individual of their overly negative performance, the individual does not engage in exercising, and as a consequence, her self-esteem drops [14], ultimately leading to cake consumption. Here, behaviour 2 was triggered because of the nudge type and not as a consequence of behaviour 1.

In this theoretical paper we conceptualise the above as a *Nudge Misfire* and argue that contrary to nudge spillovers that can be examined and mitigated through the psychological lenses proposed by relevant spillover research [13, 15], misfires and their adverse effects are primarily caused by the type of nudge employed as well as its timing [16]. We focus on the definition of Nudges as proposed by Thaler and Sunstein [3], namely, libertarian paternalism, and how the tool is informed by research on heuristics and decision-making processes. As such nudges that induce, for example, social comparisons, sequence effects, framing effects and defaults are relevant examples of the tool's application. Our focus has less to do with issues pertaining to autonomy restrictions, ethical or philosophical issues of nudges. Instead, we focus more on dimensions where nudges generate anomalous and inconsistent behaviours compared to the intentions of the choice architect that don't just position individuals in neutral situations but in worse-off ones.

This work contributes on three fronts. First, we differentiate between nudge spillovers and misfires by summarizing key empirical research that seek to explain the causes of these adverse effects, such as the role of moral licensing and ego-depletion in spillovers, and the contextual nature of misfires. We propose behavioural pathways (visual representations of behavioural trajectories following a nudge) as a design support tool that enables choice architects in identifying intended and unintended effects of nudges. Secondly, we use Dolan and Galizzi's [13] framework to expand on the causes of negative spillovers. We extend implications by proposing ways of mitigating each of the five main causes of negative spillovers. Finally, we analyse the new category of nudge misfires and provide examples of nudge types that can lead to these adverse behavioural trajectories.

2   Defining Nudge Spillovers and Misfires

Spillovers have received the attention of behavioural science and psychology literature [17] yet their application and empirical investigation specifically in Nudge theory is relatively limited. A behavioural spillover is defined as the effect an intervention that targets behaviour 1 has towards a behaviour 2 [15, 18–20]. Specifically, Dolan and Galizzi [13] base their spillover categorization on "(...) two different behaviours that take place sequentially: behaviour 1 is followed by behaviour 2". Following this logic, a nudge spillover occurs when a nudge that aims to address a behaviour also alters another, normally unaccounted, behaviour by the choice architect. Here we note that not all spillovers signify negative effects. For instance, the effects of physical activity nudges may extend to other health behaviours, such as adopting healthier nutrition (i.e., positive consistency, [21]). Our focus, nonetheless, is on spillovers that generate adverse effects on individuals - for example nudges that aimed at reducing household energy consumption through switching incandescent light bulbs to LED ones, yet lead to increased consumption, due to a follow-up change in the occupants' behaviour (e.g., leaving the lights on when away).

Nudge misfires, contrary to spillovers, lead to unintended adverse effects before the adoption of the intended behaviour. For example, a social comparison nudge that positions an individual in the lowest quartile of exercise time might not only discourage her from exercising but can also induce a worse-off psychological state that leads to calorie consumption. In the latter case two things occurred, first the nudge was ignored in the sense that the individual did not engage in exercising, and second, a worse-off position was accidentally instigated to the nudged individual via calorie consumption. Behavioural interventions that backfire is a topic touched upon by both HCI [22] and behavioural research [15] yet a distinction, at the procedural level, of adverse behavioural effects to our knowledge remains underexplored.

3   Differentiating between Nudge Spillovers and Misfires

Contrary to Spillovers, Nudge misfires occur when the individual rejects the nudged trajectory yet ends in a worse-off situation compared to the absence of that nudge. Conceptually, prior research positions the recommended term of Misfires as a type of Spillover [13] yet we argue that the two have adequate differences to justify a new taxonomy. We base this on two main premises. First, Spillovers are a consequence of the nudged behaviour while misfires are a consequence of the nudge type itself. Secondly, there is a differentiation in the stage within the behavioural process where each adverse effect occurs. A spillover leads to a new behaviour 1 as a consequence of the nudged behaviour 2. Contrary to that, a misfire occurs when the individual rejects the nudge yet the dismissed nudge leads to a new worse-off behaviour. This can be attributed to either the nudge type and/or its timing [16]. In essence, the difference between *spillovers* and *misfires* can be summarised as follows: The adverse behaviour for the spillovers occurs after accepting the nudged behaviour, while the adverse behaviour of misfires occurs after rejecting the nudge and as a consequence of it. In essence, the latter triggers a new behaviour trajectory by *missing* the behaviour it was intended to target and instigating a new negative one. Figure 1 depicts the *behavioural pathways* of each type. The visual representations demonstrate the intended and unintended behavioural changes as a result of the nudge.

1a. An intended Nudge

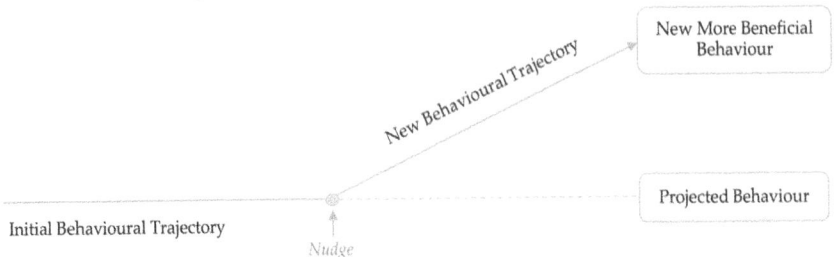

1b. A Nudge Spillover

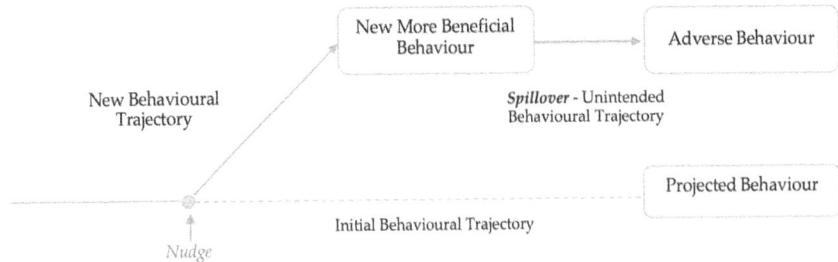

1c. A Nudge Misfire :

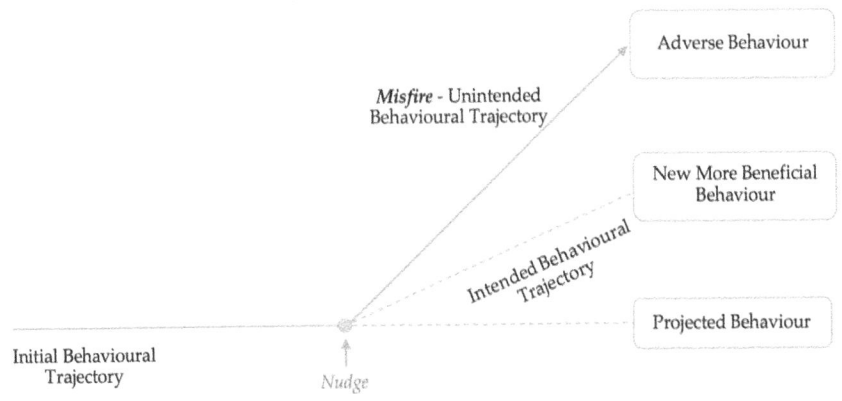

Fig. 1. Behavioural pathways for an intended Nudge (1a), a Nudge Spillover (1b) and a Nudge Misfire (1c).

4   Nudge Spillovers: Contributing Factors

Research on spillovers identifies a series of factors that create it. As negative spillovers are the present paper's focus point, we bring attention to Dolan and Galizzi [13] categorisation of permitting spillovers where inducing a positive behaviour 1 leads to a negative behaviour 2. Their categorisation focused on five identified factors that contribute to these spillovers, namely: Moral Licensing, Ego Depletion, Reverse foot-in-door, Rest-on-Laurels and Single-Action bias. The objective of this section is to reflect on each type and propose ways of mitigation for choice architects and intervention designers.

4.1 Moral licensing

Moral licensing is a psychological phenomenon where individuals feel justified in engaging in behaviours that might otherwise conflict with their moral standards after they have previously acted in a morally positive way [23, 44]. Good deeds for example serve as "licenses" that allow the person to feel they have earned the right to act less virtuously. Merritt et al. [24] mention that moral licensing occurs when "... individuals can derive confidence from their past moral behaviour, such that an impeccable track record increases their propensity to engage in otherwise suspect actions."

Consider the previously discussed LED lights example. Moral licensing suggests that the good deed of energy saving by switching to LED lamps can justify a relaxed and *deserved* attitude of not checking whether lights are unnecessarily on. Moral licensing has seen a series of empirical investigations in different contexts. For example, a prompt that led to a charity donation justified the purchase of a luxury good (designer jeans) over a necessity for an individual [25]. In a similar fashion and in the context of dieting, Fishback and Dhar [26] identify how exercising can provide licensing for consuming high-calorie chocolate over a healthy fruit alternative. Embedded in moral licensing is self-perception theory which suggests that individuals infer their own attitudes and beliefs by observing their behavior, especially when internal cues are weak or ambiguous [27]. As such after a good deed, individuals feel that their moral self-image is sufficiently strong. This can reduce the pressure to act morally in subsequent situations, as they feel they've earned the right for a moral deviation.

Handling spillovers caused by Moral Licensing: Empirical findings pertaining to moral licensing are especially valuable to nudge designers. Moral licensing is accentuated primarily in altruistic behaviours such as donations and other acts of philanthropy [25, 28]. Choice architects specifically in these domains need to be aware that individuals might indulge a nudge for a donation yet moral licensing might hinder them from more meaningful acts of charity. Default nudges with a recommended amount for a donation might be less relevant to tackle such a spillover effect. In handling this, assigning an *identity* to the individual in the form of framing and informative system 2 nudges that aim to instigate a sense of responsibility to philanthropic acts instead of being perceived as acts of generosity can mitigate this, as the latter could give *license* for other unsustainable hedonic behaviours.

4.2 Ego Depletion

Ego depletion suggests that self-control or willpower draws from a limited pool of mental resources that can be depleted with use [29]. When individuals exert significant self-control in one task, their ability to exercise self-control in subsequent tasks may be reduced, leading to diminished performance or decision-making capacity [30]. Dolan and Galizzi [13] acknowledge an association between ego depletion and spillovers especially when an ego depleting behaviour precedes one that requires willpower and cognitive energy to resist. They argue that exercising which is both a physically and mentally tiring task, can lower the individual's willpower to resist to a cake with equal (if not more) amount of calories to the ones burned by the activity. Applied to nudges, from Fig. 1b, an exercise-reminder nudge might trigger a new beneficial behaviour trajectory, yet a subsequent behaviour, that requires willpower to resist, might render the individual susceptible to it. If the second behaviour decreases the utility achieved by the nudge, we have a negative nudge spillover attributable to ego depletion.

Ego depletion has seen applications from sports [31, 32] and how tiring mental tasks affect performance, to how food choices are made following cognitively demanding tasks [33]. Nudges designed to reduce smoking renders that person's affective dimension superior over her cognitive one. This is due to the cognitive scarcity caused by the smoking reduction task. It is thus quite common for nudged smokers trying to quit, to demonstrate reduced willpower and thus lean more towards affect decisions than ones requiring cognitive effort.

Handling Spillovers Caused by Ego Depletion: Practical implications of ego deple-tion as a cause of nudge spillovers relate to the nature of behaviours affected by ego depletion. Nudging for exercising or for other willpower-demanding tasks, like quit-ting smoking, can lead to unintended spillovers like increasing sugar intake, eating more unhealthy food or buying affect-laden products. Due to the inability to predict the exact area of the spillover we propose an alternative way. Designers need to be aware of demanding behaviours that they aim to alter and perform a *willpower-demanding task audit*. As a first step, mapping the targeted behaviours will allow the avoidance of nudges that simultaneously require significant effort from the individual, for example, exercising and quitting smoking at the same time. This dual targeting can maximise the chance of ego-depleted states and by extension susceptibility to affect decisions that follow. Step two and after mapping demanding tasks, designers can utilise the right *tim-ing* for each nudge, allowing chronological space between nudges that target different willpower-demanding behaviours, one at a time.

4.3 Single-Action Bias

Single-action bias is a cognitive phenomenon where individuals take a single action in response to a perceived problem and then fail to take further necessary steps due to the emotional relief felt by the initial action [34]. Originally studied in the context of risk perception and decision-making, it has been particularly noted in environmental behaviour, health interventions, and financial decision-making [35]. When individuals face an issue, such as climate change or health risks, taking a single action can provide psychological relief, reducing the motivation for additional efforts. For instance, a person concerned about energy consumption might switch to LED bulbs but neglect further actions like reducing air travel or supporting impactful policy changes. Similar patterns emerge in health behaviour where a single preventive action, such as taking a vitamin supplement, can lead individuals to feel less urgency to adopt more impactful habits like regular exercise or a balanced diet.

Handling Spillovers Caused by Single-Action Bias: The implications of Single Action Bias are linked to how the initial action, on an issue important to the individual, leads to emotional relief. If individuals feel emotional consolation due to the initial action, nudge interventions aiming for long-term and systemic changes may be undermined. As such, one could mitigate the this by employing strategies that encourage sustained action, for example, through adjusting nudges and their frequency in a way that (i) emphasizes one's incomplete efforts, (ii) provides continuous feedback, or (iii) structures commitments that promote follow-through strategies. For instance, reframing a nudge from a "thank you for recycling" to a "Great start! Here's what you can do next", can position the initial action as a starting point to a process. With respect to timing and frequency of nudge provision, we note that one-off nudges arguably exacerbate single-action bias, and should be complemented by tailored-to-the-user well-timed nudge reminders to facilitate follow-up actions.

4.4 Rest-on-Laurels effect

The Rest-on-Laurels effect occurs when individuals reduce further effort after an initial success, believing they have already done enough. Unlike single-action bias, which is driven by emotional relief after taking a single step, Rest-on-Laurels stems from self-satisfaction and a sense of accomplishment. Amir and Ariely [36] argue that individuals break an initial goal into smaller, more manageable sub-goals. The achievement of these subgoals can lead to a sense of success resulting to complacency which gives way to behavioural stagnation hindering the completion of the initial *main* goal. The achievement of these sub-goals hinders an individual from the achievement of all sub-goals that constitute the main goal [37]. This effect is particularly evident in personal habits and social behaviour. For example, someone who sets a starting goal to exercise for a month, does so, yet the feeling of success to this goal can lead to him neglecting further workouts. The sub-goal achievement, hinders him from achieving the main goal which is about developing an exercise routine. Over time, this mindset can lead to declining motivation, missed opportunities for growth, and a false perception of long-term impact.

Handling Spillovers Caused by Rest-on-Laurels: To counteract this effect, interventions should frame achievements as steps in a process, encourage new goal-setting and provide progress-reminding nudges that mitigate this bias. Specifically, designers can capitalise on the latter and utilise nudges in the form of *visual progress indicators* that have two main dimensions: First congratulatory notes are offered to retain motivation by acknowledging subgoal achievements and secondly highlighting that such achievements constitute a part of a larger process and, by extension, that these efforts are incomplete without continuation to the next pillar of the process. For example, fitness apps can use streak tracking and/or progressive goal-setting to ensure users don't stop after achieving a few initial, short-term workout goals.

4.5 Reverse Foot-in-the-Door

The reverse foot-in-the-door spillover occurs when an individual, after completing a large or demanding action, becomes less likely to engage in smaller, follow-up actions. This contrasts with the classic foot-in-the-door effect, where a small initial action increases the likelihood of further engagement, (which is a positive spillover; [38]). Reverse foot-in-the-door is driven by effort-based exhaustion or a feeling of having already contributed enough [39]. In environmental behaviour, individuals who make a major commitment, such as installing solar panels, may neglect smaller sustainable actions like conserving daily energy [18]. Similarly, in health, someone who completes an intense workout may feel justified in skipping minor habits like taking the stairs. In charitable giving, a large one-time donation can reduce motivation for future smaller contributions.

Handling Reverse Foot-in-the-Door: The consequences of reverse foot-in-the-door spillover include behavioural stagnation and reduced long-term engagement. To counteract this, nudges should, (i) frame small actions as enhancing prior efforts, (ii) provide explanations that emphasize cumulative impact, and (iii) encourage ongoing goal-setting to sustain behaviour over time. Table 1 provides a summarisation of the mitigation strategies for each of the main five identified causes of negative spillovers.

Table 1. Mitigation strategies for the main five causes of negative spillovers.

Causes of Negative Spillovers	Mitigation Strategies	Description
Moral Licensing	*Framing Nudges* *Informative Nudges*	Framing *e.g. Philanthropic acts framed as responsibilities and not solely as acts of generosity* Informative *e.g. explanations as to the implications of systematic giving, which philanthropic acts can have the most impact, to whom and why*
Ego Depletion	*Willpower-demanding Task Audit*	Step 1. Identification of willpower-demanding tasks *e.g. quit smoking; start exercising* Step 2. Focused targeting *e.g. targeting a single willpower-demanding task at a time*
Single-Action Bias	*Progress-Reporting Nudges* *Framing Nudges*	Visual Progress Bars *e.g. use of both dynamic and static types* Framing *Framing the initial action as a part of a larger process* *e.g. Instead of "thank you for recycling" frame as "Great start! Here's what you can do next"*
Rest-on-Laurels	*Progress-Reporting Nudges* *Reminder Nudges*	Visual Progress Bars *e.g. both dynamic and static types.* Reminders *e.g. reminding users of their remaining sub-goals; reminding them of their current stage in the process.*
Reverse Foot-in-the Door	*Progress-Reporting Nudges* *Informative Nudges*	Visual Progress Bars *e.g. both dynamic and static types.* Informative *e.g. Explain the importance of cumulative impact while encouraging on-going goal setting.*

5   Nudge Misfires: Contributing Factors

When it comes to nudge misfires we argue that their causality is highly dependent on the nudge type used. Due to the case-specific nature of misfires, we review social comparison nudges as an example to analyse the nudge misfire category.

Social comparison nudges are based on Social comparison theory and the idea that individuals evaluate their own behaviors, attitudes, or abilities by comparing themselves to those of others. Social comparison nudges are prominently used in persuasive technology and beyond (see [40–42]). For example, a social comparison nudge can be used to promote exercising through comparisons. An individual's exercising performance can be contrasted to a pool of others with similar demographic characteristics, generating a descriptive statistic reflective of their performance such as: "You are currently ranked 90th compared out of 100 others in the same age and sex group in terms of weekly exercise" (see [43]). Meta-analytical data show that comparisons can have negative effects dependent on the context of application and the behaviour they are designed to alter [44] , including low self-esteem and depressing states [14]. As a result, individuals might reject the exercise prompt, but also engage in adverse health behaviours due to the adverse psychological effects of this nudge type.

Some ways to mitigate misfires for social comparison nudges include the nudge type and its timing. Consider the example of Gouveia et al. [43] who developed and field-trialed a physical activity promotion nudge that was comparing one's daily steps to that of others' sharing a similar daily goal. Every time users would check their watch, they would see two rings, representing their current and others' average performance on a 5-min resolution. They found that when users checked their watch, they were quicker to initiate a new physical activity if they were not too far behind or ahead of others (+/−500 steps).

While users check their watch on their volition, subtle prompts, being haptic, auditory or textual, could serve as attentional cues to engage with physical activity feedback. The *timing* technique would suggest increasing the frequency of those attentional cues when individuals' performance is similar to that of others. The *nudge type* technique would suggest considering what information to provide and how to frame it, in order to minimize the likelihood of misfires. For instance, and while one could question the ethics of the technique, Gouveia et al. [43] and others [39, 40] identified that artificially lowering the performance of others, or changing how it is portrayed, can communicate an opportunity for the user to catch up. Colusso et al. [46] empirically assessed its efficacy in the context of game design and found that it increased gamer performance, but only for experienced gamers, who were motivated by comparisons that deemed them closer to the leader's performance.

Furthermore, social norm nudges and the often-reported *boomerang effect*, can further lead to misfires. The boomerang effect occurs where a person who acts prosocially is led to abandon his previous behaviour when the nudge informs him that the majority does not support his prosocial behaviour. Techniques such a *"norm from the top"*[47] which provides information based on the most altruistic people in the population, can offer an effective solution. One should, however, consider that misfires can have very different causes, which, most of the time, one cannot anticipate. To effectively identify and tackle misfires, intervention designers should extensively pilot early prototypes of their nudge and carefully observe and qualitatively inquire into the likely misfires and their causes while abiding to ethical considerations.

6 Conclusions

This theoretical paper aids designers in proactively predicting potential backfires in their nudge design within a given context and reactively uncovering the causes of a nudge with adverse effects. In doing so we distinguish between two main nudge issues; Spillovers and Misfires. More importantly, we provide a clearer distinction the two, enhancing previous conceptualisations that positioned them in a single category. We argue that misfires lead to adverse behaviours because of the intervention itself (e.g. the type of the nudge) while spillovers lead to adverse situations because of both the behaviour induced by the intervention and the intervention type. This allows designers to more accurately blueprint behavioural processes and anticipate points of vulnerability in the choice architecture.

We attempt to bring forth possible explanations to this new taxonomy. We elaborate on a number of causes for Nudge spillovers, such as ego depletion, moral licensing, single-action bias, rest-on-laurels effect, and the reverse foot-in-the-door effect, while for nudge misfires we suggest considering the theory behind each nudge type as a more effective tool of analysis. The latter is especially important as nudges assessed to be ineffective do not mean that they can not be harmful.

References

1. Wall, J., Mhurchu, C.N., Blakely, T., Rodgers, A., Wilton, J.: Effectiveness of monetary incentives in modifying dietary behavior: a review of randomized, controlled trials. Nutr. Rev. **64**, 518–531 (2006)
2. Kurvers, R.H., et al.: Boosting medical diagnostics by pooling independent judgments. Proc. Natl. Acad. Sci. **113**(31). pp. 8777–8782 (2016).
3. Thaler, R.H., Sunstein, C.R.: Nudge: Improving Decisions about Wealth, and Happiness. Penguin Publications (2008).
4. Tversky, A., Kahneman, D.: Judgment under uncertainty: heuristics and biases: biases in judgments reveal some heuristics of thinking under uncertainty. Science (80-). **185**, 1124–1131 (1974)
5. Caraban, A., Karapanos, E., Gonçalves, D., Campos, R.: 23 Ways to nudge: a review of technology-mediated nudging in human-computer interaction. In: CHI Conference on Human Factors in Computing Systems Proceedings (CHI 2019), 4–9 May 2019, Glasgow, Scotland, UK
6. Broers, V.J., Breucker, C., Van den Broucke, S., Luminet, O.: A systematic review and meta-analysis of the effectiveness of nudging to increase fruit and vegetable choice. Eur. J. Public Health **27**, 912–920 (2017)
7. Arno, A., Thomas, S.: The efficacy of nudge theory strategies in influencing adult dietary behavior: a systematic review and meta-analysis. BMC Public Health **16**, 1–11 (2016)
8. Loewenstein, G., Sunstein, C.R., Golman, R.: Disclosure: psychology changes everything. Annu. Rev. Econom. **6**, 391–419 (2014)

9. Themistocleous, C., Smith, A., Wagner, C.: The ethical dilemma of implicit vs explicit data collection: examining the factors that influence the voluntary disclosure of information by consumers to commercial organizations. In: IEEE International Symposium on Ethics in Science, Technology and Engineering (2014)
10. Mertens, S., Herberz, M., Hahnel, U.J., Brosch, T.: The effectiveness of nudging: a meta-analysis of choice architecture interventions across behavioral domains. In: Proceedings of the National Academy of Sciences (2022)
11. Maier, M., Bartoš, F., Stanley, T.D., Shanks, D.R., Harris, A.J., Wagenmakers, E.J.: No evidence for nudging after adjusting for publication bias. Proc. Natl. Acad. Sci. **119**, (2022)
12. Sunstein, C.R.: Nudges that fail. Behav. Public Policy **1**, 4–25 (2017)
13. Dolan, O., Galizzi, M.: Like ripples on a pond: behavioural spillovers and their implications for research and policy. J. Econ. Psychol. **47**, 1–16 (2015)
14. White, J.B., Langer, E.J., Yariv, L., Welch, J.C.: Frequent social comparisons and destructive emotions and behaviors: the dark side of social comparisons. J. Adult Dev. **13**, 36–44 (2006)
15. Galizzi, M.M., Whitmarsh, L.: How to measure behavioral spillovers: a methodological review and checklist. Front. Psychol. **10**, 342 (2019). https://doi.org/10.3389/fpsyg.2019.00342
16. Themistocleous, C., Karapanos, E.: Precision nudging: the future of behavioural change. In: Christou, P. (ed.) AI in Social Research. p. Forthcoming. CABI Publishing (2025)
17. Lanzini, P., Thøgersen, J.: Behavioural spillover in the environmental domain: an intervention study. J. Environ. Psychol. **40**, 381–390 (2014)
18. Truelove, H.B., Carrico, A.R., Weber, E.U., Raimi, K.T., Vandenbergh, M.P.: Positive and negative spillover of pro-environmental behavior: an integrative review and theoretical framework. Glob. Environ. Chang. **29**, 127–138 (2014)
19. Nafziger, J.: Spillover effects of nudges. Econ. Lett. **190**, 109086 (2020). https://doi.org/10.1016/j.econlet.2020.109086
20. Thøgersen, J.: Spillover processes in the development of a sustainable consumption pattern. J. Econ. Psychol. **20**, 53–81 (1999)
21. Fleig, L., Lippke, S., Pomp, S., Schwarzer, R.: Intervention effects of exercise self-regulation on physical exercise and eating fruits and vegetables: a longitudinal study in orthopedic and cardiac rehabilitation. Prev. Med. (Baltim) **53**, 182–187 (2011)
22. Stibe, A., Cugelman, B.: Persuasive backfiring: when behavior change interventions trigger unintended negative outcomes. In: International Conference on Persuasive Technology, pp. 65–77. Springer, Charm (2016)
23. Lasarov, W., Hoffmann, S.: Social moral licensing. J. Bus. Ethics **165**, 45–66 (2020)
24. Merritt, A.C., Daniel, A.E., Benoit, M.: Moral self-licensing: when being good frees us to be bad. Soc. Personal. Psychol. Compass. **4**, 344–357 (2010)
25. Khan, U., Dhar, R.: Licensing effect in consumer choice. J. Mark. Res. **43**, 259–266 (2006)
26. Fishbach, A., Dhar, R.: Goals as excuses or guides: the liberating effect of perceived goal progress on choice. J. Consum. Res. **32**, 370–377 (2005)
27. Bem, D.J.: Self-perception theory. Adv. Exp. Soc. Psychol. **6**, (1972)
28. Clot, S., Della Giusta, M., Jewell, S.: Once good, always good? Testing nudge's spillovers on pro-environmental behavior. Environ. Behav. **54**, 655–669 (2022)
29. Baumeister, R.E., Bratslavsky, E., Muraven, M., Tice, D.M.: Ego depletion: is the active self a limited resource? J. Pers. Soc. Psychol. **74**, 1252–1265 (1998)
30. Muraven, M., Baumeister, R.F.: Self-regulation and depletion of limited resources: does self-control resemble a muscle? Psychol. Bull. **126**, 247 (2000)
31. Englert, C., Bertrams, A., Furley, P., Oudejans, R.R.: Is ego depletion associated with increased distractibility? Results from a basketball free throw task. Psychol. Sport Exerc. **18**, 26–31 (2015)
32. Englert, C., Wolff, W.: Ego depletion and persistent performance in a cycling task. Int. J. Sport Psychol. **46**, 137–151 (2015)

33. Shiv, B., Fedorikhin, A.: The interplay of affect and cognition in consumer decision making. J. Consum. Res. **26**, 278–292 (1999)
34. Weber, E.U.: Perception and expectation of climate change. Psychol. Perspect. Environ. Ethical Issues Manag. 314–341 (1997)
35. Choudhary, G., Dutt, V.: Analyzing single-action bias in dynamic climate change environments: insights from feedback and probability. Humanit. Soc. Sci. Commun. **11**, 1–15 (2024)
36. Amir, O., Ariely, D.: Resting on laurels: The effects of discrete progress markers as subgoals on task performance and preferences. J. Exp. Psychol. Learn. Mem. Cogn. **34**, 1158–1171 (2008)
37. Kruglanski, A.W., Shah, J.Y., Fishbach, A., Friedman, R., Chun, W., Sleeth-Keppler, D.: A theory of goal-systems. In: Zanna, M.P. (ed.) Advances in Experimental social psychology, pp. 331–376. Academic Press, New York (2002)
38. Beaman, A.L., Cole, C.M., Preston, M., Klentz, B., Steblay, N.M.: Fifteen years of foot-in-the-door research: a meta-analysis. Personal. Soc. Psychol. Bull. **9**, 181–196 (1983)
39. Guadagno, R.E., Asher, T., Demaine, L.J., Cialdini, R.B.: When saying yes leads to saying no: preference for consistency and the reverse foot-in-the-door effect. Personal. Soc. Psychol. Bull. **27**, 859–867 (2001)
40. Dijkstra, P., Gibbons, F.X., Bruunk, A.P.: Social comparison theory. In: Maddux, J.E. and Tangney, J.P. (eds.) Social Psychological Foundations of Clinical Psychology, pp. 195–211. The Guildford Press (2010)
41. Suls, J., Martin, R., Wheeler, L.: Social comparison: why, with whom, and with what effect? Curr. Dir. Psychol. Sci. **11**, 159–163 (2002)
42. Kankane, S., DiRusso, C., Buckley, C.: Can we nudge users toward better password management? An initial study. In: Extended Abstracts of the 2018 CHI Conference on Human Factors in Computing Systems, pp. 1–6 (2018)
43. Gouveia, R., Pereira, F., Karapanos, E., Munson, S.A., Hassenzahl, M.: Exploring the design space of glanceable feedback for physical activity trackers. In: Proceedings of the 2016 ACM International Joint Conference on Pervasive and Ubiquitous Computing, pp. 144–155 (2016)
44. Gerber, J.P., Wheeler, L., Suls, J.: A social comparison theory meta-analysis 60+ years on. Psychol. Bull. **144**, 177 (2018)
45. Adar, E., Tan, D.S., Teevan, J.: Benevolent deception in human computer interaction. In: Proceedings of the SIGCHI Conference on Human Factors in Computing Systems, pp. 1863–1872 (2013)
46. Colusso, L., Hsieh, G., Munson, S.A.: Designing closeness to increase gamers' performance. In: Proceedings of the 2016 CHI Conference on Human Factors in Computing Systems, pp. 3020–3024 (2016)
47. Rouillé, A.: Norm from the top: a social norm nudge to promote low-practiced behaviors without boomerang effect. Socioecon. Challenges. **8**, 123–142 (2024)

Laughing at Bias: An Exploratory Study on Generation Z's Persuasion and Skepticism Toward AI- vs. Human-Generated Sexist Humorous Ads

Maria C. Voutsa[1]([⊠]) [iD], Dimitra Kerkidou[1], and Leonidas Hatzithomas[2] [iD]

[1] Cyprus University of Technology, Limassol, Cyprus
maria.voutsa@cut.ac.cy, dv.kerkidou@edu.cut.ac.cy
[2] University of Macedonia, Thessaloniki, Greece
hatzithomas@uom.edu.gr

Abstract. In today's fast-changing digital world, the question *"Is this real?"* comes up often, especially as consumers interact with ads—many of which use humor or artificial intelligence (AI)-generated content. This study explores how disparagement in humor, particularly in the form of sexist advertising, affects consumer skepticism perceptions when the content is generated by AI compared to human sources. As AI becomes a prominent actor in the creative process, its capacity to produce emotionally charged, humorous content presents opportunities and ethical challenges for persuasive technologies. Using the Persuasion Knowledge Model (PKM) framework, the research focuses on Generation Z, known for their tech-savviness and awareness of social issues, to see how they react to AI- versus human-generated ads containing sexist humor. The results reveal that consumers' skepticism increases when AI is disclosed in ads, leading to more negative attitudes toward the ad. In the case of sexist humor, this skepticism further reduces the perceived humorousness, which worsens overall advertising evaluations. The study makes three key contributions: (1) it advances theoretical insights into AI-driven persuasive communication, (2) it provides actionable guidance for designers and marketers working with persuasive technologies, and (3) it highlights the ethical imperatives of transparency and social responsibility in algorithmically mediated persuasion, especially as the boundaries between human and machine-generated content continue to blur.

Keywords: AI disclosure · skepticism · persuasion · Advertising · Sexist Humor · Artificial Intelligence · Generation Z

1 Introduction

The increasing use of AI-generated advertising presents opportunities and challenges for marketers, particularly in persuasive technologies. As synthetic content becomes increasingly prevalent, questions around credibility, transparency, and consumer trust

© The Author(s), under exclusive license to Springer Nature Switzerland AG 2026
I. Wiafe et al. (Eds.): PERSUASIVE 2025, CCIS 2542, pp. 71–85, 2026.
https://doi.org/10.1007/978-3-031-97177-8_6

are intensifying [1, 2]. In practice, synthetic ads seem to be becoming more prevalent, not only as creative tools but often as the central subject of advertisements. Many recent campaigns reference AI, acknowledging its growing role even when not AI-generated. For example, OpenAI's Super Bowl ad showcased human evolution while teasing AI's future potential, while Virgin Voyages' "Jen AI" campaign used humor to reveal that a glamorous Jennifer Lopez ad was an AI-generated version portrayed by a man named Kyle. This humorous twist made the campaign memorable and encouraged audience interaction through the brand's AI-powered customization tool. Similarly, Apple's "Apple Intelligence" campaign framed AI as a seamlessly integrated, practical tool for everyday life, reinforcing its accessibility and reducing consumer skepticism.

While humor is increasingly used in AI-related advertising, combining AI and disparaging humor remains rare. So far, AI itself has been the target rather than humans, as seen in Burger King's campaign mocking AI's creative limitations [3]. This suggests a strategic approach where brands use AI as a safe comedic subject to foster engagement without risking offense. How AI is framed in advertising directly ties into persuasion knowledge—consumers' awareness of marketing tactics. When humor in synthetic ads must be carefully designed to avoid perceptions of manipulation, as persuasion knowledge can trigger skepticism [4].

Persuasion knowledge in advertising has been extensively studied through both quantitative and qualitative approaches, with various measures assessing consumer responses [4]. We focus on ad skepticism, originally conceptualized by Obermiller and Spangenberg [5], as a key component of situational persuasion knowledge. Ad skepticism primarily reflects consumer mistrust toward marketers' persuasive messages and has been used to represent negative attitudes toward persuasion attempts [4]. For example, skepticism is commonly triggered by disclosures such as "Paid Ad" or #ad in native advertising [6]. Furthermore, Chen et al. [7] explored agentic vs. communal appeals in synthetic vs. human-generated ads, finding that synthetic ads with agentic appeals lead to more favorable ad attitudes and higher purchase intentions. This suggests that while AI-generated humor raises trust concerns, strategic message framing and transparency can enhance effectiveness. Our study contributes to these studies by exploring how AI vs. non-AI disclosure, presented via a low-cognitive-load logo, influences ad skepticism and subsequently affects ad attitude in the context of sexist humorous ads.

A low-cognitive-load (i.e., a simple visual design that requires minimal mental effort to process) logo is essential for Generation Z (hereinafter Gen Z), a highly sought-after yet challenging audience for marketers. In 2023, Gen Z made up 23% of the global population, representing a tech-savvy yet skeptical generational cohort that is difficult to target through traditional marketing approaches [8]. A key factor shaping Gen Z's response to AI in advertising is technology dissonance—the psychological discomfort caused by rapid advancements and their perceived risks. This generation navigates a paradox between valuing AI-driven convenience and prioritizing privacy, making AI disclosure a critical yet delicate element in brand communication [9].

Thus, this study has a twofold aim: (1) to examine how AI disclosure influences consumer skepticism and ad attitude, and (2) to investigate the role of ad skepticism and humor perception in shaping responses to AI-generated sexist humorous ads, particularly among Generation Z. By weaving together insights from AI disclosure, persuasion knowledge, and humor in advertising, this study sheds light on a largely uncharted intersection. To the best of our knowledge, no prior research has brought these threads together, offering a meaningful step toward understanding how technology, persuasion, and humor shape Gen Z's reactions toward synthetic advertisements.

2 Theoretical Framework and Literature Review

2.1 AI Disclosure and Persuasion Knowledge in Advertising

The Persuasion Knowledge Model (PKM) in marketing examines how consumers respond to marketers' persuasion attempts [10], influenced by individual factors (e.g., age) and contextual cues (e.g., culture) [11]. Several persuasion elements moderate the relationship between consumer persuasion knowledge and marketer-intended outcomes (e.g., attitudes, behavior) and unintended effects (e.g., resistance, skepticism). These elements include the source, the message, the channel, and the receiver [11]. This study focuses on three key moderating persuasion elements: the source (human vs. AI-generated ad), the message (sexist humorous vs. non-humorous ad), and the receiver (focus on Gen Z).

While AI-driven advertising enhances efficiency, personalization, and scalability, it also triggers skepticism, consumers may question machine-generated content's authenticity and persuasive intent [1, 2]. Unlike human-created advertisements, AI-generated ads lack social intuition and emotional nuance, which may make them appear less authentic and more mechanical [12]. Prior research highlights that AI disclosure significantly impacts consumer perception, often negatively affecting credibility. Baek et al. [12], drawing on the PKM and advertising disclosure literature, found that AI disclosure reduces perceived credibility and lowers donation intentions, particularly in contexts that rely on empathy and emotional engagement, such as charitable giving ads. While synthetic ads are increasingly legitimized in nonprofit advertising, consumers may exhibit skepticism toward AI-generated content in for-profit advertising [13]. This suggests that trust in AI-driven marketing depends heavily on context, where AI-generated content may be accepted in certain domains while raising concerns in others.

Furthermore, ad disclosure is a key trigger for persuasion knowledge activation, as it enhances ad recognition and exposes marketers' persuasive intent [14]. In the commercial sector, AI disclosure frequently increases skepticism and negatively affects ad attitudes, as AI-generated content is often perceived as less persuasive, less authentic, and potentially manipulative [12]. Research indicates that when a persuasion attempt comes from a credible source, consumers are more likely to trust both the message and the messenger [15]. However, AI disclosure may weaken source credibility, leading to higher skepticism toward the ad. Thus, the following hypothesis is formulated:

H1: AI (vs. non-AI) disclosure increases ad skepticism.

According to PKM, consumers learn to recognize persuasive attempts based on past experiences, enabling them to evaluate advertiser credibility, intentions, and strategies [16]. This knowledge informs cognitive and emotional responses to ads, determining whether consumers will accept or resist a message. According to Friestad and Wright

[10], PKM outlines three dimensions of persuasion knowledge that shape consumer-advertiser interactions: (1) topic knowledge (i.e., consumer's familiarity with the advertised product or content), (2) agent knowledge (i.e., perceptions of the advertiser's credibility), and (3) persuasion knowledge (i.e., understanding the scope of marketers' strategies). Persuasion knowledge is not automatically activated; instead, it depends on the consumer's motivation and ability to detect persuasive intent [10]. In the context of AI disclosure, when consumers become aware that an ad is AI-generated, they are likely to activate agent knowledge, leading to increased persuasion knowledge activation and higher skepticism toward the ad. This ad skepticism plays a critical role in ad effectiveness, as it influences cognitive processing and consumer resistance. In their meta-analysis, Eisend and Tarrahi [11] found that persuasion knowledge negatively impacts attitude toward the ad and general ad effectiveness, as consumers who are more skeptical tend to resist persuasion attempts. Ad skepticism is a key barrier to advertising success, so it is expected to diminish consumers' attitudes toward AI-generated ads. Thus, the following hypothesis is proposed:

H2: Ad skepticism negatively influences attitude toward the ad.

2.2 Humor in Human-Machine (H2M) Interaction

The effectiveness of AI-generated humor depends on humor type, source perception, audience traits, and context. Non-disparaging humor is perceived as funnier and less offensive when delivered by humans, whereas disparaging humor (e.g., racist or sexist jokes) is judged similarly regardless of source, indicating that content matters more than the source [17]. Trust and rapport shape engagement, with human communication proving more effective than AI-driven exchanges [18]. AI attribution can reduce humor perception, though repeated exposure may lessen this bias [19].

The role of anthropomorphism in AI humor perception is also significant. Mirnig et al. [20] found that perceived humorousness in H2M communication depends on the level of robot anthropomorphism, suggesting that more human-like AI may enhance humor reception. Additionally, human laughter itself can act as a social trigger for better H2M interaction. Similarly, Oliveira et al. [21] demonstrated that robot-generated humor positively influences H2M communication, improving both the robot's likability and human enjoyment during interactions. Researchers also explored how humor reception depends on human psychological traits. Individuals who fear being laughed at (gelotophobes) are more sensitive to malicious humor, even from AI sources, while AI-driven laughter can enhance engagement but not necessarily cheerfulness [22, 23]. Mood shifts before and after AI interaction further shape responses, making it crucial to assess AI's emotional impact [24].

Context also plays a critical role. People exhibit different personality traits when interacting with AI versus humans, showing more openness and self-disclosure with humans and higher neuroticism with AI [25]. Decision-making context matters as AI-generated humor is judged more critically in sexist cases where cognitive processing overrides initial biases [26]. Given that humor is a deeply human form of social bonding, AI struggles to replicate the emotional nuance and timing that make human humor engaging.

Humor is a widely used persuasive tool in marketing, enhancing advertising effectiveness. However, its impact depends largely on the type of humor employed. Among various humor strategies, disparagement humor remains particularly controversial yet frequently utilized. Voutsa [27] identified disparaging humorous advertising (DHA) as a growing but underexplored area, often leveraged to mask controversial content while aiming to improve brand perception and purchase intention. By its nature, disparagement humor—targeting individuals or groups—can evoke both amusement and offense, making it a polarizing advertising approach.

A subcategory of DHA, sexist humorous advertising, is often conflated with sexually humorous advertising. Sexually humorous ads incorporate themes of sex, sexuality, or sex-related elements in a humorous manner [28]. However, when such ads embed sexist themes, they align with disparagement theory, which suggests that humor at the expense of others can reinforce stereotypes, provoke negative emotional responses, and shape brand perception [28]. The superiority-inferiority theory further explains that humor often stems from the perceived inferiority of its target, meaning that audience identification with the victim can trigger negative reactions—even when humor is used as a veil [29]. This is particularly relevant in sexist humorous ads, where gender-based stereotypes may alienate certain audience segments, ultimately diminishing the ad's effectiveness. From an ethical standpoint, Grougiou et al. [30] found that female-disparaging ads are perceived as less ethical, leading to less favorable ad and brand attitudes. These perceptions vary based on gender and benevolent sexism, indicating that audience characteristics significantly influence ad effectiveness. This suggests that when humor reinforces gender biases, it may fail to entertain and instead provoke resistance, particularly if the audience perceives it as an unethical persuasion attempt. Given that persuasion knowledge influences skepticism toward ads [11], AI-generated humor in a sexist context may heighten ad skepticism, negatively impacting humor perception. Thus, the following research hypotheses are formed. The conceptual model is also represented in Fig. 1.

H3: In sexist humorous ads, higher ad skepticism reduces perceived humorousness.

H4: Ad skepticism and perceived humorousness serially mediate the relationship between AI disclosure and ad attitude.

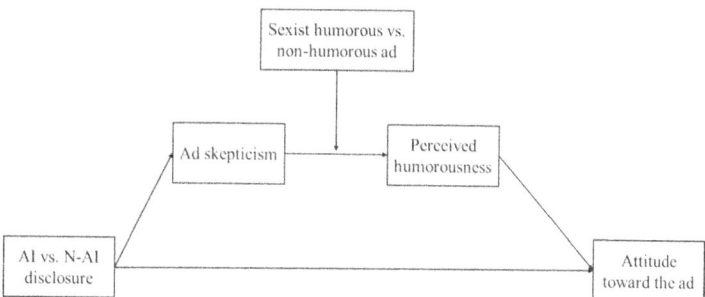

Fig. 1. Conceptual model.

3 Methodology

3.1 Sample

This study examines Generation Z's reactions to sexist humorous ads under AI or non-AI disclosure conditions. Given the specificity and challenges associated with the target audience, a convenience sampling approach was initially employed, followed by the snowball sampling technique to expand participation. A total of 263 Gen Z individuals—the majority being undergraduate students—completed a questionnaire designed in Qualtrics. After excluding 44 participants due to invalid responses or completion times of less than four minutes, the final sample comprised 219 individuals (38.4% male, 61.6% female) born between 1997 and 2007 ($M = 2003$, $SD = 1.5$). The average questionnaire completion time was 675.52 s.

3.2 Study Design and Procedure

We conducted an online experiment using a 2 (AI disclosure: AI vs. human-created) × 2 (type of ad: non-humorous vs. sexist humorous) between-subjects design for a fictitious headphone brand (see Fig. 2). The experimental stimuli consisted of four variations of a DigiVerse headphones advertisement, systematically manipulated along two dimensions: source disclosure (AI vs. human) and humor (non-humorous vs. sexist humorous). In the AI condition, an "AI" label was included to indicate that the advertisement was machine-generated, whereas in the human-created condition, an "N-AI" label was used. Both labels were designed in orange, a neutral yet attention-grabbing color, ensuring that participants noticed the disclosure without associating it with positive or negative connotations. Humor was manipulated through the tagline; the humorous version read, "So you don't have to hear her!" suggesting that the headphones could help the user ignore conversations, incorporating a gendered, potentially sexist undertone. The non-humorous version used "For high-quality listening!" emphasizing product features. All the participants were randomly allocated to one of four identical self-reported online questionnaires.

All four versions of the static ad were pre-tested with 46 Gen Z undergraduate students, who did not participate in the final experiment. The goal of the pre-test was to ensure the successful manipulation of sexist humor, perceived humorousness, and AI vs. non-AI disclosure. Participants evaluated the ads based on perceived humorousness [31], perceived sexism, and perceived AI-generated content. The pre-test results confirmed that the sexist humorous ad was perceived as more sexist than the non-humorous ad ($t(12.49) = -2.751$, $p = .017$) and that the AI-labeled ad was perceived as AI-generated to a greater extent than the non-AI version ($t(21) = -4.562$, $p < .001$). Additionally, while the sexist humorous ad was rated as more humorous than the non-humorous version, this difference was not statistically significant ($t(21) = -0.043$, $p = .356$). This may be attributed to the sample composition (74% female, 26% male), as prior research suggests that women may have lower perceived humorousness in sexist ads targeting their gender. Despite this, manipulation was considered successful.

Stimulus	Copy in English

Non-AI disclosure condition & Non-humorous ad

ΓΙΑ ΑΚΡΟΑΣΗ ΥΨΗΛΗΣ ΠΟΙΟΤΗΤΑΣ!

Με προηγμένη τεχνολογία ακύρωσης θορύβου, καθαρό ήχο υψηλής ποιότητας και άνετη εφαρμογή, τα ακουστικά DigiVerse είναι ιδανικά για να απολαμβάνεις τη μουσική σου κάθε στιγμή.

DIGIVERSE

FOR HIGH-QUALITY LISTENING!
With advanced noise-canceling technology, clear high-quality sound, and a sleek design, DigiVerse headphones are ideal for enjoying your music anytime.

AI disclosure condition & Disparaging humorous ad

ΓΙΑ ΝΑ ΜΗΝ ΤΗΝ ΑΚΟΥΣ!

Με προηγμένη τεχνολογία ακύρωσης θορύβου, καθαρό ήχο υψηλής ποιότητας και άνετη εφαρμογή, τα ακουστικά DigiVerse είναι ιδανικά για να απολαμβάνεις τη μουσική σου κάθε στιγμή.

DIGIVERSE

SO YOU DON'T HAVE TO HEAR HER!
With advanced noise-canceling technology, clear high-quality sound, and a sleek design, DigiVerse headphones are ideal for enjoying your music anytime

Fig. 2. Examples of experimental stimuli.

3.3 Measures

For AI disclosure, participants were first presented with an introductory text explaining the meaning of the AI disclosure logos, clarifying that "AI" indicated an ad created by AI, while "N-AI" signified human-created content. To ensure comprehension, they were asked a multiple-choice question to select the correct interpretation of the logos. Participants who provided an incorrect response and did not understand the AI disclosure were excluded from the study.

All continuous variables in this experiment were measured using 5-point Likert scales. Attitude toward the ad was assessed using a six-item scale [32] ($\alpha = .86$), with items such as "I liked this ad." Ad skepticism was measured using a three-item bipolar scale (e.g., This ad was (1) = non-deceptive to (5) = deceptive) from Hossain and Saini [33] ($\alpha = .723$), which specifically captures advertising skepticism. Given the multiple ways to assess persuasion knowledge identified by Eisend and Tarrahi [11], we selected this concise scale to accommodate Generation Z's lower likelihood of completing lengthy questionnaires. Perceived humorousness was evaluated using a four-item scale [31] (α = .889), including statements such as "This ad was funny."

For manipulation checks, perceived AI-created content and perceived sexism were measured using bipolar single-item scales. Participants rated the extent to which they believed the advertisement was AI-generated on a scale from (1) human-created to (5) AI-created, and perceived sexism on a scale from (1) non-sexist to (5) sexist. Product seeking, frequency of AI use, ad familiarity, and brand familiarity were also measured as potential covariates.

4 Results

4.1 Manipulation Checks

Manipulation checks confirmed that participants recognized the AI-generated advertisements when an AI disclosure was present ($M = 4.45$), whereas they perceived the ads with no AI disclosure as human-created ($M = 1.38$; $t(191.88) = -20.957$, $p < .001$). Additionally, sexist humorous stimuli were rated as more sexist ($M = 2.71$) compared to non-humorous stimuli ($M = 1.5$; $t(176.37) = -6.645$, $p < .001$) and were also perceived as more humorous ($M = 2.36$) than non-humorous ones ($M = 1.85$; $t(189.23) = -3.974$, $p < .001$). These results confirm the effectiveness of the manipulations.

4.2 Normality Tests and Inferential Statistics

None of the dependent variables followed a normal distribution, as indicated by the Kolmogorov-Smirnov test ($D_{sexist}(219) = .329$, $p < .001$; $D_{humor}(219) = .131$, $p < .001$; $D_{skepticism}(219) = .093$, $p < .001$; $D_{ad\_attitude}(219) = .089$, $p < .001$). However, given that the sample size (N = 219) exceeds 200, the Central Limit Theorem suggests that deviations from normality are less problematic, allowing for valid statistical [34].

Regardless of the experimental condition, acknowledgment of the source as AI showed a positive statistically significant correlation with ad skepticism ($r(219) = .325$, $p < .001$) and a negative statistically significant correlation with ad attitude ($r(219) = -.162$, $p = .017$). Ad skepticism also had a negative statistically significant correlation with perceived humorousness ($r(219) = -.178$, $p = .008$) and ad attitude ($r(219) = -.451$, $p < .001$), and a positive statistically significant correlation with perceived sexism ($r(219) = .321$, $p < .001$). Ad attitude, the primary outcome variable, correlated positively only with ad familiarity ($r(219) = .186$, $p = .006$) (see Table 1). Thus, ad familiarity was included as a covariate in subsequent analyses. Additionally, there was no statistically significant gender difference regarding AI acknowledgment ($t(217) = -.883$, $p = .378$). However, statistically significant gender differences emerged for ad skepticism ($t(217) = -3.067$, $p < .001$), perceived humorousness ($t(143.07) = 4.027$, $p < .001$), perceived sexism ($t(213.5) = -2.776$, $p = .006$), and ad attitude ($t(217) = 2.656$, $p = .008$). Specifically, males reported higher perceived humorousness and ad attitude, while females demonstrated higher ad skepticism and perceived sexism. Although gender appears important, a detailed analysis of gender differences lies outside the scope of this research. Thus, gender was also included as a covariate. Finally, although beyond the study's scope, the interaction between AI disclosure and ad type was not statistically significant for ad skepticism ($\beta = -.031$, $p = .636$), perceived humorousness ($\beta = -.042$, $p = .510$), and ad attitude ($\beta = -.045$, $p = .386$).

4.3 Hypotheses Testing

To test the research hypotheses, Model 91 of the PROCESS macro [35] was employed, with ad attitude as the dependent variable, AI disclosure as the independent variable, ad skepticism, and perceived humorousness as mediators, ad type (sexist humorous vs. non-humorous) as the moderator, and gender and ad familiarity as covariates. AI disclosure positively influences ad skepticism ($\beta = .196$, $p = .003$). In turn, ad skepticism negatively affects perceived humorousness ($\beta = -.168$, $p = .009$), while sexist humorous ads lead to a higher level of perceived humorousness ($\beta = .283$, $p < .001$). Additionally, the interaction between ad skepticism and ad type has a statistically significant effect on perceived humorousness ($\beta = -.176$, $p = .004$). More specifically, in the case of sexist humorous ads, ad skepticism has a significant negative effect on perceived humorousness ($\beta = -.348$, $p < .001$). However, in non-humorous ads, ad skepticism does not significantly affect perceived humorousness ($\beta = .003$, $p = .971$) (Fig. 3). Furthermore, AI disclosure does not have a statistically significant direct effect on ad attitude ($\beta = .034$, $p = .387$). However, ad skepticism negatively impacts ad attitude ($\beta = -.281$, $p < .001$), whereas perceived humorousness has a positive effect on ad attitude ($\beta = .412$, $p < .001$) (Table 2). Finally, the total index of the moderated mediation analysis at a 95% bootstrap confidence interval is statistically significant (B $= -.028$, SE $= .014$, 95% CI $= [-.06, -.006]$) only for sexist humorous ads (Table 3).

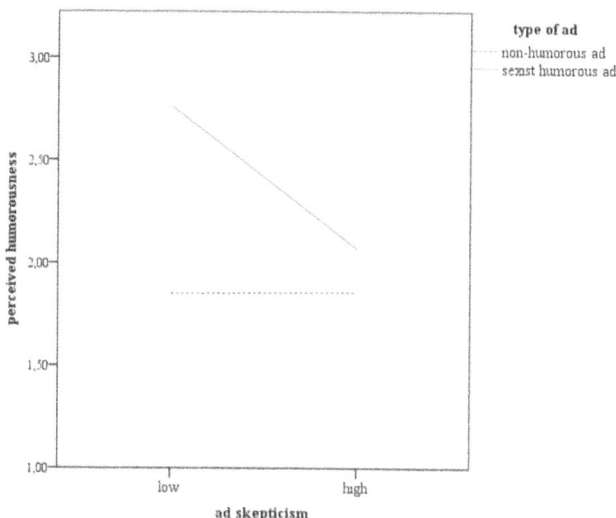

Fig. 3. Interaction effect.

Table 1. Correlation matrix.

Variable	1	2	3	4	5	6	7	8	9
1. AI acknowledgment									
2. ad skepticism	.325**								
3. Perceived humor	−.075	−.178**							
4. Perceived sexist	.030	.321**	−.012						
5. ad attitude	−.162*	−.451**	.585**	−.186**					
6. Birth year	−.011	.142*	−.231**	.009	−.068				
7. ad familiarity	-.021	−.100	.098	−.047	.186**	−.101			
8. Brand familiarity	−.070	−.092	.171*	.009	.104	.040	.109		
9. AI frequency use	−.109	−.046	.006	−.061	.004	.159*	.091	.127	
10. Product seeking	−.026	.013	−.081	.023	.053	.137*	−.002	.015	−.052

Note. **p < .001; *p < .05; AI acknowledgment: (1) source = human to (5) source = AI

Table 2. Hierarchical Regression Analysis (via PROCESS).

Variable	B	SE	t-value	p-value	LLCI	ULCI
DV: ad skepticism						
constant	−.542	.250	−2.169	.031	−1.034	−.049
AI disclosure	.196	.066	2.986	.003	.067	.325
gender (1M/2F)	.405	.134	3.030	.003	.142	.669
ad familiarity	−.078	.070	−1.115	.266	−.215	.060
DV: perceived humorousness						
constant	2.765	.231	11.950	.000	2.309	3.221
AI disclosure	−.003	.061	−.051	.959	−.124	.118
ad skepticism	−.168	.064	−2.636	.009	−.294	−.042
type of ad	.283	.061	4.632	.000	.162	.403
ad skepticism X type of ad	−.176	.061	−2.886	.004	−.296	−.056
gender (1M/2F)	−.451	.125	−3.593	.000	−.698	−.203
ad familiarity	.063	.064	.987	.325	−.063	.190
DV: ad attitude						
constant	1.595	.187	8.548	.000	1.227	1.963
AI disclosure	.034	.039	.867	.387	−.043	.111
ad skepticism	−.281	.040	−7.022	.000	−.360	−.202
perceived humorousness	.412	.041	10.069	.000	.332	.493
gender (1M/2F)	.072	.082	.874	.383	−.090	.234
ad familiarity	.085	.041	2.075	.039	.004	.166

Table 3. Moderated mediation analysis.

Mediation effect	B	SE	LLCI	ULCI
AI disclosure -- > ad attitude	.034	.039	−.043	.111
AI disclosure -- > ad skepticism -- > ad attitude	−.055	.020	−.095	−.018
AI disclosure -- > perceived humorousness -- > ad attitude	−.001	.025	−.050	.047
AI disclosure -- > ad skepticism -- > perceived humorousness -- > ad attitude (for non-humorous ad)	.000	.007	−.013	.014
AI disclosure -- > ad skepticism -- > perceived humorousness -- > ad attitude (for sexist humorous ad)	−.028	.014	−.060	−.006

Discussion

This study explores how AI disclosure, ad skepticism, and humor perception influence consumer attitudes toward advertisements, particularly in the context of sexist humorous versus non-humorous ads. The results highlight that AI disclosure increases skepticism, meaning that when consumers are aware that an ad is AI-generated, they tend to question its credibility more. This skepticism, in turn, reduces the perceived humorousness of the ad, especially when the ad contains sexist humor. Interestingly, while sexist humorous ads are generally perceived as more humorous than non-humorous ads, this effect weakens when skepticism is high. In contrast, skepticism does not significantly impact humor perception in non-humorous ads. This suggests that skepticism can interfere with effectiveness when an ad relies on humor, particularly controversial humor.

4.4 Theoretical Contributions

This study advances the literature at the intersection of AI disclosure, disparaging humorous advertising (DHA), and human-to-machine (H2M) communication, focusing on persuasive technologies. First, the relationship between DHA and persuasion knowledge—particularly advertising skepticism—has received limited attention in the literature. In a bibliometric literature review, Voutsa [27] identified key research areas on DHA, including cross-cultural differences, audience characteristics, and the role of perceived humor. However, no studies have yet examined AI disclosure or consumer perceptions of AI in the context of DHA. Additionally, research on advertising skepticism within disparaging humor remains scarce. The only identified study in this domain explored brandjacking—an anti-commercial ad parody that subverts corporate or political messages to reveal underlying truths about products [36]. To our knowledge, this is the first study to examine AI disclosure and persuasion knowledge through the lens of DHA. Second, this study confirms that advertising skepticism negatively affects attitudes toward ads, reinforcing that skeptical consumers are less likely to respond favorably to advertisements. Conversely, perceived humor enhances attitude toward the ad, highlighting humor as an effective engagement tool when well-received. However, AI disclosure does not directly influence ad attitudes. This finding aligns with Baek et al. [12], who observed that while AI disclosure can undermine ad credibility, its impact varies by context. Specifically, AI-generated donation ads tend to suffer in credibility, influencing consumer attitudes toward charitable appeals. Third, AI disclosure has primarily been studied in the context of non-profit organizations. Interestingly, AI disclosure in charity advertising legitimizes synthetic ads, suggesting a growing consumer acceptance despite initial skepticism [13]. However, AI disclosure increases skepticism in for-profit advertising and negatively influences ad attitudes. This indicates that consumer trust in AI-generated content depends heavily on the ad's purpose and context. Lastly, humor and H2M communication have largely been studied [17, 18, 25, 26] through the Computers Are Social Actors (CASA) paradigm [37], which suggests that principles of human-to-human (H2H) communication also apply to human-to-machine (H2M) interactions. However, based on this study's findings, this framework does not fully apply to humor—particularly sexist humor. These results challenge the assumption that AI can effectively mimic human humor in all contexts, revealing significant differences in consumer responses to humor generated by AI versus human sources.

4.5 Practical Implications

Humor remains one of the last strongholds of H2H communication, making it essential for practitioners to exercise caution with synthetic content. Fully automating ad creation carries risks, as AI-generated humor may backfire and harm brand perception [27, 29, 30, 38, 39]. Practitioners should always review and refine AI-generated content to ensure alignment with brand values and audience expectations. These findings also have important implications for persuasive technologies like chatbots, virtual agents, and virtual influencers. AI-driven humor in these systems should be personalized to match user expectations, maintaining engagement while avoiding consumer resistance. A hybrid AI-human collaboration approach can enhance humor effectiveness, balancing authenticity with AI's efficiency. To optimize AI disclosure without compromising ad effectiveness, industry-wide efforts should focus on AI literacy education, equipping consumers with a clearer understanding of AI's role, capabilities, and risks in advertising. Research suggests that ad disclosure alone is insufficient in activating persuasion knowledge, highlighting the crucial role of consumer education in fostering transparency and trust [14]. Beyond education, establishing a unified global synthetic content logo would standardize AI disclosure across markets, helping consumers critically evaluate AI-generated content while also protecting brands from potential AI-related errors. However, AI disclaimers must be applied consistently, as selective disclosure could erode trust and raise regulatory concerns.

5 Limitations and Future Research

This study is exploratory in nature, which inherently comes with certain limitations that may serve as a foundation for future research to investigate further and address these gaps. First, the ads used in our study were not real synthetic ads but rather static images with AI disclosure. Future research should explore consumer responses to fully AI-generated ads to examine how synthetic content influences perceptions beyond disclosure alone and the role of the source's perceptions of credibility [15]. Additionally, future research could extend beyond AI vs. non-AI disclosure to explore the level of human involvement in decision-making. This includes human-only decisions, AI-only decisions (where AI is fully responsible for ad creation, placement, and promotion), augmented human decisions (where a human makes the final choice with AI recommendations), and augmented AI decisions (where AI makes the final decision with human input as a reference) [40]. Understanding how perceived human–AI collaboration influences ad credibility and persuasion will be critical for designing effective persuasive technologies. Furthermore, studies could investigate the different levels of synthetic ad, distinguishing between narrow AI, generative AI, and super AI [41].

Although perceived humorousness and sexism scores were relatively low, this is a known limitation of experiments using static images, as humor often relies on dynamic elements [29, 38]. In advertising, humor intensity is often moderated to avoid negative reactions, aligning with the inverted U-shaped relationship between humor intensity and ad effectiveness. Furthermore, while our study examines sexist humor through verbal text, future research could extend this by exploring its effects in controlled (cognitive) laughter, auditory laughter (e.g., prolonged syllable duration), and body laughter (e.g., high-intensity movements), as these factors may influence perceived maliciousness and shape AI users' reactions [22].

In addition, in our study, the victim in the ad was female, reflecting a common marketing tactic [30]. Future research could examine reversed roles, exploring how audience perceptions change when a male becomes the target of humor. Future studies could investigate other forms of disparaging humor, such as racist ads, and analyze gender differences in responses to AI- vs. human-generated disparaging humor as well. Further research could also consider personality traits like gelotophobia, gelotophilia, and katagelasticism [27, 29, 38] or benevolent sexism [30] to better understand individual differences in humor perception.

Finally, this research focuses on Gen Z's perceptions, a tech-savvy group with relatively uniform AI usage and familiarity. Our convenience sample was based in Cyprus, which may limit generalizability. Future research should adopt cross-cultural and cross-generational approaches to examine variation in AI acceptance, humor perception, and ad skepticism, thereby refining the global applicability of persuasive technologies.

References

1. Wu, L., Jing Wen, T.: Understanding AI advertising from the consumer perspective. J. Advert. Res. **61**, 133–146 (2021)
2. Kim, D., Wang, Z.: Social media influencer vs. virtual influencer: the mediating role of source credibility and authenticity in advertising effectiveness within AI influencer marketing. Comput. Hum. Behav. Artif. Hum. **2** (2024)
3. ADWEEK. https://www.adweek.com/creativity/why-burger-king-is-proudly-advertising-a-moldy-disgusting-whopper/
4. Ham, C.-D., Nelson, M.R., Das, S.: How to measure persuasion knowledge. Int. J. Advert. **34**, 17–53 (2015)
5. Obermiller, C., Spangenberg, E.R.: Development of a scale to measure consumer skepticism toward advertising. J. Consum. Psychol. **7**, 159–186 (1998)

6. Jing Wen, T., Kim, E., Wu, L., Dodoo, N.A.: Activating persuasion knowledge in native advertising: the influence of cognitive load and disclosure language. Int. J. Advert. **39**, 74–93 (2020)
7. Chen, Y., Wang, H., Rao Hill, S., Li, B.: Consumer attitudes toward AI-generated ads: Appeal types, self-efficacy and AI's social role. J. Bus. Res. **185** (2024)
8. Euromonitor International. https://www.euromonitor.com/article/future-of-consumption-unlocking-gen-z-behaviour
9. Wang, Z., Yuan, R., Luo, J., Liu, M.J., Yannopoulou, N.: Does personalized advertising have their best interests at heart? A quantitative study of narcissists' SNS use among Generation Z consumers. J. Bus. Res. **165** (2023)
10. Friestad, M., Wright, P.: The persuasion knowledge model: how people cope with persuasion attempts. J. Consum. Res. **21**, 1–31 (1994)
11. Eisend, M., Tarrahi, F.: Persuasion knowledge in the marketplace: a meta-analysis. J. Consum. Psychol. **32**, 3–22 (2021)
12. Baek, T.H., Kim, J., Kim, J.H.: Effect of disclosing AI-generated content on prosocial advertising evaluation. Int. J. Advertising 1–22 (2024)
13. Arango, L., Singaraju, S.P., Niininen, O.: Consumer responses to AI-generated charitable giving ads. J. Advert. **52**, 486–503 (2023)
14. Jung, A.R., Heo, J.: Ad disclosure vs. ad recognition: how persuasion knowledge influences native advertising evaluation. J. Interact. Advertising **19**, 1–14 (2019)
15. Isaac, M.S., Grayson, K.: Priming skepticism: Unintended consequences of one-sided persuasion knowledge access. Psychol. Mark. **37**, 466–478 (2019)
16. Evans, N.J., Park, D.: Rethinking the persuasion knowledge model: schematic antecedents and associative outcomes of persuasion knowledge activation for covert advertising. J. Curr. Issues Res. Advertising **36**, 157–176 (2015)
17. Tay, B.T.C., Low, S.C., Ko, K.H., Park, T.: Types of humor that robots can play. Comput. Hum. Behav. **60**, 19–28 (2016)
18. Van Pinxteren, M.M.E., Pluymaekers, M., Lemmink, J.G.A.M.: Human-like communication in conversational agents: a literature review and research agenda. J. Serv. Manag. **31**, 203–225 (2020)
19. Joshi, N.N.: Evaluating human perception and bias in AI-generated humor. In: Proceedings of the 1st Workshop on Computational Humor (CHum), pp. 79–87 (Year)
20. Mirnig, N., Stadler, S., Stollnberger, G., Giuliani, M., Tscheligi, M.: Robot humor: how self-irony and Schadenfreude influence people's rating of robot likability. In: 2016 25th IEEE International Symposium on Robot and Human Interactive Communication (RO-MAN), pp. 166–171. IEEE, (Year)
21. Oliveira, R., Arriaga, P., Axelsson, M., Paiva, A.: Humor-robot interaction: a scoping review of the literature and future directions. Int. J. Soc. Robot. **13**, 1369–1383 (2020)
22. Ruch, W.F., et al.: Gelotophobia and the challenges of implementing laughter into virtual agents interactions. Front. Hum. Neurosci. **8**, 928 (2014)
23. Hofmann, J., Platt, T., Ruch, W., Niewiadomski, R., Urbain, J.: The influence of a virtual companion on amusement when watching funny films. Motiv. Emot. **39**, 434–447 (2015)
24. Platt, T., Hofmann, J., Ruch, W., Niewiadomski, R., Urbain, J.: Experimental standards in research on AI and humor when considering psychology. In: AAAI Fall Symposium: Artificial Intelligence of Humor (Year)
25. Mou, Y., Xu, K.: The media inequality: Comparing the initial human-human and human-AI social interactions. Comput. Hum. Behav. **72**, 432–440 (2017)
26. Hong, J.-W., Choi, S., Williams, D.: Sexist AI: an experiment integrating CASA and ELM. Int. J. Hum. Comput. Interact. **36**, 1928–1941 (2020)
27. Voutsa, M.C.: Disparaging humorous advertising: A bibliometric review. J. Mark. Commun. 1–25 (2024)

28. Mayer, J.M., Kumar, P., Yoon, H.J.: Does sexual humor work on mars, but not on Venus? An exploration of consumer acceptance of sexually humorous advertising. Humor Advertising 92–116. Routledge (2021)

29. Hatzithomas, L., Voutsa, M.C., Boutsouki, C., Zotos, Y.: A superiority–inferiority hypothesis on disparagement humor: the role of disposition toward ridicule. J. Consum. Behav. **20**, 923–941 (2021)

30. Grougiou, V., Balabanis, G., Manika, D.: Does humour influence perceptions of the ethicality of female-disparaging advertising? J. Bus. Ethics **164**, 1–16 (2018)

31. Zhang, Y.: The effect of humor in advertising: an individual-difference perspective. Psychol. Mark. **13**, 531–545 (1996)

32. Baker, S.M., Kennedy, P.F.: Death by nostalgia: a diagnosis of context-specific cases. Adv. Consumer Res. **21** (1994)

33. Hossain, M.T., Saini, R.: Suckers in the morning, skeptics in the evening: time-of-Day effects on consumers' vigilance against manipulation. Mark. Lett. **25**, 109–121 (2014)

34. Field, A.: Discovering statistics using IBM SPSS statistics. Sage publications limited (2024)

35. Hayes, A.F.: Partial, conditional, and moderated moderated mediation: quantification, inference, and interpretation. Commun. Monogr. **85**, 4–40 (2018)

36. Thota, S.C.: What is brandjacking? Origin, conceptualization and effects of perceived dimensions of truth, mockery and offensiveness. Int. J. Advert. **40**, 292–310 (2021)

37. Nass, C., Fogg, B.J., Moon, Y.: Can computers be teammates? Int. J. Hum. Comput. Stud. **45**, 669–678 (1996)

38. Voutsa, M.C., Hatzithomas, L., Tsichla, E., Boutsouki, C.: Face reading the emotions of gelotophobes toward disparaging humorous advertising. Eur. J. Humour Res. **10**, 88–112 (2022)

39. Karpinska-Krakowiak, M.: Gotcha! Realism of comedic violence and its impact on brand responses: what's so funny about that bloody ad? The moderating role of disposition to laughter. J. Advert. Res. **60**, 38–53 (2020)

40. Zhang, Y., Gosline, R.: Human favoritism, not AI aversion: People's perceptions (and bias) toward generative AI, human experts, and human–GAI collaboration in persuasive content generation. Judgment Decis. Making **18** (2023)

41. Huang, M.-H., Rust, R.T.: A strategic framework for artificial intelligence in marketing. J. Acad. Mark. Sci. **49**, 30–50 (2021)

Poster Presentations

Evaluating and Influencing Strategy in Real-Time: Example of a Collaborative Strategy Game

Marie Morelle-Gerritsen[1,2,3], Damien Marion[2], Julien Cegarra[4], Hélène Unrein[3], Théodore Letouzé[3], and Jean-Marc André[3(✉)]

[1] University of Bordeaux, 351 Cours de la Libération, 33400 Talence, France
marie.morelle@ensc.fr
[2] THALES LAS France, 1 bis rue Louis Braille, 35136 Saint Jacques de la Lande, France
[3] IMS Laboratory, 109 Avenue Roul, 33400 Talence, France
jean-marc.andre@ensc.fr
[4] Champollion National University Institute, Place de Verdun, 81000 Albi, France

Abstract. This research explores real-time strategy evaluation in crisis management using the collaborative game Hellapagos. Situational awareness, as defined by Endsley, is central to this research, focusing on detecting early cues to anticipate situational changes. Using a decision tree methodology inspired by the ANTICIPE planning and decision-support software, the study aims at automatically identifying the player's dominant strategy from four types: individualistic, pragmatic, collaborative and irrational. The goal is to assess the methodology's ability to identify a situation, track its evolution in real-time and suggest appropriate tactics to guide the situation in the chosen direction. While the decision tree has been developed and validated with preliminary results presented, tests on real-time strategy identification are still ongoing.

Keywords: Situational Awareness · decision support tools · real-time strategy assessment · influence

1 Introduction

1.1 Situational Awareness and Crisis Management

Endsley [1] defines Situational Awareness (SA) as "the perception of elements in the environment within a volume of time and space, the comprehension of their meaning, and the projection of their status in the near future". Prébot [2] emphasizes that a sufficient level of SA is crucial for anticipating changes and adapting decisions accordingly. Endsley [1] outlines three levels of SA: perceiving environmental information, comprehending its meaning, and the projecting its short-term evolution.

This study focuses on situation comprehension, detecting early clues of situational change. It aims to develop a persuasion system that uses suggestions and self-monitoring [3] to recommend justified corrective actions aligned with the user's desired outcome.

© The Author(s), under exclusive license to Springer Nature Switzerland AG 2026
I. Wiafe et al. (Eds.): PERSUASIVE 2025, CCIS 2542, pp. 89–93, 2026.
https://doi.org/10.1007/978-3-031-97177-8_7

1.2 Aim of the Study

This study evaluates real-time strategy implementation in crisis management using the semi-collaborative game Hellapagos [4]. Clear and concise situational updates are crucial for decision-makers to make rapid choices based on reliable and relevant information. Leveraging the ANTICIPE planning and decision-support software developed by THALES for Command & Control, we aim to extend its methodology to various applications to enhance and accelerate decision-making. The software uses a three-level decision tree to detect situational change through data-mining on the surveillance points at the tree's lowest level (cues) and proposes actions to address identified issues [5].

The study has two primary goals: 1) assess whether this decision tree methodology can objectively detect and identify strategies and their changes in real-time by monitoring predefined cues; 2) test the feasibility of orienting a player's strategy using pre-conceived messages.

2 Study Methodology

In Hellapagos, shipwrecked survivors on a desert island must build a raft to escape, managing limited food and water supplies. Players choose actions between fishing, collecting water or gathering wood. Teamwork is essential, but players may need to sacrifice crew members in times of scarcity. We modified the rules to include systematic card draws, where players look at a card before deciding to keep it or discard it and collect resources instead. This offers better insight into player strategies, as cards can have individualistic, pragmatic or collaborative effects.

2.1 Developing the Decision Tree

The first stage of this study involved listing game strategies and significant player actions, mapping actions to corresponding strategies. We conducted focus sessions with five expert Hellapagos players and studied games. After identifying the possible strategies based on their own experience, the experts played with different game scenarios and assigned roles to determine which actions were significant to identify each strategy.

We identified four main strategy types: individualistic (prioritizing personal survival), pragmatic (ensuring group survival if possible, if not oneself), collaborative (prioritizing group survival), or irrational (illogical actions benefiting no one). Actions considered include gameplay decisions, information sharing, cards kept or discarded and eliminating another player. The resulting decision tree has three levels: at the top, the four identified strategy types; at the bottom, cues representing significant actions, such as keeping or discarding a card, using a card for themselves or for others, collecting wood (evaluated as more significant than collecting water or food because it involves a risk for the player), voting to eliminate a specific person (including themselves); in between, a level that groups actions into a particular identified player trait, for example being dishonest, self-sacrificing or using cards logically. Some cues can indicate several strategies depending on context: when a cue is ambiguous, other detected cues can specify which strategy is dominant. Each cue has a weight reflecting its significance in the trait it is linked to. For example, using the revolver card strongly indicates individualistic behavior but can also reflect pragmatism if it benefits group survival: it is thus linked to an individualistic trait with a high weight and to a pragmatic trait with a lower weight. When enough cues are detected, the trait is triggered and a percentage of activation is assigned to each strategy based on the number and weight of associated cues. A result might be 70% individualistic and 30% pragmatic.

2.2 Validating and Refining the Decision Tree

The second stage aims to validate the decision tree developed in the first stage. Three groups of four experienced players played a game without knowing the initial hypotheses about possible strategies. Their only instruction was to "leave the island", which they could interpret as winning alone or with the group. We then conducted collective interviews with each group to identify strategies as well as the reasoning behind each action. Participants also completed personality [6], metacognitive [7] and decision-making style [8] questionnaires, along with a questionnaire about their ideal initial set of cards.

The questionnaire about the ideal set of cards, game observations and interviews allowed us to confirm the four strategy types and refine the decision tree. Notably, the assumption that individualistic players would collect less wood was not confirmed, as action choices were rather influenced by the cards in hand. This cue was removed from the decision tree. While individualistic players did keep and use individualistic cards, collaborative cards were used by all players, contradicting another assumption.

In a last validation step, expert players played games with random card draws and assigned strategies. Cues in the decision tree were selected based on these games to verify if the system could detect the assigned strategy.

A preliminary prediction model of player strategy, based on personality, metacognitive, and decision-making style questionnaires, was developed but requires further validation. The questionnaires calculate scores of different traits of the participant, some of which may predict their strategy. If confirmed, the scores could be added as new cues and traits in the decision tree, providing initial insight into a player's strategy.

2.3 Attempting to Identify and Influence Strategy in Real-Time

This final stage is currently being prepared. It aims to determine if the decision tree methodology can effectively identify player strategies and real-time changes.

Participants complete the same questionnaires as in the previous stage, to further develop the potential strategy prediction model based on their profiles. They then play several games on a digital version of the game with two simulated players, one collaborative and one individualistic, controlled by an experimenter following strict rules about the cards to keep or play and actions to take. Participants believe they are playing with other participants to avoid authority bias. During the games, a software implementing the decision tree receives real-time information from the game and selects corresponding cues; the cues that cannot be deduced logically are selected manually. Players communicate via in-game chat, which also delivers messages indicated as "coming from a social network offering seemingly relevant information to improve game-play". Initially neutral, these messages are directed to attempt to influence the player during the last two games towards a strategy opposite to the one observed with the decision tree. A self-confrontation interview [9] follows to confirm or refute strategy assessments and evaluate the influence messages' effectiveness. We also assess whether the experimenter's choices and communication during the game affected the participant's decisions and check for potential bias.

Post-experiment, the player's strategy is evaluated using their "ideal initial set of cards" questionnaire answers, debriefing questionnaires on group dynamics and personal goals, and interview responses. If the deduced strategy aligns with the system's findings, the system will be considered validated.

3 Prospects for This Principle of Situation Assessment Using a Decision Tree

3.1 Benefits of the Methodology

This methodology, which tracks weak signals across predefined monitoring points, seems to have potential for broader applications. For example, the concept could be adapted for sports strategy and training, energy consumption, skills development or investment strategies, with the suggestion of actions to undertake tailored to the observed and target situation. Additionally, studying the relationship between user's psychological, metacognitive and decision-making profile and their preferred strategies could enhance the analysis. This could provide additional cues for the decision tree and suggest more effective persuasion methods tailored to general (psychological, metacognitive, decision-making) and task-specific user profile (e.g., investor profile or learning preferences).

3.2 Steps to Adapt the System

Adapting the system to a new use involves two main steps. First, develop the decision tree with experts to define strategy types or user profile and identify cues reflecting each strategy. Second, identify approaches and actions to assist the user in adjusting their strategy with incentive messages adapted to their profile, the situation and targeted strategy. The data mining feature of the ANTICIPE software developed by THALES could then be reintroduced to automatically select appropriate cues in the decision tree.

4 Conclusion

This study explores the potential for real-time strategy evaluation and influence using a decision tree model within a collaborative game context. We believe that this approach could enhance situational awareness and decision-making, with potential applications in various strategic domains. Future research will aim to validate these observations and explore the model's adaptability across various contexts.

Acknowledgments. This PhD research is funded by THALES LAS France and the French Ministry of Defense - Defense Innovation Agency (AID).

Disclosure of Interests. This PhD research is funded by THALES LAS France and the French Ministry of Defense - Defense Innovation Agency (AID).

References

1. Endsley, M.R.: Toward a theory of situation awareness in dynamic systems. Hum. Factors **37**(1), 32–64 (1995)
2. Prébot, B.: Représentation partagée et travail collaboratif en contexte C2: monitoring d'opérateurs en situation simulée de command and control. Bordeaux University, PhD diss. (2020)
3. Fogg, B.J.: Chapter 3-Computers as persuasive tools. Persuasive Technol. 31-59 (2003)
4. Gigamic Hellapagos Homepage. https://www.en.gigamic-adds.com/game/hellapagos/index. Accessed 21 Feb 2025
5. NATO STO video Using artificial intelligence to enhance military decision-making. https://www.youtube.com/watch?v=A2ZAHrT3UwM. Accessed 21 Feb 2025
6. John, O.P., Donahue, E.M. and Kentle, R.L.: Big five inventory. J. Pers. Soc. Psychol. (1991)
7. Wells, A., Cartwright-Hatton, S.: A short form of the metacognitions questionnaire: properties of the MCQ-30. Behav. Res. Ther. **42**(4), 385–396 (2004)
8. Scott, S.G., Bruce, R.A.: Decision-making style: the development and assessment of a new measure. Educ. Psychol. Measur. **55**(5), 818–831 (1995)
9. Theureau, J.: Les entretiens d'autoconfrontation et de remise en situation par les traces matérielles et le programme de recherche «cours d'action». Revue d'anthropologie des connaissances **2**, 287–322 (2010)

Who Plays? The Tension Between User Autonomy and Designer Control in Gamified Systems

A Theoretical Framework - Work in Progress

Elad Orr[2]([⊠]), Ganit Richter[1,3]([⊠]) [iD], and Sheizaf Rafaeli[1,2] [iD]

[1] University of Haifa, 199 Abba Khoushy Avenue Mount Carmel, 3103301 Haifa, Israel
`grichter@univ.haifa.ac.il, sheizaf@rafaeli.net`
[2] Shenkar: Engineering, Design, Art, 12 Anne Frank Street, 5252626 Ramat Gan, Israel
`orrelad@yahoo.com`
[3] The College of Management Academic Studies, 7549071 Rishon LeTsiyon, Israel

Abstract. This study introduces a theoretical perspective for understanding gamification through the lens of autonomy transfer. Drawing on Self-Determination Theory (SDT) and game research, we propose that gamification can be viewed as a process where player autonomy shifts from the user to the system designer.

While play traditionally involves voluntary participation driven by intrinsic motivation, gamified experiences often introduce external rewards and feedback mechanisms, potentially diminishing user autonomy. This study explores the implications of this shift for user motivation, ethical concerns, and the design of persuasive technologies. Using the example of the Olympic Games as a case study, we discuss how professional sports represent a reduction in autonomy and affect intrinsic motivation. This perspective offers theoretical advancement and practical implications for designing ethical persuasive systems that balance motivation with user autonomy.

We address a gap in existing literature by explicitly focusing on the ethical implications of autonomy transfer, a concept underexplored in gamification. By offering a framework for understanding how system designers gain control over user behavior, we contribute a novel perspective to discussions on motivation, ethics, and user agency.

Keywords: Game research · Gamification · Motivation · Autonomy · Persuasive Technology · Ethics

1 Introduction

Gamification is an increasingly prevalent strategy for enhancing user engagement across sectors, such as business, education, healthcare and entertainment [1, 2]. While traditional play is characterized by voluntary participation, gamification- by integrating game mechanics into non-game contexts, often results in a reduction of user autonomy. According to Self-Determination Theory (SDT) autonomy is a core psychological

I. Wiafe et al. (Eds.): PERSUASIVE 2025, CCIS 2542, pp. 94–98, 2026.
https://doi.org/10.1007/978-3-031-97177-8_8

need necessary for intrinsic motivation [3, 4]. This study examines the process through which gamification shifts decision-making power from users to designers, often altering motivation and behavior.

Persuasive technologies are intentionally designed to shape user behavior, often incorporating gamified elements to sustain engagement. [5]. While such systems may promote positive outcomes (e.g., encouraging exercise or financial literacy), they also raise ethical concerns regarding autonomy and consent. We explore the intersection of gamification and persuasive design by analyzing how autonomy transfer impacts motivation. SDT [3], which differentiates between various motivation types, serves to highlight the transition of control from players to system designers.

In contrast to prior work that focuses primarily on motivation or engagement outcomes, this study foregrounds the control dynamics embedded in persuasive systems and how they unfold through autonomy transfer.

2 Play as an Act of Autonomy

Game scholars generally agree that play is defined by voluntary participation and intrinsic motivation [6–8]. They argue that:

- Play is released from serious needs; it is not intended for survival.
- Play is self-rewarding and not undertaken for extrinsic rewards beyond those intrinsic to the game.
- Play is voluntary and occurs under no pressure or coercion.

These principles set play apart from externally regulated activities and highlight the centrality of autonomy in the player's experience (Fig. 1).

SDT identifies autonomy as a fundamental component of motivation, alongside competence and relatedness [3, 9]. Yet, persuasive design and gamification often shift autonomy from the user to the system by introducing external incentives such as rewards, leaderboards, and push notifications [9]. For example, fitness applications like Strava or e-learning platforms like Duolingo use reward structures to encourage continued engagement. While motivating, these mechanisms can exert pressure that may gradually undermine intrinsic motivation over time.

3 Case Study: The Olympic Games and Professionalized Play

To ground the concept of autonomy transfer, we present a structured case analysis of the Olympic Games, illustrating how the transition from informal play to professional sport reflects key dynamics of autonomy loss.

Whereas informal play is self-motivated, professionalized sports, such as the Olympic Games, demonstrate how structured rules and external rewards can diminish player autonomy. The ancient Olympic Games held cultural and social significance [10], while modern Olympics are shaped by financial, social, and institutional forces. In both cases, play becomes a structured, externally regulated activity [6].

For example, running can be an autonomous and playful activity, as in chasing games or 'tag'. In contrast, Olympic running is a structured competitive event shaped by social status, expectations, and financial incentives [10]. Athletes may enjoy running, but their participation is largely driven by these external pressures. Although athletes can theoretically choose not to compete, in practice, these forces constrain that decision.

The transition from self-motivated play to high-stakes competition exemplifies how autonomy is diminished in structured systems. As Caillois' [6] noted, "clearly they are not players but workers". Though rooted in traditional play, the Olympic have evolved into a system where performance, recognition and structured incentives override voluntary participation. This pattern extends beyond sports, as illustrated next.

4   The Autonomy Transfer Framework in Gamified Systems

We propose the "Autonomy Transfer Framework" (Fig. 1) as a conceptual tool to assess how gamified systems shift decision-making power from users (voluntary play) to designer-driven control (controlled motivation). The vertical axis reflects how game elements (like rewards and rules) affect motivation. Categories include play, gamified activity, professional play, and involuntary activity.

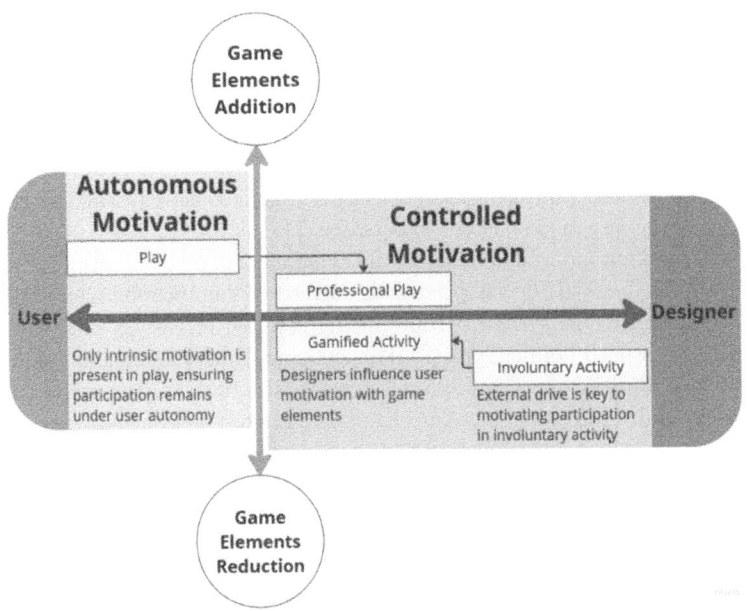

Fig. 1. Autonomy spectrum in gamified systems - from user autonomy to designer control

Gamification, as well as persuasive technologies, operate by balancing intrinsic and extrinsic motivation elements [9, 11, 12] such as scoring, rewards, and social communities to increase relatedness and competence. As intrinsic motivation declines, designers may add gamification to drive engagement. Yet, once users opt in, designers gain behavioral control via mechanics such as notifications, feedback loops, and engagement algorithms, gradually transferring autonomy from the player to the system. Indicators include external rewards, nudges, habit loops, and reduced choice. Identifying these patterns can support empirical evaluation of user autonomy.

Autonomy represents a form of power distribution [12]. As users lose autonomy, designers gain influence over behavior, raising ethical concerns about the limits of persuasive design. Table 1 outlines autonomy across activity types, designer influence and key indicators (system characteristics).

Table 1. Autonomy transfer in gamified systems - from player choice to system control

Activity Type	User/player experience	Designer influence	Indicators
Voluntary play	Full autonomy, intrinsic motivation, playful	Minimal - user-initiated activity	No external rewards, no external goals
Gamified engagement	Semi-voluntary, mixed motivations	Moderate - rewards, nudges, leaderboards	Notifications, points, progress bars
Persuasive control	Reduced autonomy, external pressure	High - behavior shaping design	Habit loops, social pressure, limited choice
Involuntary activity	Little / no autonomy, obligation to perform	Maximal - system dictates behavior	Mandatory tasks, penalties, fixed goals

5 Ethical Implications and Design Considerations

Gamification blends play with external incentives. While this can enhance engagement, it also raises ethical concerns related to autonomy and consent, especially when used with vulnerable populations [13]. Autonomy is often where users and designers diverge most: users prefer to maintain control, while designers aim to sustain participation. This tension arises as designers aim to maximize engagement without entirely undermining autonomy, pushing the boundaries between persuasion and control.

Autonomy loss is often masked by playful design and rewarding feedback. In this sense, users who "opt in" to play may, paradoxically, be the ones being played. Some researchers argue that excessive gamification can cross ethical lines, becoming manipulative or even abusive [12]. At some point, users may realize that their autonomy has diminished, even when their needs for relatedness or competence are being met.

Ethical design should inform users of persuasive mechanisms, allow customization of preferences, support autonomy, competence, and relatedness, and assess autonomy transfer, including opt-out mechanisms and adaptable rewards.

6 Conclusion and Future Research

The autonomy transfer framework, grounded in self-determination theory, offers a novel lens for understanding gamification. It invites researchers and designers to locate their system along the autonomy spectrum and consider how to promote ethical design practices. Future research will examine how varying autonomy levels affect user motivation and engagement. While the model offers conceptual clarity, it also faces limitations—particularly in measuring autonomy. By exploring the nuanced balance between autonomy and engagement, this work can contribute to the development of practical tools that respect user agencies while achieving design goals.

References

1. Deterding, S., Dixon, D., Khaled, R., Nacke, L.: From game design elements to gamefulness: defining gamification. In: Proceedings of the 15th International Academic MindTrek Conference: Envisioning Future Media Environments, pp. 9–15. ACM, New York, NY, USA (2011)
2. Richter, G., Raban, D.R., Rafaeli, S.: Tailoring a points scoring mechanism for crowd-based knowledge pooling. In: 51st Hawaii International Conference on System Sciences, pp. 1128–1137 (2018)
3. Deci, E.L., Ryan, R.M.: Self-determination theory: a macrotheory of human motivation, development, and health. Can. Psychol. **49**, 182–185 (2008)
4. Ryan, R.M., Rigby, C.S., Przybylski, A.K.: The motivational pull of video games: a self-determination theory approach. Motiv. Emot. **30**, 347–363 (2006)
5. Vaijayanthi, I., Marur, M.: Persuasive design for energy saving behavior through social gaming. In: Ramírez, E.R. (ed.) Design and Semantics of Form and Movement (DeSForM) Conference, pp. 33–42 (2012)
6. Caillois, R., Barash, M.: Man, play, and games. Univ of Illinois Pr (2001)
7. Dissanayake, E.: A hypothesis of the evolution of art from play. Leonardo **7**, 211 (1974). https://doi.org/10.2307/1572893
8. Huizinga, J.: Homo Ludens Ils 86. Routledge (2014)
9. Richter, G., Raban, D.R., Rafaeli, S.: Studying Gamification: The Effect of Rewards and Incentives on Motivation. In: Reiners, T., Wood, L. (eds.) Gamification in Education and Business, pp. 21–46. Springer, Cham (2015)
10. Allen, D.W., Lantinova, V.: The ancient olympics as a signal of city-state strength. Econ. Governance **14**, 23–44 (2013). https://doi.org/10.1007/s10101-012-0119-5
11. Deterding, S.: Gamification: designing for motivation. Interactions **19**, 14–17 (2012)
12. Fuchs, M., Fizek, S., Ruffino, P., Schrape, N. eds: Rethinking Gamification. meson press, Hybrid Publishing Lab, Leuphana University of Lüneburg, Germany (2014). https://doi.org/10.14619/001
13. Packin, N.G.: Financial Inclusion Gone Wrong: Securities and Crypto Assets Trading For Children. Hastings Law Journal (2024)

Tailoring Gamification in Mobility-as-a-Service Apps

Célia Vancaemelbecke(✉) ⓘ, Céline Lemercier ⓘ, and Loïc Caroux ⓘ

CLLE Laboratory, University of Toulouse and CNRS, Toulouse, France
celia.vancaemelbecke@univ-tlse2.fr

Abstract. Gamification, the use of game elements in non-game contexts, has been widely studied in education, but its impact on Mobility-as-a-Service (MaaS) apps is less understood. While research suggests that gamification can enhance the intention to use MaaS, its effectiveness in sustaining long-term engagement seems limited. Tailoring gamification to users appears to be a promising start to sustain engagement and motivation. Moreover, some studies highlight hedonic motivation as a key predictor of intention to use MaaS. In our experimental study ($n = 159$ participants), we examined how tailored gamification influences intention to use MaaS, with hedonic motivation as a mediator. Participants were either in a coherent tailoring condition (i.e., matched to the participants' Hexad profile) or an incoherent condition. The results showed that tailored gamification significantly increased hedonic motivation but did not directly or indirectly affect intention to use MaaS. However, hedonic motivation itself did directly predict intention. We conclude that tailored gamification is promising, but further research is needed to refine its implementation.

Keywords: Gamification · Mobility-as-a-Service · Intention to Use

1 Introduction

Gamification refers to the use of game-like elements in non-game contexts, and its potential to enhance user engagement and performance has been widely explored in domains such as education and environmental awareness [4, 8]. Several studies highlighted positive effects of gamification [3, 11], while others pointed to negligible or even adverse outcomes due to pointsification [8], which is the overuse of points as game elements, and the over-justification effect [5]. The over-justification effect appears when intrinsically motivated users experience a decline in motivation due to expectation of extrinsic rewards. To address these challenges, scholars have increasingly emphasized the value of tailored gamification, which customizes game elements based on user profiles [19]. Studies have shown that tailoring gamification can improve user engagement and performance [16].

The HEXAD model [17], built on Self-Determination Theory [14], classifies individuals into six gamification player types: Achievers, Players, Free Spirits, Disruptors, Philanthropists, and Socializers. Studies demonstrated that tailoring game elements based

I. Wiafe et al. (Eds.): PERSUASIVE 2025, CCIS 2542, pp. 99–103, 2026.
https://doi.org/10.1007/978-3-031-97177-8_9

on HEXAD profiles improves motivation and engagement by aligning with basic psychological needs [9]. Competence (i.e., the need to feel effective), autonomy (i.e., the need to have control), and relatedness (i.e., the need to feel connected to others) are key motivators for Achievers, and are therefore more attracted to challenges and levels game elements [10]. Meanwhile, Players are primarily driven by extrinsic rewards like points and leaderboards. Tailored gamification strategies have the potential to enhance hedonic motivation. Hedonic motivation is an intrinsic factor defined as the enjoyment derived from using a technology-based system [18]. It is a key predictor of behavioral intention in technology use models, and particularly in intention to use Mobility-as-a-Service (MaaS) apps [15].

In the transportation and mobility sector, MaaS platforms have begun integrating gamification to promote sustainable travel behaviors [12]. However, recent studies indicated that current MaaS solutions lack sufficient user-centered design to retain users [6]. The current implementation of one-size-fits-all (OSFA) gamification in MaaS has shown mixed results [2], suggesting a need for tailored approaches [6]. Tailored gamification could play a key role in enhancing the intention to use MaaS, particularly by the indirect effect of hedonic motivation apps [15].

This study investigated whether and how tailored gamification has an effect on the intention to use MaaS solutions, and whether and how hedonic motivation mediates the relationship between tailored gamification and the intention to use MaaS solutions.

2   Method

Participants. We conducted an experimental study using a between-participants design with 170 participants categorized as either Achievers or Players according to the HEXAD model. To evaluate how tailoring game elements to player types influences hedonic motivation and intention to use, participants were randomly assigned to either a profile-coherent or profile-incoherent condition. After removing implausible data, as the study was conducted online, our final sample was of 159 participants. Almost 34% were between 26 and 34 years old, and 30% were between 18 and 25 years old. Regarding gender distribution, 64% participants identified as men.

Materials and Procedure. First, participants completed the HEXAD questionnaire to identify their player profile. We had translated the 24-item HEXAD questionnaire (Tondello et al., 2016) from English to French. As no validated French version of the HEXAD currently exists, we relied on our translation with inputs from two native English speakers. Reliability was satisfactory for most subscales, except for Free Spirit ($\alpha <$ 0.60). Participants were then introduced to the concept of MaaS through an explanation similar to previous studies.

Afterwards, they were presented with a context where they needed to act as interns working for an organization promoting street art. Their task involved visiting artists daily to sign contracts, starting from a pop-up store. This context provided the setting for the travel scenarios they would evaluate. The main task involved completing 12 fictional journeys using a dummy MaaS app, each showing two travel options that varied by transport modes, travel time, and carbon dioxide emissions. The app displayed the mode of transport, journey duration, and a non-interactive map for each option. Participants had to select between a low-carbon option and a high-carbon option for each journey. They were randomly assigned to either an Achiever-oriented or Player-oriented gamification style based on their experimental condition (i.e., coherent or incoherent to their Hexad's profile). Progress was tracked using a leveling-up system for Achievers or a leaderboard for Players. To level up or climb the leaderboard, participants needed to select at least three low-carbon options.

Afterward, they completed two questionnaires. The first one measured their intention to use MaaS and hedonic motivation, and the second one collected socio-demographic data. For hedonic motivation and intention to use MaaS, we adapted items from previous studies [15] and translated them into French. Both translated scales demonstrated very good reliability ($\alpha > 0.70$). Participants could also provide qualitative feedback if they wished at the end of the experiment. The experiment had an average duration of approximately 12 min.

3   Results and Discussion

The mediation model displayed weak variance for both hedonic motivation and intention to use, indicating that a significant portion of the variability was not explained by the model's predictors. Significant effects were found for tailored gamification on hedonic motivation and for hedonic motivation on intention to use MaaS. While the effect size of hedonic motivation on intention to use was large, the effect of tailored gamification on hedonic motivation was small. No significant direct effect of tailored gamification on intention to use MaaS was detected. Similarly, the indirect effect of tailored gamification on intention to use, mediated by hedonic motivation, was not significant. The total effect was significant, but it is likely due to the strong relationship between hedonic motivation and the intention to use MaaS. This suggests that while tailored gamification may influence hedonic motivation, its role in directly or indirectly driving MaaS adoption is limited. According to our power analysis, all significant effect sizes were higher than minimum direct effect sizes detectable with 80% of power. Conversely, the non-significant effect of tailored gamification on intention to use MaaS was lower than the minimum direct effect size detectable with 80% of power.

In sum, our results support previous findings [15] which dentified hedonic motivation as a key predictor of the intention to use MaaS. Yet, we observed that tailored gamification had only a small effect on hedonic motivation, with no direct or indirect effect on the intention to use MaaS. This last finding is contradictory to other studies who investigated the impact of gamification on intention to use in other contexts [1, 13].

The limited effect on hedonic motivation may be explained by the fact that we tailored gamification solely based on the participants' dominant player profile. Previous studies suggested that tailoring gamification should consider additional factors [7, 10]. To the best of our knowledge, no studies have yet determined which game elements are suitable for combinations of profiles. Due to technical constraints, we could not allow participants to customize the gamification themselves and had to predefine which gamified features would suit them. As a result, the proposed gamification may have been disappointing or misaligned with their preferences. Additionally, the French translation of the HEXAD scale exhibited low reliability for the Free Spirits subscale, suggesting that some Free Spirits may have been misclassified or excluded from the study.

The absence of direct and indirect effects of tailored gamification on the intention to use MaaS could also be attributed to insufficient sample size. Our initial power analysis indicated that at least 300 participants were required to detect small effects with 80% power, but we were only able to recruit 170 participants in total, with only 159 participants having plausible data. Furthermore, the low variance explained by the model suggests that factors such as perceived usefulness or ease of use may be stronger predictors. Qualitative feedback from participants revealed that the non-interactive nature of the dummy MaaS app hindered their ability to assess its usability. The lack of cost information was also highlighted as a limitation. Although the study did not focus on participants' travel choices, this missing information could have influenced their intention to use MaaS.

Overall, our study contributes to the literature on persuasive technologies, particularly on tailored gamification in MaaS applications. We provide insights into the challenges of tailoring gamification and the relevance of user typologies, such as HEXAD, for practical implementation.

Acknowledgments. We would like to thank all undergraduate students and participants who participated in this study, as well as other graduates from the CLLE laboratory who helped in pre-testing this experiment. *CV*: Conceptualization, Methodology, Data Curation, Formal analysis, Investigation, Resources, Writing – original draft, Writing – editing. *CL*: Supervision, Funding acquisition, Writing – review & editing. *LC*: Conceptualization, Methodology, Supervision, Funding acquisition, Resources, Writing – review & editing.

Disclosure of Interests. This research was carried out with the support of the French government as part of the "Territoire d'Innovation" program, an action of the "Grand Plan d'Investissment" backed by France 2030, Toulouse Métropole and the GIS neOCampus.

References

1. Anam Akhtar, M., Sarea, A., Khan, I., Khan, K.A., Singh, M.P.: The moderating role of gamification towards intentions to use mobile payments applications in Bahrain: An integrated approach. Emerald Insights (2024). https://doi.org/10.1108/prr-06-2022-0074/full/pdf
2. Avril, E., Picco, A., Lescarret, C., Lemercier, C., Arguel, A., Caroux, L.: Gamification in the transport and mobility sector: a systematic review. Transport. Res. F: Traffic Psychol. Behav. **104**, 286–302 (2024). https://doi.org/10.1016/j.trf.2024.06.004
3. Bitrián, P., Buil, I., Catalán, S.: Enhancing user engagement: the role of gamification in mobile apps. J. Bus. Res. **132**, 170–185 (2021). https://doi.org/10.1016/J.JBUSRES.2021.04.028
4. Boncu, Ş., Candel, O.S., Popa, N.L.: Gameful Green : A systematic review on the use of serious computer games and gamified mobile apps to foster pro-environmental information, attitudes and behaviors. Sustainability (Switzerland) **14**(16) (2022). https://doi.org/10.3390/su141610400
5. Dah, J., Hussin, N., Zaini, M.K., Isaac Helda, L., Senanu Ametefe, D., Adozuka Aliu, A.: Gamification is not Working : Why? Games Cult. (2024). https://doi.org/10.1177/15554120241228125

6. Douglas, B.D., Brauer, M.: Gamification to prevent climate change: a review of games and apps for sustainability. Curr. Opin. Psychol. **42**, 89–94 (2021). https://doi.org/10.1016/J.COPSYC.2021.04.008

7. Hallifax, S., Serna, A., Marty, J., Lavoué, G., Lavoué, E., Assoc Comp Machinery. Factors to Consider for Tailored Gamification (WOS:000518632600046), pp. 559-572 (2019). https://doi.org/10.1145/3311350.3347167

8. Hellberg, A.S., Moll, J.: A point with pointsification ? Clarifying and separating pointsification from gamification in education. Front. Educ. **8** (2023). https://doi.org/10.3389/feduc.2023.1212994

9. Kirchner-Krath, J., et al.: Uncovering the theoretical basis of user types: an empirical analysis and critical discussion of user typologies in research on tailored gameful design. Int. J. Hum. Comput. Stud. **190** (2024). https://doi.org/10.1016/j.ijhcs.2024.103314

10. Klock, A.C.T., Gasparini, I., Pimenta, M.S., Hamari, J.: Tailored gamification: a review of literature. Int. J. Hum. Comput. Stud. **144**, 102495 (2020). https://doi.org/10.1016/J.IJHCS.2020.102495

11. Minnich, A.: Gamification in the transport sector: quasi-experimental evidence from a bicycle navigation app. Transp. Res. Part A: Policy Pract. **167**, 103552 (2023). https://doi.org/10.1016/J.TRA.2022.11.012

12. Pasca, M.G., Guglielmetti Mugion, R., Di Pietro, L., Renzi, M.F.: Unveiling the role of gamification in shared mobility services. Environ. Dev. Sustain. **2024**, 1–40 (2024). https://doi.org/10.1007/S10668-024-04465-0

13. Rodrigues, L.F., Oliveira, A., Costa, C.J.: Playing seriously – how gamification and social cues influence bank customers to use gamified e-business applications. Comput. Hum. Behav. **63**, 392–407 (2016). https://doi.org/10.1016/j.chb.2016.05.063

14. Ryan, R.M., Deci, E.L.: Self-determination Theory. Am. Psychol. **55**(1), 68–78 (2000). https://doi.org/10.1037/0003-066X.55.1.68

15. Schikofsky, J., Dannewald, T., Kowald, M.: Exploring motivational mechanisms behind the intention to adopt mobility as a service (MaaS): Insights from Germany. Transp. Res. Part A: Policy Pract. **131**, 296–312 (2020). https://doi.org/10.1016/J.TRA.2019.09.022

16. Tondello, G.F., Nacke, L.E.: Validation of user preferences and effects of personalized gamification on task performance. Front. Comput. Sci. **2**, 29 (2020). https://doi.org/10.3389/fcomp.2020.00029

17. Tondello, G.F., Wehbe, R.R., Diamond, L., Busch, M., Marczewski, A., Nacke, L.E.: The gamification user types Hexad scale. In: Proceedings of the 2016 Annual Symposium on Computer-Human Interaction in Play, pp. 229–243 (2016). https://doi.org/10.1145/2967934.2968082

18. Venkatesh, V., Thong, J.Y.L., Xu, X.: Consumer acceptance and use of information technology : extending the unified theory of acceptance and use of technology. MIS Quarterly, **36**(1), 157 (2012). https://doi.org/10.2307/41410412

19. Xiao, Y., Hew, K.: Personalized gamification versus one-size-fits-all gamification in fully online learning: effects on student motivational, behavioral and cognitive outcomes. Learn. Individ. Differ. **113** (2024). https://doi.org/10.1016/j.lindif.2024.102470

Demonstrations and Artefacts

APOLLO: An Open Platform for LLM-Based Multi-agent Interaction Research

Abel Johny[1][✉][iD], Eike Schneiders[2][iD], and Jeremie Clos[1][iD]

[1] University of Nottingham, Nottingham, UK
{psxaj3,jeremie.clos}@nottingham.ac.uk
[2] University of Southampton, Southampton, UK
eike.schneiders@soton.ac.uk

Abstract. Traditional decision-making processes often struggle to capture diverse stakeholder perspectives and anticipate potential outcomes. Complex decisions and persuasions might rely on insights and perspectives which might not be available. In this paper, we leverage recent advances in large language models and retrieval-augmented generation to introduce APOLLO—an Architecture and oPen-source system that Orchestrates Large Language mOdels. APOLLO coordinates multiple LLMs by engaging them in collaborative discourse to reach a consensus on user-defined prompts. This system enables HCI and AI researchers and practitioners, and allows them to explore and experiment with LLM-based multi-agents systems in a user-configurable and customisable manner. By providing this flexible platform, APOLLO enables new avenues for studying and designing human-AI interactions, investigating the impact of multi-agent interaction on human behaviour, and ultimately facilitates a deeper understanding of how AI-driven collaboration can enhance human-AI interaction and decision making.

Keywords: Human-AI Interaction · Multi-Agent Systems · Large Language Models · LLM · Research Software · Decision-Making · Generative AI

1 Introduction

Since the release of ChatGPT in November 2022 the HCI community has demonstrated an interest in investigating the implications on human interactions, behaviours, and reliance using Large Language Models (LLM) [10,12]. However, as a community, we still lack flexible open-access tools allowing us to investigate multi-agent interaction with LLMs. To address this, we present an Architecture and oPen-source platform that Orchestrates Large Language mOdels

---

Supplementary Information The online version contains supplementary material available at https://doi.org/10.1007/978-3-031-97177-8_10.

I. Wiafe et al. (Eds.): PERSUASIVE 2025, CCIS 2542, pp. 107–112, 2026.
https://doi.org/10.1007/978-3-031-97177-8_10

(APOLLO). We developed APOLLO to enable researchers and practitioners to customise the behaviour of multiple large language models, and subsequently study user interaction with these systems. This is increasingly relevant for tasks such as AI supported medical [1] and legal [9] decision making, problem solving [7], and persuasion or interaction with opposing viewpoints online [13].

In this paper, we present APOLLO, an Architecture and oPen-source system that Orchestrates Large Language mOdels (LLMs) for autonomous decision making[1]. The APOLLO system provides a platform that enables LLMs to function autonomously, effectively transforming them into autonomous AI agents, capable of pursuing complex user-specified goals with or without human interaction. These agents are orchestrated by APOLLO to engage in collaborative discourse aimed at reaching consensus. This agent-based deliberation process mirrors the complexity of real-world decision-making environments but allows for a more thorough exploration of potential solutions and their implications by providing options to model complex alternative scenarios. With this platform we provide HCI and AI researchers and practitioners the means to investigate interaction with LLM-based multi-agent systems in a user configurable way.

2   The APOLLO System

In this key part of this demonstrator paper, we briefly introduce the Architecture and oPen-source system that Orchestrates Large Language mOdels, in short: the APOLLO system. We designed and implemented APOLLO to facilitate researchers and practitioners in investigating decision-making, problem solving, persuasion strategies, and human-LLM interaction by orchestrating multiple Large Language Models (LLMs) in collaborative scenarios. By enabling multiple AI agents to engage in structured discourse, for instance in an effort to reach consensus or persuade, APOLLO bridges a critical gap between single-agent AI systems and the multi-faceted nature of real-world AI-interactions. The system integrates diverse perspectives and reasoning approaches, similar to human group deliberations[2].

2.1   System Personalisation Through Configuration

A key feature of APOLLO is its ability to manipulate the behaviour of the LLMs without the need for technical expertise. APOLLO facilitates this through the configuration of key system behaviours and characteristics. The System Parameter Configuration component is the primary interface for engaging with AI agents in the system. It allows researchers to configure the system. Amongst others, APOLLO users have the option to enter custom textual prompts, define the behaviour of the LLM agents, as well as supplement their knowledge base by uploading domain-specific PDFs and text files. The interaction back-end provides a number of parameters for tuning and personalisation of the interaction environment. Specifically, the parameters can be configured:

---

[1] APOLLO as open-source on github: https://github.com/abeljohny/apollo.
[2] A brief APOLLO demo: https://www.youtube.com/watch?v=TqA7yZXAPBo.

1. **System Prompt:** All LLM agents share a common protocol through a centrally maintained system prompt. This shared foundation serves as the "common vocabulary", as described by Allan et al. [3]. The system prompt is exposed to the APOLLO user to allow personalisation of the agents through customisation of LLM agents behaviour during the discourse.
2. **Maximum Number of Turns:** A turn is defined as a complete cycle of responses from all participating agents. To ensure a balance in representation of all agents [11], we ensured that each agent contributed during each turn. Providing the option to limit the amount of turns prevents indefinite conversations while providing users with a predictable timeframe for discourse completion. Should the LLM agents reach consensus before the user-defined maximum number of turns, the conversation will conclude early.
3. **Harmfulness Detection:** To ensure the safety and appropriateness of LLM responses, a label can be displayed after every response classifying it as *Harmful* or *Harmless*. Harmful responses include a toxicity metric and a percentage indicating their level of toxicity [5].
4. **Domain-Specific Mode (e.g., Lawyer Mode):** APOLLO repurposes LLMs for specific domains by modifying the system prompt. In this mode, agents act as virtual legal strategists, analysing documents and formulating legal strategies. Users can upload court cases to enhance the LLMs knowledge. Agents collaborate to extract relevant details and generate responses, showcasing APOLLO's adaptability[3].
5. **Select Model:** APOLLO detects locally available LLMs and allows users to add models via the Ollama [8] API. Users select models from a drop-down menu; if none is chosen, APOLLO defaults to Gemma 2 (9B) and Llama 3.1 (8B). If unavailable, the system selects two random models or duplicates one.
6. **Agent Behaviour:** APOLLO supports two response formats: *Round-Robin Discussion* and *Summarised Discussion*. In the former, LLMs provide responses based on a sequence. Each response is displayed through a chat-based GUI. In the latter, a concise turn-level summary is generated by the first agent in the sequence, starting from the second turn. Subsequent turns use only these summaries instead of the individual agent responses to continue the discourse.
7. **Only Show Final Consensus:** This option configures APOLLO to present only the final consensus. Each LLM will respond individually, however, these responses will not be shown and only the final consensus will be summarised.

2.2   Auxiliary Utilities

Alongside the core components that define the behaviour of the LLM agents, which can be personalised by the user (see Sect. 2.1), APOLLO incorporates several auxiliary utilities. These utilities are coordinated by the orchestrator which acts as link between the user interface, the system configuration, and

---

[3] LLM agents should not be relied upon for legal advice; this context serves as an example of APOLLO's capabilities only.

the auxiliary utilities. The system's orchestrator follows a game loop model [4] to simulate the continuous, turn-based interactions among LLMs. It manages critical state variables such as the discussion topic, references to persistence mechanisms (database and file system), and a list of participating LLMs, as well as auxiliary functions such as prompt formatting and context-aware responses via Retrieval-Augmented Generation (RAG) [2,6].

1. **Retrieval-Augmented Generation (RAG):** The open source Haystack framework is integrated to allow LLMs to query external knowledge sources using natural language. This utility extends the model's memory limits, allowing the agents to work with information from external documents without requiring the entire text to fit within their limited context capacity. The RAG subsystem thus serves as a bridge between the extensive knowledge contained in uploaded documents and the processing capabilities of lightweight LLMs.
2. **Harmfulness Classifier:** To ensure the safety and appropriateness of agent responses, we integrated the Detoxify classifier [5] to identify potentially harmful content in text. Each agent's response is analysed across multiple toxicity categories, including insults, threats, and sexually explicit comments, with toxicity thresholds set to a default value (50%) for each category. This threshold is customisable. When an agent's response exceeds the threshold in any category, the system flags the response as potentially harmful and displays to the user both the specific toxicity metric that triggered the flag and the percentage at which the classifier assessed the harmfulness.
3. **Persistence (Database & File System):** Upon completion of the discussion, when all LLM agents have reached a consensus, the entire conversation chain is maintained in a database, preserving the reasoning chain and ensuring accountability and traceability.

2.3   Example Cases for Research with APOLLO

1. **Case 1: Can LLM-based multi-agent interaction persuade to healthier life choices?** Imagine a smoker considering quitting but lacking a supportive network to reinforce their decision. The APOLLO system allows researchers to explore whether LLM-based multi-agent systems can persuade users to make healthier choices and provide the support needed to follow through on their decision to quit.
2. **Case 2: Nudge towards Friendlier Online Discourse.** Imagine an online forum where discussions frequently become hostile, discouraging constructive dialogue. The APOLLO system allows researchers to explore whether LLM-based multi-agent systems can guide conversations toward more positive and respectful interactions, fostering a friendlier and more inclusive online environment.

3   Conclusion

In this demonstration paper, we introduced APOLLO, a configurable multi-agents system which enables HCI and AI researchers and practitioners to manipulate the behaviour of multiple large language models, and subsequently study user interaction. The APOLLO system thereby facilitates future research investigating human-AI interaction within various use cases such as, AI-supported decision making, persuasions using agent based discussions, and problem-solving. The system overcomes the limitations of a model's memory limits by allowing it to work with information from external documents without requiring the entire text to fit within its limited context capacity.

Acknowledgement. This project was supported by the Engineering and Physical Sciences Research Council Responsible AI UK [grant number EP/Y009800/1].

References

1. Barabucci, G., Shia, V., Chu, E., Harack, B., Laskowski, K., Fu, N.: Combining multiple large language models improves diagnostic accuracy. NEJM AI **1**(11), AIcs2400502 (2024)
2. Chang, C.C., Chang, H.P., Lee, H.S.: Leveraging retrieval-augmented generation for culturally inclusive hakka chatbots: design insights and user perceptions. In: 2024 IEEE International Conference on Recent Advances in Systems Science and Engineering (RASSE), pp. 1–6 (2024). https://doi.org/10.1109/RASSE64357.2024.10773731
3. Dafoe, A., Bachrach, Y., Hadfield, G., Horvitz, E., Larson, K., Graepel, T.: Cooperative AI: machines must learn to find common ground. Nature **593**(7857), 33–36 (2021). https://doi.org/10.1038/d41586-021-01170-
4. Gregory, J.: Game Engine Architecture, 2nd edn. A. K Peters, Ltd., Natick (2014)
5. Hanu, L., Unitary, T.: Detoxify (2020). https://github.com/unitaryai/detoxify
6. Lewis, P., et al.: Retrieval-augmented generation for knowledge-intensive nlp tasks. Adv. Neural. Inf. Process. Syst. **33**, 9459–9474 (2020)
7. Li, G., Hammoud, H., Itani, H., Khizbullin, D., Ghanem, B.: Camel: communicative agents for "mind" exploration of large language model society. Adv. Neural. Inf. Process. Syst. **36**, 51991–52008 (2023)
8. Morgan, J., Chiang, M.: Ollama (2023). https://ollama.com/
9. Schneiders, E., et al.: Objection overruled! lay people can distinguish large language models from lawyers, but still favour advice from an llm. In: Proceedings of the 2025 CHI Conference on Human Factors in Computing Systems, CHI '25. ACM, New York (2025). https://doi.org/10.1145/3706598.3713470
10. Seabrooke, T., et al.: A survey of lay people's willingness to generate legal advice using large language models (llms). In: Proceedings of the Second International Symposium on Trustworthy Autonomous Systems, TAS '24. ACM, New York (2024). https://doi.org/10.1145/3686038.3686043
11. Tennent, H., Shen, S., Jung, M.: Micbot: a peripheral robotic object to shape conversational dynamics and team performance. In: 2019 14th ACM/IEEE International Conference on Human-Robot Interaction (HRI), pp. 133–142 (2019). https://doi.org/10.1109/HRI.2019.8673013

12. Wang, C., et al.: Lami: large language models for multi-modal human-robot inter-
    action. In: Extended Abstracts of the CHI Conference on Human Factors in Com-
    puting Systems, CHI EA '24. ACM, New York (2024). https://doi.org/10.1145/
    3613905.3651029
13. Zhang, Y., et al.: See widely, think wisely: toward designing a generative multi-
    agent system to burst filter bubbles. In: Proceedings of the 2024 CHI Conference on
    Human Factors in Computing Systems, CHI '24. ACM, New York (2024). https://
    doi.org/10.1145/3613904.3642545

A Demo of Google Inject

Loukas Konstantinou$^{(\boxtimes)}$ (iD) and Evangelos Karapanos (iD)

Cyprus University of Technology, Limassol, Cyprus
lok.konstantinou@edu.cut.ac.cy, evangelos.karapanos@cut.ac.cy

Abstract. We present a demo of *Google Inject*, a technology-mediated nudge aimed at increasing users' engagement with fact-checks by injecting fact-checking articles, relevant to one's query, at the top of Google search results. We elaborate on the problem that *Google Inject* aims to address, the design and development of the tool, and our ongoing and future empirical work to test its effectiveness in changing individuals' behaviors.

Keywords: Online Misinformation · Nudging · Fact-Checking

1 Introduction

Fact-checking, defined as the *task of assessing the truthfulness of claims made by public figures such as politicians and pundits* [20], has emerged as a principal component of news reporting over the last decade [10]. Digital outlets, such as PolitiFact, Snopes.com, and FactCheck.org, have received considerable attention, while reports have identified over 400 active fact-check organizations verifying claims in more than 100 countries and 69 languages [18].

Prior studies have suggested that fact-checking can hold public figures accountable, and educate the public while correcting false claims; fact-checkers deeming a statement as false causes a 9.5% reduction in the probability that a political figure repeats the claim [11], while implementation intentions interventions (*i.e.*, an *"if-then"* plan of fact-checking a story before sharing it on social media: *"If I want to share a story on social media, then I will check its validity on Snopes.com."*), alongside educational ones (*i.e.*, informing users about fake news, and strategies for verifying information credibility), can significantly boost fact-checking behavior (*e.g.*, validating a story through a fact-checking site) [2].

Despite the prevalence of fact-checking organizations, interaction with fact-checks is limited. Evidence suggests that users are unfamiliar with the work of fact-checking sites and fact-checkers, such sites are rarely visited, a limited number of people share fact-checks, and when they do so, they serve particular purposes (*i.e.*, political reasons) [16]. In a recent study, only about one in ten individuals reported using fact-checking services, and to verify claims made during pre-election periods [10].

Recent attempts have concentrated on facilitating the search for relevant fact-checks - *making the task less daunting* - by bringing fact-checks together,

I. Wiafe et al. (Eds.): PERSUASIVE 2025, CCIS 2542, pp. 113–117, 2026.
https://doi.org/10.1007/978-3-031-97177-8_11

from diverse sources and formats, in particular spaces. As a case in point, *Google Fact Check Explorer* provides an easy search interface for fact-check search and retrieval [22], while *MisinfoMe* taps into a dataset of (approximately) 100,000 fact-checking reviews of claims, from 86 registered fact-checkers, to highlight tweets that point to reliable or unreliable sources and content [12].

Nonetheless, even if all fact-checks can be easily accessible through a single search engine, several behavioral barriers may arise, as users need to pause their ongoing task (*e.g.*, reading through a news piece) and initiate a new fact-checking inquiry on their own volition. This, in turn, may result in *behavioral inertia* as the new fact-checking task will impose increased cognitive load and, possibly, even derail users' former, primary (reading) task [15].

2 Google Inject

Google Inject[1] (see Fig. 1) aims at increasing users' engagement with fact-checks by injecting fact-checking articles, relevant to one's query, at the top of the Google search results page. *Google Inject* was one of 21 concepts that came out of a workshop that aimed at exploring the design space of technology-mediated nudges against misinformation [9]. *Nudges*, defined as "*any aspect of the choice architecture that alters people's behavior in a predictable way without forbidding any option or significantly changing their economic incentive*" [19], exploit knowledge around cognitive biases (*i.e.*, systematic ways in which people err), to guide the design of, among others, digital information consumption environments. While empirical evidence on their effectiveness for mitigating misinformation is limited, early studies have shown promise (*i.e.*, see [7] for a review of digital behavioral interventions against misinformation). For instance, a social norms nudge (*i.e.*, reminding users of others' online behavior), was found to reduce users' likelihood of sharing noncredible articles within their social network [1].

Google Inject was designed as a *transparent* (*i.e.*, clearly conveying its purpose and means of behavior change) and *Type 2* (*i.e.*, targeting reflective cognitive processing) nudge, presenting *multiple viewpoints* to tackle users' *confirmation bias* (*i.e.*, individuals' tendency to interpret new evidence as a confirmation of their existing beliefs), and promote more critical content consumption while browsing search results (see [8] for an elaboration on the design and evaluation of Google Inject).

By integrating articles from fact-checking organizations and sites directly into search results, *Google Inject* provides an opportunity for *situated learning* [5]. This approach may boost interaction with fact-checking content, even among users who lack prior awareness or positive attitudes toward fact-checking, potentially bypassing such stages for engagement [8,9].

---

[1] "*Google Inject*" is an independent term, not affiliated with or endorsed by Google LLC. The nudge was independently developed and is not associated with any Google product or service.

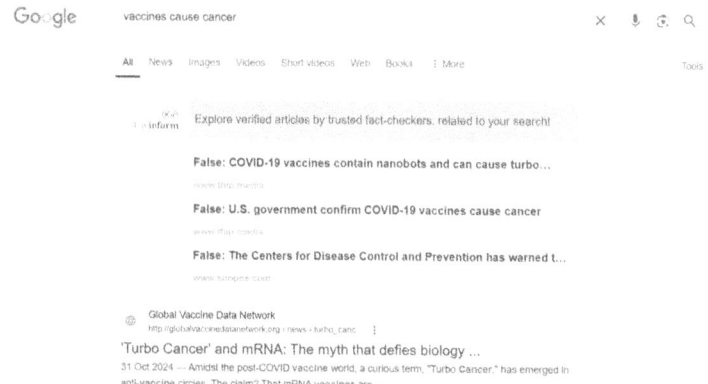

Fig. 1. An instance of *Google Inject* presenting three fact-check articles relevant to a user's query "*vaccines cause cancer*".

3   Implementation

Google Inject is developed on JavaScript, as a Google Chrome browser plugin. Using one's Google search query, it retrieves relevant fact-checks from a repository containing the most recent *ClaimReview* dataset: a collection of false claims and their corresponding fact-checks, issued by at least 70 registered fact-checking organizations that are signatories of the International Fact-Checking Network, from over 32 countries and spanning 23 languages [4,12,13]. ClaimReview is a standardized way to markup fact-checks (*e.g.*, who made the false claim, what the claim was, the fact-check verdict, the fact-checking organization, the link pointing to the fact-check verdict, the validation rating, etc.), so search engines and other digital platforms can swiftly recognize and display verified fact-checking information [12]. If relevant articles are found within the dataset, debunking false claims in English, *Google Inject* inserts them within the Google search engine results page, attempting to dispel misinformative narratives.

4   Future Work

In a study currently under review [8], we have explored how different design variations of *Google Inject*, as a result of manipulating four design variables (*i.e.*, the number of fact-checking articles injected, their positioning, concealment and seamlessness), affected *users' experience and proximal behaviors* (*e.g.*, visual attention, article selection, and nudge preference). In a controlled laboratory environment, 21 participants were sequentially exposed to each variation of the *Google Inject* nudge. For each variation, they were presented with a pre-formed query related to a vaccination-oriented topic and were then asked to select the search item they deemed most suitable and relevant. The search results included articles from the nudge design variation and standard Google search results. Preliminary findings revealed significant variation in engagement with recommended nudge articles across different *Google Inject* interventions. For instance, when nudge articles were seamlessly integrated into the first position of search results, they accounted for 57% of selections, with some participants raising concerns about being coerced or manipulated into engaging with such articles and others praising seamless integration for boosting engagement with fact-check articles [8]. In contrast, when the nudge articles were hidden and only revealed after user interaction, no selections were detected, with most of the participants expressing concern that hiding mechanisms make fact-check articles easy to overlook and ignore [8].

Our future work will examine whether *Google Inject* influences *biases and beliefs*, particularly in the context of vaccine hesitancy. Prior studies have indicated that psychological antecedents, such as confidence, complacency, constraints, calculation of risk and collective responsibility, are significant predictors of vaccine hesitancy, often surpassing demographic variables in their predictive power. [6]. Online misinformation has been shown to affect these psychological antecedents and, in turn, increase vaccine hesitancy. For example, exposure to vaccine-related misinformation and conspiracy theories can negatively impact confidence in vaccines, hence boosting vaccine hesitancy [3,14,21]. Likewise, misinformation can increase complacency, with individuals perceiving a lower risk of contracting vaccine-preventable diseases, hence lowering their intention to get vaccinated [17]. All in all, by examining how *Google Inject* may impact these antecedents through fact-checking, our future work intends to determine whether we can effectively reduce vaccine hesitancy.

Funding Information. The study was partially funded by the Co-Inform project (770302), under the Horizon 2020 call "H2020-SC6-COCREATION-2016-2017 (CO-CREATION FOR GROWTH AND INCLUSION)" of the European Commission.

References

1. Andı, S., Akesson, J.: Nudging away false news: evidence from a social norms experiment. Digit. Journal. **9**(1), 106–125 (2020)
2. Armeen, I., Niswanger, R., Tian, C.: Combating fake news using implementation intentions. Inf. Syst. Front. 1–14 (2024)
3. Betsch, C., et al.: Sample study protocol for adapting and translating the 5c scale to assess the psychological antecedents of vaccination. BMJ Open **10**(3), e034869 (2020)
4. Burel, G., Mensio, M., Peskine, Y., Troncy, R., Papotti, P., Alani, H.: Cimplekg: a continuously updated knowledge graph on misinformation, factors and fact-checks. In: International Semantic Web Conference, pp. 97–114. Springer, Heidelberg (2024). https://doi.org/10.1007/978-3-031-77847-6_6
5. Clancey, W.J.: A tutorial on situated learning. In: Proceedings of the International Conference on Computers and Education (Taiwan), pp. 49–70. AACE, Charlottesville (1995)
6. Eitze, S., Felgendreff, L., Horstkötter, N., Seefeld, L., Betsch, C.: Exploring pre-pandemic patterns of vaccine decision-making with the 5c model: results from representative surveys in 2016 and 2018. BMC Public Health **24**(1), 1205 (2024)

7. Konstantinou, L., Karapanos, E.: Behavior change interventions combating online misinformation: a scoping review. In: Proceedings of CHI Conference on Human Factors in Computing Systems (CHI'25), Yokohama, Japan, 26 April–1 May 2025 (2025)

8. Konstantinou, L., Karapanos, E.: Google inject: increasing engagement with fact-checks through nudging. Behav. Inf. Technol. (2025)

9. Konstantinou, L., Panos, D., Karapanos, E.: Exploring the design of technology-mediated nudges for online misinformation. Int. J. Hum.–Comput. Interact. 1–28 (2024)

10. Kyriakidou, M., Cushion, S., Hughes, C., Morani, M.: Questioning fact-checking in the fight against disinformation: an audience perspective. Journal. Pract. 17(10), 2123–2139 (2023)

11. Lim, C.: Can fact-checking prevent politicians from lying? Disponible en (2018)

12. Mensio, M., Alani, H.: Misinfome: who's interacting with misinformation? (2019)

13. Mensio, M., Burel, G., Farrell, T., Alani, H.: Misinfome: a tool for longitudinal assessment of twitter accounts' sharing of misinformation. In: Adjunct Proceedings of the 31st ACM Conference on User Modeling, Adaptation and Personalization, pp. 72–75 (2023)

14. Ngaybe, M., et al.: Association of vaccine intention against covid-19 using the 5c scale and its constructs: a pima county, arizona cross-sectional survey. PeerJ 12, e18316 (2024)

15. Opgenhaffen, M.: Fact-checking interventions on social media using cartoon figures: lessons learned from "the tooties." Digit. Journal. 10(5), 888–911 (2022)

16. Robertson, C.T., Mourão, R.R., Thorson, E.: Who uses fact-checking sites? The impact of demographics, political antecedents, and media use on fact-checking site awareness, attitudes, and behavior. Int. J. Press/Politics 25(2), 217–237 (2020)

17. See, K.C.: Enhancing covid-19 vaccination awareness and uptake in the post-pheic era: a narrative review of physician-level and system-level strategies. Vaccines 12(9), 1038 (2024)

18. Stencel, M., Ryan, E., Luther, J.: Misinformation spreads, but fact-checking has leveled off: 10th annual fact-checking census from the reporters' lab tracks an ongoing slowdown (2023). https://reporterslab.org/misinformation-spreads-but-fact-checking-has-leveled-off/. Accessed 21 Jan 2025

19. Thaler, R.H., Sunstein, C.R.: Nudge: improving decisions about health, wealth, and happiness (2018)

20. Vlachos, A., Riedel, S.: Fact checking: task definition and dataset construction. In: Proceedings of the ACL 2014 Workshop on Language Technologies and Computational Social Science, pp. 18–22 (2014)

21. Wismans, A., Thurik, R., Baptista, R., Dejardin, M., Janssen, F., Franken, I.: Psychological characteristics and the mediating role of the 5c model in explaining students' covid-19 vaccination intention. PLoS ONE 16(8), e0255382 (2021)

22. Yang, Q., Christensen, T., Gilda, S., Fernandes, J., Oliveira, D.: Are fact-checking tools reliable? An evaluation of google fact check. arXiv preprint arXiv:2402.13244 (2024)

Doctoral Consortium Papers

Role of Family, School Environments, and Barriers to Reporting Behavior: A Research Proposal on Combating Cyberbullying Through Online Forum Theater

Salem Bafjaish[✉]

College of Science and Engineering, Hamad Bin Khalifa University, Doha, Qatar
saba56819@hbku.edu.qa

Abstract. In the digital era, cyberbullying has emerged as a significant issue with adverse impacts on adolescents. This research proposal aims to investigate the influence of family and school environments on adolescents' vulnerability to cyberbullying. It proposes studies that evaluate the potential of online interactive forum theater as an innovative intervention to foster empowerment and resilience. This research will employ a mixed-methods approach, combining quantitative surveys and qualitative interviews to explore how family dynamics and school environments can mitigate adolescents' susceptibility to cyberbullying victimization. Additionally, it will explore barriers and motivators for reporting cyberbullying, including cultural factors. The research also proposes to study the potential of online interactive forum theater in promoting active discourse and coping mechanisms among adolescents, as well as the motivations and deterrents for participating in physical forum theater among adolescents, and the potential of adapting these interventions to an online setting to reduce barriers. The findings from this research are expected to inform the development of targeted interventions that consider environmental and cultural factors, with the goal of enhancing the resilience and safety of adolescents online.

Keywords: Cyberbullying · Adolescents · Family Environment · School Environment · Resilience · Role Playing · Online Forum Theater

1 Introduction

In the digital age, adolescents are increasingly exposed to online interactions through social media, gaming, and messaging apps, which pose risks like cyberbullying. Factors influencing an adolescent's susceptibility to cyberbullying include family and school environments. Poor family relationships and negative school environments are linked to higher rates of Internet addiction [1]. Adolescents are more likely to be dependent on the Internet if their parents are also dependent Internet users [2]. A supportive family environment can protect against cyberbullying, while a negative family environment can heighten vulnerability [3, 4]. Open communication within families can empower adolescents to seek help and report bullying [5, 6].

I. Wiafe et al. (Eds.): PERSUASIVE 2025, CCIS 2542, pp. 121–133, 2026.
https://doi.org/10.1007/978-3-031-97177-8_12

A positive school environment, characterized by respect and empathy, serves as a protective factor against cyberbullying [7]. Teachers play a pivotal role in cultivating this environment by promoting respectful interactions and addressing inappropriate behaviors swiftly [8]. Peer support in schools is also crucial, students who feel connected to their peers are less likely to engage in or fall victim to cyberbullying, highlighting the importance of robust social networks within educational settings [9]. Conversely, when supportive networks falter or schools fail to enforce anti-bullying policies effectively, the school environment can deteriorate, becoming a breeding ground for cyberbullying and peer aggression.

Cultural norms and societal expectations significantly influence how cyberbullying incidents are reported and managed. In many cultures, there is a stigma associated with being a victim of bullying, which can prevent adolescents from coming forward [10]. This reluctance is often compounded by fears of familial and social retaliation or misunderstanding, making cultural sensitivity crucial in cyberbullying prevention and intervention strategies. Differences in cultural perceptions of authority and communication within families and schools can also affect the effectiveness of reporting mechanisms [11]. In some cultural contexts, strict hierarchies may discourage students from reporting bullying incidents to authorities, necessitating approaches that consider these cultural dimensions to encourage open communication and reporting.

Participatory interventions like forum theater have shown promise in addressing bullying by fostering empathy and empowerment [12, 13]. However, adolescents often hesitate to participate due to fear of judgment and cultural stigmas [14]. Online interactive forum theater can mitigate these barriers by providing a safe, anonymous environment for role-playing and discussing cyberbullying scenarios [15]. This research proposes developing such interventions to guide adolescents through simulations, enhancing their resilience and ability to confront cyberbullying.

2 Related Work

This section reviews the current research related to the influence of family and school environment factors that impact susceptibility to cyberbullying victimization among adolescents. It is divided into several sub-sections, each addressing different aspects of the environments that influence cyberbullying behavior. Section 2.1 discusses the role of family environment factors (e.g., parenting style, poor supervision, poor communication). Section 2.2 examines the influence of school environment factors (e.g., school climate, teacher-student interactions, and peer relationships). Section 2.3 explores barriers to reporting cyberbullying, highlighting cultural and social dynamics. Finally, Sect. 2.4 considers the potential of forum theater as an innovative intervention to empower adolescents against cyberbullying.

2.1 Family Environment Factors

Informative guidance from parents about the dangers of the internet and how to behave online positively affects adolescents' awareness and reduces their propensity to engage in risky online behaviors [16], it also helps them to manage academics pressure and reduce the likely of developing IA (Internet Addiction) [17]. Additionally, restrictions on online interactions such as limiting access to certain sites and supervising online time can mitigate the risks associated with cyber interactions and decrease the likelihood of becoming a cyberbullying victim [18]. Family dysfunction, characterized by conflict, neglect, or poor communication, significantly increases the risk of cyberbullying victimization. The lack of emotional support found in such family environments makes adolescents less resilient to the challenges of cyberbullying [19]. Conversely, families that foster open and effective communication are likely to protect their children from cyber threats, as this encourages children to discuss their online experiences and learn coping strategies [20]. In contract, negative communication patterns can lead to psychological distress and problematic social media usage, further increasing vulnerability to cyberbullying [21]. Moreover, the quality of communication between parents and adolescents is crucial for providing the guidance and education needed to prevent cyberbullying. Inadequate communication can lead to behavioral deviations among adolescents, as identified by [22]. Similarly, [23] noted that suboptimal communication might make adolescents more susceptible to deviant influences. Furthermore, [24] emphasized that positive parenting and communication within the family can bolster interpersonal relationships, thereby reducing the IA (Internet Addiction) and the likelihood that adolescents will engage in negative activities prompted by their peers. Research underscores the importance of nurturing relationships within the family, where children feel secure and valued, thereby significantly reducing their risk of encountering cyberbullying [25]. Discussions about online risks within these supportive settings can further decrease a child's involvement in cyberbullying incidents [18]. The style of parenting adopted can have profound effects on children's online behaviors. Authoritative parenting, which balances high responsiveness with appropriate demands, supports children in ways that shield them from cyberbullying, fostering responsible and respectful online interactions [26]. In contrast, authoritarian parenting may inadvertently encourage aggressive behaviors due to its restrictive nature, which could translate into bullying tendencies online [27]. Permissive parenting, characterized by a lack of supervision, allows for greater exposure to cyber risks, thus increasing the likelihood of cyberbullying [16]. Finally, neglectful parenting is particularly detrimental as it fails to provide the necessary guidance and supervision needed to navigate the online world safely, leaving children exceptionally vulnerable to cyber threats.

2.2 School Environment Factors

The overall climate of a school plays a critical role in shaping students' perceptions of safety and belonging, which directly influences their behavior and vulnerability to cyberbullying. Positive school climates are characterized by supportive peer interactions, clear rules, fair enforcement, and responsive teacher behavior, all of which contribute to a lower incidence of cyberbullying [28]. Studies such as those by [29] and [30] have documented that schools with a positive climate not only see enhanced academic outcomes but also a significant reduction in violence and cyberbullying, thus highlighting the crucial role of the educational environment in promoting student well-being. The quality of the school environment significantly impacts students' academic success and psychological health. Schools that succeed in creating such environments see higher GPAs and better test performance among students [31]. These positive educational outcomes are critical as they also correlate with reduced engagement in risky behaviors, including cyberbullying. The interactions between teachers and students, as well as among peers, are foundational to a school's environment. Supportive teacher behaviors and positive peer interactions are integral to fostering a school climate that combats cyberbullying. Teachers who engage positively with students and enforce rules fairly contribute to a sense of justice and respect among students, which deters aggressive behaviors like cyberbullying [32].

2.3 Barriers to Reporting Cyberbullying

Cultural norms and values deeply influence attitudes towards reporting cyberbullying. In societies where collectivism and community cohesion are valued, there is a significant reluctance to report cyberbullying due to the potential social repercussions. The fear of disrupting group harmony or attracting negative attention can deter victims from speaking out, leading to a culture of silence where cyberbullying goes unreported [33]. This silence is often compounded by the normalization of aggressive behaviors within certain cultural contexts, where such actions may be viewed as rites of passage or forms of social bonding, reducing the likelihood that these actions are recognized and reported as cyberbullying [34]. The dynamics of power and authority within social structures can also create barriers to reporting cyberbullying. Victims may feel disempowered to report incidents involving perpetrators who hold a perceived authority, such as senior students or educators. This disempowerment is often exacerbated by fears of retaliation or not being believed, which can discourage victims from reporting the abuse they encounter [35]. Additionally, the fear of punishment from authority figures or losing internet privileges at home can prevent young people from discussing their experiences with cyberbullying, particularly when they anticipate negative consequences [36]. A lack of clear communication or trust between parents and children can significantly impact the reporting of cyberbullying. Children who do not feel comfortable discussing their online experiences with their parents may choose to handle the situation independently or with peers, avoiding adult intervention. This can be due to various reasons, including a fear of being misunderstood, judged, or not taken seriously by adults [37]. The absence of open communication channels within the family can hinder the effective reporting and handling of cyberbullying incidents. Many victims of cyberbullying may choose to keep their experiences private due to feelings of shame, embarrassment, or fear of being seen as vulnerable. This reluctance is often reinforced by social expectations and the stigmatization associated with being a victim. Adolescents may prefer to deal with cyberbullying independently, employing strategies like blocking perpetrators or ignoring harmful messages, rather than seeking help from adults or authorities [38]. This self-reliance can limit the effectiveness of interventions and reduce the likelihood that cyberbullying is addressed in a timely and supportive manner.

2.4 Forum Theater Against Bullying

Forum theater is an interactive form of performance, originally developed by Augusto Boal as part of the Theatre of the Oppressed [12]. It is designed to promote social change by engaging participants in the exploration and enactment of real-life issues. In the context of cyberbullying, this participatory approach allows adolescents to enact and resolve cyberbullying scenarios, enhancing resilience and encouraging open discussions about their experiences [13]. Previous studies have highlighted Cognitive Rehearsal as an effective strategy to counteract bullying within nursing contexts [39] and extend its application to nursing education [40]. However, not all instances can be adequately addressed through pre-rehearsed responses. Other research underscores the benefits of theater as a pedagogical tool, enhancing communication, critical thinking, and interpersonal skills through dramatized scenarios that reflect real-life interactions and power dynamics [41]. In terms of the combating cyberbullying and bullying students engage in a scripted performance that depicts a bullying interaction, which allows them to step into roles that challenge the status quo and propose alternative responses. This method not only opens space for vulnerability and experimentation without fear of real-world repercussions but also fosters a democratic environment where students can practice and reflect on their responses to bullying [42]. Together, these integrated approaches offer a robust framework for addressing bullying in educational settings, empowering students with both the theoretical understanding and practical skills necessary to navigate and influence challenging social interactions. However, the effectiveness of these interventions is often hindered by cultural stigma against public self-expression and peer judgment, suggesting the need for supportive environments that foster engagement in such creative activities [43]. To address these barriers, this research proposal suggests the implementation of online interactive forum theater. This innovative approach leverages digital platforms to create a virtual space where students can participate using avatars, text-based chats, and other interactive tools to intervene in cyberbullying scenarios. By moving the forum theater experience online, students can engage in a more anonymous and less intimidating environment, reducing the fear of judgment and stigma associated with public self-expression. This virtual format not only mitigates cultural and social barriers but also allows for broader participation, enabling students to experiment with alternative responses to bullying in a safe and supportive setting. Through this method, the research aims to empower students with the skills and confidence to address cyberbullying effectively, while fostering a culture of empathy and collaboration in digital spaces.

3   Aim and Research Questions

The aim of this research is to explore the influence of family and school environments on adolescents' vulnerability to cyberbullying. It also seeks to evaluate the potential of online interactive forum theater as an innovative intervention to foster empowerment and resilience among adolescents. The research questions these studies intend to address are:

RQ1. How do family and school environments influence an adolescent's susceptibility to cyberbullying victimization?

This question delves into how family dynamics and school environment collectively shape the vulnerability of adolescents to becoming victims of cyberbullying incidents.

RQ2. How do social and cultural factors deter adolescents from reporting cyberbullying incidents?

This inquiry focuses on the influence of social norms, cultural values, and societal attitudes on adolescents' willingness to disclose instances of cyberbullying.

RQ3. What preventive measures can be employed to enhance adolescents' resilience against cyberbullying victimization and empower them to report such incidents?

This question investigates potential strategies and interventions that could increase resilience against cyberbullying and inspire adolescents to come forward about such incidents.

4 Research Objectives and Methods

4.1 Research Objectives

We aim to achieve the following objectives:

RO 1: Explore how family dynamics and school environments shape adolescents' vulnerability to cyberbullying victimization (addresses RQ1).

RO 2: Explore the cultural and social barriers that deter adolescents from reporting cyberbullying, especially in Arab GCC (Gulf Cooperation Council) and UK contexts (addresses RQ2).

RO 3: Explore the potential of online interactive forum theater as a preventive intervention to build resilience and empower adolescents to report cyberbullying (addresses RQ3).

4.2 Participants and Sampling

This study will involve two participant groups: adolescents (13–16 years) and parents from GCC (Gulf Cooperation Council) countries. Adolescents will be recruited through schools in Qatar, targeting 400 participants to ensure diversity in gender, age, and cultural backgrounds (e.g., Qatari nationals and long-term expatriate families from (Saudi Arabia, UAE, Kuwait, Bahrain, Oman). Qatar's schools serve as a strategic hub, reflecting the region's multinational demographics while simplifying logistical coordination. For parents' participants, 400 Arab parents from all six GCC countries (Qatar, Saudi Arabia, UAE, Kuwait, Bahrain, Oman). The data collection for this survey will be conducted using CINT Research [44] for the GCC region and Prolific research [45] for the UK. For qualitative insights, 30 adolescents (15 Arab GCC and 15 UK nationals) and their parents will be recruited from the original surveys group. Parents will be recontacted to request permission for their child to participate in semi-structured interviews, exploring the potential of online interactive forum theater as a tool to address cyberbullying. This approach efficiently captures cultural variations in parenting practices, socioeconomic factors, and digital access across the GCC countries. The sample size accounts for statistical power, potential attrition, and subgroup analyses (e.g., comparing parenting styles by country). Cross-cultural comparisons between Qatar and the UK will also be explored, leveraging Qatar's unique position as a regional crossroads.

4.3 Instruments Development

A structured questionnaire will gather quantitative data on key variables aligned with the research objectives, primarily using 6-point Likert-scale items alongside a few multiple-choice and demographic questions. Where feasible, validated measures from prior studies will be adapted to ensure reliability and validity. Table 1 outlines the adolescents' survey, and Table 2 summarizes the parents' survey.

Table 1. Survey Design and Sections for Adolescents' Survey

Section	Description	Measurement Objective
Demographics	Basic profile of participants for diverse representation.	Measure demographic variability
Family Environment [46, 47]	Family relationships and their impact on cyberbullying experiences.	Measure influence of family dynamics on cyberbullying susceptibility using a 4-point Likert scale e.g., We can express our feelings openly in my family.
School Environment [48]	School's role in shaping cyberbullying experiences.	Measure impact of school environments on cyberbullying using a 5-point Likert scale e.g., I feel that my teachers accept me as I am.
Cyberbullying Experience	Prevalence and nature of cyberbullying among participants.	Measure direct cyberbullying experiences and correlate with environmental factors, e.g., How often have you personally experienced cyberbullying on social media platforms? (1 = Very Frequently, 5 = Very Infrequently).
Cultural Impact [49]	Specific cultural dimensions (e.g., religion, family honor, collectivism)	Measure cultural influences on attitudes and behaviors toward cyberbullying, e.g., "When thinking about reporting cyberbullying, how much do cultural factors motivate or deter you? (1 = Highly Motivating, 6 = Not Motivating at All).
Reporting Behavior [49]	Barriers and facilitators in reporting cyberbullying incidents.	Measure factors influencing the likelihood of reporting cyberbullying using a 6-point Likert scale e.g., I don't think my parent/guardian would understand or believe me.

The semi-structured interviews will be divided into six sections to explore key aspects of the research. Section 1 will collect demographic information and confirm consent, while also assessing participants' understanding of bullying and familiarity with forum theatre. Section 2 will explore their experiences with in-person forum theatre, including roles played, feelings, and classmates' reactions. Section 3 will identify barriers (e.g., peer pressure, cultural norms) and motivators (e.g., supportive environments) to participating in in-person activities. Section 4 will examine how transitioning to an online platform might reduce barriers, leveraging anonymity and virtual interactions to encourage engagement. Section 5 will gather input on designing an online forum theatre platform, including preferred interaction methods and tools for addressing bullying.

Table 2. Survey Design and Sections for Parents' Survey

Section	Description	Measurement Objective
Demographics	Age, gender, profession, family structure, financial status, education, employment	Measure background and characteristics of respondents and their families
Family Dynamics [46, 50]	Family environment, parenting styles, emotional/functional dynamics	Measure influence of family dynamics on cyberbullying susceptibility using a 4-point Likert scale e.g., We can express our feelings openly in my family
Child Behavior and Cyberbullying	Child's behavior, cyberbullying experiences, and emotional/behavioral impacts	Measure direct cyberbullying experiences and correlate with environmental factors, e.g., How frequently do cyberbullying incidents occur to your child? (1 = Never, 5 = Very Often)
Cultural Influences [49]	Specific cultural dimensions (e.g., religion, family honor, collectivism)	Measure cultural influences on attitudes and behaviors toward cyberbullying, e.g., When thinking about reporting cyberbullying, how much do cultural factors motivate or deter your child? (1 = Highly Motivating, 6 = Not Motivating at All)
Sources of Information [51]	Parents' current and preferred sources of internet safety information	Measure where parents get information and their preferences for future guidance

Finally, Sect. 6 will compare online and in-person formats, discussing strengths, weaknesses, and comfort levels in each setting. The interviews will ensure confidentiality and voluntary participation, providing valuable insights for developing effective, culturally sensitive interventions.

4.4 Data Collection Procedures

Data collection will occur in multiple phases as shown in Fig. 1. After obtaining ethical approvals and school permissions, the adolescent survey will be administered during school sessions using SurveyMonkey in activity classes, supervised by school administration. The survey for adolescents will take approximately 10–15 min to complete. Research staff and teachers will be present to answer questions and ensure a quiet environment. Prior to the survey administration, informed consent and assent forms will be collected from both parents and their children to ensure compliance with ethical standards. For parents, the survey will be available in two versions: Arabic for Arabic-speaking parents and English for others, taking approximately 18–20 min. For parents, the survey will be available in Arabic for Arabic-speaking parents and in English for others, taking about 18–20 min to complete. Informed consent forms will also be collected from parents, ensuring they are fully aware of the study's purpose, procedures, and the measures taken to protect their confidentiality. Additionally, 30 adolescents (15 GCC, 15 UK) and their parents will participate in semi-structured interviews to explore the effectiveness of online interactive forum theater in addressing cyberbullying. Interviews, lasting 45–60 min, will be recorded (with consent) and transcribed for analysis.

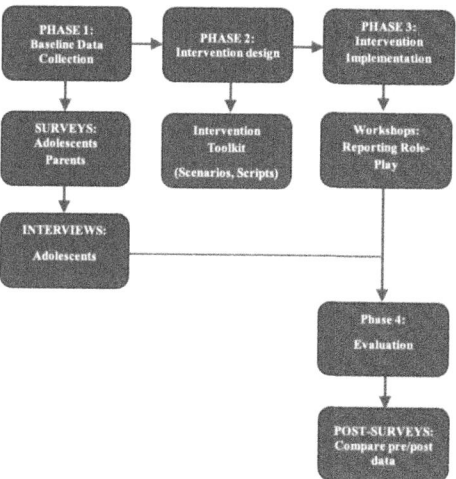

Fig. 1. Shows the structured flow of the research

4.5 Analytical Approaches

For analytical approaches, we will apply statistical analysis techniques such as T-test, ANOVA, and Regression using data analysis tools such as JASP and R. For the survey data collected from adolescents and parents, these techniques will help us identify significant relationships and differences in the data, such as the impact of family and school environments on cyberbullying susceptibility and the influence of cultural factors on reporting behavior. For the semi-structured interviews, qualitative analysis methods will be employed to explore themes and patterns related to the potential of online interactive forum theater as an intervention against bullying and cyberbullying.

4.6 Ethical Considerations

This research will secure approvals from an Institutional Review Board (IRB) and the relevant Ministry of Education for school access. Informed consent from parents and assent from adolescents will be required. Privacy and confidentiality of participants will be rigorously maintained throughout the research.

4.7 Evaluation

To ensure data quality, participants must meet pre-selection criteria and pass attention check questions to confirm they are reading the surveys carefully. Those who fail these checks or complete the survey too quickly will be excluded. Interview transcripts will be analyzed thematically to identify key patterns and insights. Pre- and post-surveys will assess changes in adolescents' reporting behavior, attitudes toward cyberbullying, and resilience. Workshop participation metrics will be analyzed to measure the intervention's effectiveness and identify areas for improvement. The expected outcomes include implementing online forum theater, which involves creating role-playing scenarios where participants can take on roles such as victim, bystander, or bully. Participants can select avatars and intervene through various interactive methods like chat, comments, and emojis. The online platform should support these features to facilitate realistic and engaging simulations, allowing participants to explore different perspectives and responses to cyberbullying in a safe and anonymous environment. This approach helps build resilience and encourages open communication among adolescents. It provides a clear understanding of the intervention's impact on behavior and attitudes.

5 Conclusion

This research proposal aims to explore the significant impact of family and school environments on adolescents' vulnerability to cyberbullying. By employing a mixed-methods approach, the study will investigate how supportive family dynamics and positive school climates can mitigate the risks associated with cyberbullying. Additionally, the research will delve into the cultural and social barriers that deter adolescents from reporting cyberbullying incidents. The innovative use of online interactive forum theater as an intervention is proposed to empower adolescents, fostering resilience and encouraging open communication about their experiences. The findings from this research are expected to inform the development of targeted intervention that consider environmental and cultural factors, ultimately enhancing the safety and well-being of adolescents in the digital age.

Acknowledgments. I gratefully acknowledge my supervisor Prof. Raian Ali, Prof. Aiman Erbad and Dr. Diana Alsayed Hassan for their valuable suggestions and guidance. This publication was supported by NPRP 14 Cluster grant # NPRP 14C-0916–210015 from the Qatar National Research Fund (a member of Qatar Foundation). The findings herein reflect the work and are solely the responsibility of the authors.

References

1. Chemnad, K., et al.: Adolescents' Internet addiction: does it all begin with their environment? Child Adolesc. Psychiatry Ment. Health **17**(1) (2023). https://doi.org/10.1186/s13034-023-00626-7
2. Chemnad, K., et al.: Is it contagious? does parents' internet addiction impact their adolescents' internet addiction? Soc. Sci. Comput. Rev. **41**(5), 1691–1711 (2023). https://doi.org/10.1177/08944393221117408

3. Baldry, A.C., Sorrentino, A., Farrington, D.P.: Cyberbullying and cybervictimization versus parental supervision, monitoring and control of adolescents' online activities. Child Youth Serv. Rev. **96**, 302–307 (2019). https://doi.org/10.1016/j.childyouth.2018.11.058

4. Hinduja, S., Patchin, J.W.: Cyberbullying: an exploratory analysis of factors related to offending and victimization. Deviant Behav. **29**(2), 129–156 (2008). https://doi.org/10.1080/016396 20701457816

5. Zhang, Y., Hu, Y., Yang, M.: The relationship between family communication and family resilience in Chinese parents of depressed adolescents: a serial multiple mediation of social support and psychological resilience. BMC Psychol. **12**(1) (2024). https://doi.org/10.1186/ s40359-023-01514-7

6. Wright, M.F.: Parental mediation, cyberbullying, and cybertrolling: the role of gender. Comput. Human Behav. **71**, 189–195 (2017). https://doi.org/10.1016/j.chb.2017.01.059

7. Suárez-García, Z., Álvarez-García, D., García-Redondo, P., Rodríguez, C.: The effect of a mindfulness-based intervention on attention, self-control, and aggressiveness in primary school pupils. Int. J. Environ. Res. Public Health **17**(7) (2020). https://doi.org/10.3390/ijerph 17072447

8. Sulkowski, M.L., Simmons, J.: The protective role of teacher–student relationships against peer victimization and psychosocial distress. Psychol. Sch. **55**(2), 137–150 (2018). https:// doi.org/10.1002/pits.22086

9. Thornberg, R., et al.: Associations between student-teacher relationship quality, class climate, and bullying roles: a Bayesian multilevel multinomial logit analysis. Vict. Offender **17**(8), 1196–1223 (2022). https://doi.org/10.1080/15564886.2022.2051107

10. Ahad, A.A., Sanchez-Gonzalez, M., Junquera, P.: Understanding and addressing mental health stigma across cultures for improving psychiatric care: a narrative review. Cureus (2023). https://doi.org/10.7759/cureus.39549

11. Ranjith, P.J., Vranda, M.N., Kishore, M.T.: Barriers to mental health support in cyberbullying. Indian J. Psychol. Med. (2024). https://doi.org/10.1177/02537176241253390

12. Boal, A.: Legislative Theatre: Using Performance to Make Politics. 2nd edn. Taylor and Francis, London (1995). https://doi.org/10.4324/9780203984895

13. Briones, E., Gallego, T., Palomera, R.: Creative drama and forum theatre in initial teacher education. Teach. Teach. Educ. **117** (2022). https://doi.org/10.1016/j.tate.2022.103809

14. Logie, C.H., et al.: Participatory theatre to reduce stigma and promote health equity. Health Educ. Behav. **46**(1), 146–156 (2019). https://doi.org/10.1177/1090198118760682

15. McGrath, D., et al.: Online forum theatre training with domestic abuse victims. Adv. Simul. **7**(1) (2022). https://doi.org/10.1186/s41077-022-00208-1

16. Chen, L., Ho, S.S., Lwin, M.O.: Cyberbullying perpetration and victimization: a meta-analysis. New Media Soc. **19**(8), 1194–1213 (2017). https://doi.org/10.1177/146144481663 4037

17. Chemnad, K., Alharahsheh, S., Abdelmoneium, A., Baghdady, A., Ali, R.: School pressure and academic performance versus internet addiction in early and middle adolescents: the mediating role of family relationship. Behav. Inf. Technol. 1–17 (2024). https://doi.org/10. 1080/0144929X.2024.2396434

18. Mesch, G.S.: Parent-child connections and cyberbullying. Youth Soc. **50**(8), 1145–1162 (2018). https://doi.org/10.1177/0044118X16659685

19. Slonje, R., Smith, P.K., Frisén, A.: Cyberbullying: nature and prevention strategies. Comput. Human Behav. **29**(1), 26–32 (2013). https://doi.org/10.1016/j.chb.2012.05.024

20. López-Castro, L., Priegue, D.: Family variables and cyberbullying. Soc. Sci. **8**(3) (2019). https://doi.org/10.3390/socsci8030098

21. Martínez-Ferrer, B., et al.: Parental socialization and cyber-aggression. Int. J. Environ. Res. Public Health **16**(20) (2019). https://doi.org/10.3390/ijerph16204005

22. Octavia, D., et al.: Parental communication, self-esteem, and cyberbullying. J. Ners **17**(1), 42–46 (2022). https://doi.org/10.20473/jn.v17i1.24539
23. Luk, J.W., et al.: Parent-child communication and adolescent substance use. Addict. Behav. **35**(5), 426–431 (2010). https://doi.org/10.1016/j.addbeh.2009.12.009
24. Mousa, O., et al.: Good technology requires a good environment. In: Proceedings of ACM, pp. 143–150. ACM, New York (2024). https://doi.org/10.1145/3677525.3678654
25. Ok, S., Aslan, S.: Bullying and parental style. In: Proceedings of Social Behav. Sci., pp. 536–540. Elsevier (2010). https://doi.org/10.1016/j.sbspro.2010.07.138
26. Rajendran, K., et al.: Parenting style influences bullying. J. Child Psychol. Psychiatry **57**(2), 188–195 (2016). https://doi.org/10.1111/jcpp.12433
27. Stavrinides, P., et al.: Parental knowledge, bullying, and victimization. J. Soc. Pers. Relat. **32**(2), 180–196 (2015). https://doi.org/10.1177/0265407514525889
28. Izaguirre, L.A., et al.: School climate, positive psychology, and life satisfaction. Br. J. Educ. Psychol. **93**(1), 318–332 (2023). https://doi.org/10.1111/bjep.12557
29. Berkowitz, R.: Positive school climate and educational equity. Youth Soc. **54**(3), 372–396 (2022). https://doi.org/10.1177/0044118X20970235
30. Massetti, G.M., et al.: Implementation of violence prevention programs. J. Community Health **41**(4) (2016). https://doi.org/10.1007/s10900-016-0156-z
31. Makaremi, N., et al.: Classroom environment and student wellbeing. Build. Environ. (2024). https://doi.org/10.1016/j.buildenv.2024.111958
32. Konold, T., et al.: School climate and academic achievement. AERA Open **4**(4) (2018). https://doi.org/10.1177/2332858418815661
33. Park, M.S.A., et al.: Adolescent cyberbullying in East Asia. Cyberpsychology **15**(1), 1–19 (2021). https://doi.org/10.5817/CP2021-1-5
34. Evans, M.: Normalize bullying prevention. Online J. Zines About Soc. Movements **5**, 4 (2023). https://digitalscholarship.tnstate.edu/creating_change/vol5/iss1/4
35. Herry, E., et al.: Bystander intervention online. J. Appl. Dev. Psychol. **76** (2021). https://doi.org/10.1016/j.appdev.2021.101322
36. eSafety: Mind the Gap – Parental awareness of children's exposure to risks online (2020). https://esafety.gov.au/research. Accessed: 12 Aug 2023
37. Wójcik, M., Rzeńca, K.: Disclosing or hiding bullying victimization. Sch. Ment. Health **13**(4), 808–818 (2021). https://doi.org/10.1007/s12310-021-09447-5
38. Görzig, A., Machackova, H.: Cyberbullying from a socio-ecological perspective: a contemporary synthesis of findings from EU Kids Online. Media LSE Working Pap. Ser. 36 (2015)
39. Clarke, C.M., et al.: Bullying in nursing education. J. Nurs. Educ. **51**(5), 269–276 (2012). https://doi.org/10.3928/01484834-20120409-01
40. Gillespie, G.L., et al.: Nurses eat their young. J. Nurs. Educ. Pract. **7**(7), 11 (2017). https://doi.org/10.5430/jnep.v7n7p11
41. Taylor, S.S., Taylor, R.A.: Theatre-based status work in nursing. Nurse Educ. Pract. (2017). https://doi.org/10.1016/j.nepr.2017.06.003
42. Rodricks, D.J.: Drama education as restorative. Res. Drama Educ. **20**(3), 340–343 (2015). https://doi.org/10.1080/13569783.2015.1059742
43. Orkibi, H., et al.: Drama therapy and mental illness stigma. Arts Psychother. **41**(5), 458–466 (2014). https://doi.org/10.1016/j.aip.2014.08.006
44. Noman, M., et al.: Challenging misinformation: UK vs. Arab comparison. Behav. Inf. Technol. (2023). https://doi.org/10.1080/0144929X.2023.2298306
45. Schoenebeck, S., et al.: Online harassment across countries. In: CHI '23 Proceedings of ACM, New York (2023). https://doi.org/10.1145/3544548.3581020
46. Epstein, N.B., Baldwin, L.M., Bishop, D.S.: The McMaster assessment device (1983)

47. Gross, T.J., et al.: Alabama Parenting Questionnaire–9. Assessment **24**(5), 646–659 (2017). https://doi.org/10.1177/1073191115620839
48. Inchley, J., et al.: HBSC Study Protocol 2017/18 (2018). http://www.hbsc.org. Accessed 10 Apr 2025
49. Delara, E.W.: Why adolescents don't disclose bullying. J. Sch. Violence **11**(4), 288–305 (2012). https://doi.org/10.1080/15388220.2012.705931
50. Kliem, S., et al.: Parenting scale short form (PS-8). J. Child Fam. Stud. **28**(1), 30–41 (2019). https://doi.org/10.1007/s10826-018-1257-3
51. Livingstone, S., Mascheroni, G.: Children's online risks and opportunities (2014). https://www.researchgate.net/publication/313017175. Accessed 10 Apr 2025

Towards Personalisation and User-Agent Similarity in Persuasive Agents for Sustainability

Elena Minucci(✉) ⓘ

University of Glasgow, Glasgow, UK
elena.minucci@glasgow.ac.uk

Abstract. In order to achieve large scale behaviour change, persuasive technology should look beyond the minority of users who already behave sustainably and aim to involve larger segments who are willing to behave more sustainably, but are not doing so yet. There is strong consensus that effective persuasive agents should be personalised; people tend to be more persuaded by messages that are relevant to their circumstances and that are delivered in a way that is relatable to them. Several open questions remain in relation to what the optimal persuasive language looks like for different users, and whether an agent is more persuasive if it speaks like its different users. Through a series of studies, this research proposal sets out to develop a persuasive agent with personalised dialogue to help people behave more sustainably. We specifically explore how different people write persuasively, and look for possible user-chatbot similarity effects to enhance persuasion. Preliminary results which isolated personality markers in persuasive language are presented, followed by a proposed methodology for subsequent studies.

Keywords: Persuasive Technology · Behaviour Change · Personalisation · User Model · User Profiling · Conversational Agent

1 Introduction

Reports from the United Nations state that we have a "rapidly closing" window to preserve a sustainable future [54]. Tackling the environmental crisis requires significant changes in infrastructure as well as a significant behavioural shift in society at large. The main challenge with facilitating simultaneous behaviour change amongst many individuals is that the changes required are not a one-size-fits-all. Firstly, not every user can implement every sustainable behaviour; for each user, some behaviours will come easier than others and it is important to suggest behaviours that are within a user's *latitude of acceptance* [26]. In addition, as demonstrated by over a decade of research in persuasive technology, not all users are persuaded to change their behaviour in the same way. In fact, differences between users may be so strong that what is motivating to one user is actively discouraging to another [3, 35].

Research in persuasive technology has long identified the need for personalised interventions. While there still is not a unified framework for personalising persuasive

© The Author(s), under exclusive license to Springer Nature Switzerland AG 2026
I. Wiafe et al. (Eds.): PERSUASIVE 2025, CCIS 2542, pp. 134–147, 2026.
https://doi.org/10.1007/978-3-031-97177-8_13

technologies, many follow the same personalisation process: building a user model and delivering a behaviour change intervention based on that user model.

First, the system collects and stores information about the user, which is a process commonly referred to as "user modelling" or "user profiling". Persuasive technologies have considered various user characteristics that could be relevant predictors of behaviour change, such as user personality [6], the user's current habits [5, 7, 9], their motivation for changing their behaviour [8, 22], their health needs (where appropriate) [30, 41], and even their susceptibility to different persuasive techniques, based on widely used frameworks such as the Persuasive System Design model [34] or Cialdini's principles of persuasion [14]. Information about the user may be either given by the user directly, for example through completing a health needs assessment or a susceptibility questionnaire, or it may be inferred automatically from the user's previous behaviour. For example, some persuasive applications may keep track of the user's context, such as triggering a reminder to log food at the user's meal time, which is inferred from the time of previous food logs into the app.

Once a persuasive system has collected information about the user, it uses this information to deliver a suitable intervention. Persuasive technologies vary widely in terms of what a personalised intervention looks like. Some persuasive technologies may personalise the goals that they set for the user [2, 10]; for example, the technology may propose a daily step count goal that is 10% higher than the user's current daily step count. Other persuasive technologies personalise the way they speak to the user [17, 19, 22]; for example, motivating the user through social competition or by providing support if the goals are not met.

User feedback from various persuasive technologies paints a clear picture: personalisation is not just important for effective persuasion, it may be in fact necessary. Personalised interventions are overwhelmingly reported as more effective than one-size-fits-all. For example, adaptive goals based on the user's abilities are met significantly more often than static goals [2, 42], and reminders which are timed around the user's schedule are significantly more effective than generic reminders [21, 38]. Users commonly wish for their persuasive technologies to be even more personalised, and may distrust advice that is perceived to be "too general" [37]. Relatability plays a crucial role: advice coming from relatable sources is consistently rated as more persuasive than advice from 'credible' or 'expert' sources [16, 35–37]. In addition, participants in usability interviews often compare persuasive technology to humans [9, 10, 29]. Some users express a lack of human presence accompanying them through change [9], while others report the feeling of "forming a bond" with their persuasive technology [10]. Conversational persuasive technologies are a largely unexplored avenue which holds potential for offering personalised support in behaviour change, both in terms of giving advice in a way that the user finds relatable, as well as supporting users who may struggle to change despite wanting to. Building on theories from social psychology [44, 45], my research sets out to explore what exactly it means to build persuasive conversational agents that the user finds relatable, specifically exploring how different people communicate persuasively, and whether users are more likely to take advice from a conversational agent that speaks like them.

1.1 Building Persuasive Agents that Speak like Their Users: Key Gaps and Research Questions

Research in human-human interaction emphasizes the role of language style as a means to establish rapport [15, 33] and promote trust and credibility [28, 52]. According to the social identity theory [43, 45], people tend to routinely categorize themselves and others into social groups. People trust advice more if it comes from someone who speaks in a similar way to them, because they perceive them to be part of their own social group. Linguistic mirroring has been previously explored in the context of therapy [1], negotiation [47], and police interrogations [39], as a means to build trust and encourage prosocial behaviour [48]. The phenomenon of liking, trusting, and generally gravitating towards people who we perceive as similar to us is known as *similarity-attraction paradigm* [44]. In the context of human-computer interaction, similarity-attraction has previously been explored as a proxy for trust in autonomous systems [49], but it has not yet been fully explored in agent-human persuasion.

Currently, there is no general framework for adapting language style in persuasive agents. Previous research has explored tweaking single dimensions of language, for example dominance or single traits of agent personality [27, 50], but there is no comprehensive model of how different people persuade each other, which can then be used to train an agent. Building a persuasive agent that portrays different 'persuasion types' falls into the field of category-aware natural language processing (NLP) [40, 51], which deals with understanding, manipulating and generating bodies of text that fit the characteristics of predefined categories. Category-aware NLP presents recurring challenges, relating to sourcing category-labelled data, solving issues with category definition, such as granularity and overlap, and appropriately evaluating how well the models understands and generates category-specific text [31]. All of these challenges are highly relevant to the context of a persuasive agent that adapts to different categories of users.

Firstly, there is currently no dataset explicitly linking persuasive texts with several individual characteristics. The relationship between user characteristics and persuasion has mostly been investigated in terms of how people with different characteristics *respond to* persuasive attempts [23, 25], rather than how people with different characteristics *produce* persuasive attempts. In order to investigate whether the similarity-attraction paradigm applies to agent-human persuasion, both sides need to be explored.

Secondly, current user profiling methods only take into consideration the characteristics of the user, for example their personality traits or their susceptibility to different topics. This approach assumes that people will be persuaded by a certain type of advice, no matter who delivers it. In line with the similarity-attraction paradigm, we posit that we are likely more persuaded by people who are similar to us. Thus, a better approach to user profiling would be to consider the characteristics of the persuader and the persuadee in tandem. Our research questions are as follows:

RQ1: *How do different people attempt to persuade others?*

RQ2: *Are we more persuaded by people who write like us?*

RQ3: *Are we more persuaded by conversational technology if it writes like us?*

2 Preliminary Results

As a first step in investigating how different people persuade others, we investigated personality markers in persuasive text. Out of many possible user characteristics, this first study focused on personality because personality traits are a stable predictor of behaviour change across different contexts [4] and have been extensively employed in persuasive technologies across different domains [3, 6]. We considered two different dimensions of persuasive text: content (*what* is said) and linguistics (*how* it is said). We explored the following research questions:

RQ1: *How do people with different personality attempt to persuade others, based on linguistic or content features of their writing?*

RQ2: *Is it possible to predict personality traits from persuasive writing? Which features matter?*

2.1 Study 1 Methodology

The dataset collected for this study, together with the writing prompts and materials used, has been made publicly available [32]. We collected a dataset of 137 participants through Prolific [53]. To be included in the study, participants needed to be native English speakers over 18 years of age. We recruited a gender-balanced sample to reduce potential bias. Participation was on a voluntary basis and participants were paid an average of £8.45/hr for their time. As part of the study, participants were administered a personality questionnaire, a demographic questionnaire and five writing prompts. The chosen personality questionnaire was the 44-items Big Five Inventory, assessed on a 1–5 Likert scale. This is one of the most widely used personality questionnaires and has been extensively validated across cultures [20, 24]. Other participant demographics were collected as control variables, such as participant's gender, age, nationality and environmental concern, assessed through the New Environmental Paradigm questionnaire [18]. To assess individual differences in persuasive attempts, participants were administered five persuasive writing prompts. In each prompt, a fictitious character (e.g., "Your neighbour Susan") would share their plan to engage in a sustainable behaviour and ask for the participant's advice on it. These prompts were designed to explore how people support others to meet their goals, which is a central role of persuasive technology. The prompts used are available at [32]. This study was approved by the Ethics Committee at University of Glasgow.

To answer RQ1, linguistic features of the text were extracted using Linguistic Inquiry and Word Count (LIWC) software [11]. Five linguistic features were selected for analysis: Word Count, Analytical Language, Certitude, Self-references and Lexical Diversity. We ran a 5x5 multivariate regression model on R exploring whether personality traits scores predicted our chosen linguistic features. We then extracted content features by running a thematic analysis on the participants' text entries. Eleven total content themes emerged, clustered around three categories: people gave a mix of different reasons to carry out sustainable behaviours, practical advice on starting a sustainable behaviour, and evaluations on different sustainable behaviours, such as using praise or asking questions. To explore whether personality predicted differences in content features, we ran a 5 x 11 multivariate regression model. To answer RQ2, we chose a machine learning (ML) approach as this had been previously used in personality prediction tasks for general-purpose text [13]. We predicted personality from three characteristics of the text: its linguistic features, its content features, which were both defined in RQ1, and using the features resulting from a TF-IDF vectorisation. We also compared three different ML models for the same task: Random Forest (RF), XGBoost (XGB) and Support Vector Machine (SVM), using 5-fold validation for each. We predicted all Big Five personality traits as continuous variables, using Mean Absolute Error (MAE) as performance metric. We then ran a 5 (Big Five traits) x 3 (ML models) x 3 (sets of text features) ANOVA to find which models and sets of features would lead to higher predictions across each trait, checking for both main effects and interactions.

2.2 Study 1 Results

Data Description. We excluded participants who wrote less than 100 words, resulting in a final sample of N = 128. Descriptive statistics of our sample's linguistics variables, content variables and personality traits are reported in Tables 1, 2 and 3 respectively.

Table 1. Definition, means and SDs of selected linguistic features used to answer RQ1.

Linguistic features descriptives		
Feature	Definition	*Mean (SD)*
Word Count (WC)	Total word count	324.70 (184.08)
Analytical Language	Metric of logical, formal thinking	33.81 (18.86)
Certitude	Words relating to certitude (really, actually, of course, real) as a % of word count	0.74 (0.67)
Self-References	Use of "I" + "we" pronouns as a % of word count	3.04 (2.19)
Lexical Diversity	Unique words / total words	0.58 (0.06)

Table 2. Examples, definitions, means and SDs for content features. Means are reported as counts (the average participant mentioned environmental reasons 2.80 times).

Content features descriptives				
Theme	Feature	Definition	Example	*Mean (SD)*
Reasons	Environmental Reasons	Used when a participant mentions environmental reasons to carry out the target behaviour	"You should be buying second hand clothes because it reduces your carbon footprint"	2.80 (2.40)

(continued)

Table 2. (*continued*)

Content features descriptives

Theme	Feature	Definition	Example	*Mean (SD)*
	Financial Reasons	Used when a participant mentions financial reasons to carry out the target behaviour	"Think at how much money you can save"	1.80 (1.23)
	Health Reasons	Used when a participant mentions health reasons to carry out the target behaviour	"a bonus of eating less meat is the health benefits you will most likely reap"	0.90 (0.96)
	Easy to Do	Used every time a participant mentions that the target behaviour is easy to carry out	"Super easy way to help reduce pollution"	0.54 (0.67)
Advice	Offers to Help	Used when the participant suggests to seek help from others, or directly offers to help	"I recycle a lot. Let me help you"	1.17 (1.68)
	Alternatives	Used when a participant suggests an alternative sustainable behaviour that is not in the prompt	"You could start with electricity consumption. I shut off a lot of my household electronics."	0.43 (0.88)
	Start Small	Used when a participant suggests a starting step that is easier to achieve than the target behaviour	"Start small – try to walk or cycle to work one day a week and then try to build it up."	0.80 (0.99)
Evaluations	Praise	Used when a participant uses words of praise or encouragement	"I'm so proud of you for thinking of this"	1.62 (1.73)
	Criticism	Used when a participant criticises the target behaviour	"Eating less meat doesn't necessarily reduce your carbon footprint, some fruit and veg may need to travel just as far"	0.17 (0.43)

(*continued*)

Table 2. (*continued*)

Content features descriptives				
Theme	Feature	Definition	Example	*Mean (SD)*
	Scoping Questions	Used when a participant asks a question about circumstances that affect the target behaviour	"Is there much public transportation infrastructure near you?"	0.54 (0.99)
	Barriers	Used when a participant mentions obstacles to the target behaviour	"It's tough because fast fashion is convenient"	1.10 (1.29)

Table 3. Characteristics, means and SDs of Big Five personality traits in our dataset.

Personality trait descriptives		
Trait	*Characteristics*	*Mean (SD)*
Extraversion	Low: reserved, thoughtful High: sociable, fun-loving	3.04 (0.85)
Agreeableness	Low: suspicious, uncooperative High: trusting, helpful	3.85 (0.58)
Conscientiousness	Low: impulsive, disorganized High: disciplined, careful	3.73 (0.72)
Openness	Low: prefers routine, practical High: imaginative, spontaneous	3.74 (0.66)
Neuroticism	Low: calm, confident High: anxious, pessimistic	2.83 (0.87)

RQ1. Do personality traits predict differences in persuasive writing? Our multivariate models showed that personality traits did not significantly predict differences in the linguistic characteristics of persuasive writing, Pillai's $V = 0.23$, $F(25, 610) = 1.19$, $p = 0.237$, but they did instead significantly predict differences in the content of persuasive writing, Pillai's $V = 0.65$, $F(55, 580) = 1.58$, $p = 0.006$. Specifically, higher openness scores predicted more frequent mentions of health reasons ($B = 0.51$, $SE = 0.13$, $\beta = 0.26$, $t(116) = 3.79$, $p < 0.001$), while higher extraversion ($B = 0.30$, $SE = 0.15$, $\beta = 0.25$, $t(116) = 1.99$, $p = 0.049$), and lower conscientiousness ($B = -0.58$, $SE = 0.19$, $\beta = -0.47$, $t(116) = -2.94$, $p = 0.004$) both predicted more frequent mentions of barriers to adopt a sustainable behaviour.

RQ2. Is it possible to predict personality traits from persuasive writing? We ran a total of 45 machine learning models, each predicting the five personality traits from one of three sets of predictors (linguistic variables, content variables, TF-IDF vectorized text), using one of three ML models (RF, SVM, XGBoost). Mean Average Errors for each model are reported in Fig. 1.

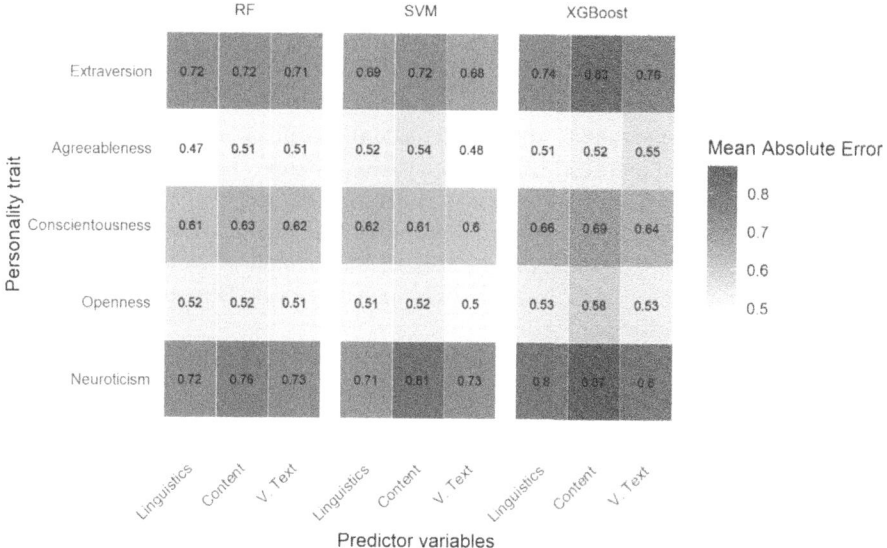

Fig. 1. Faceted heatmap of Mean Absolute Error by personality trait (Y axis), predictor (X axis) and ML model used (facets). Lighter colour indicates better performance.

Follow-up ANOVA results indicated that error margin was significantly lower in agreeableness (M = 0.51, SD = 0.36) and openness (M = 0.52, SD = 0.42) compared to all other traits, closely followed by conscientiousness (M = 0.63, SD = 0.44). In addition, we found that linguistic features (M = 0.61, SD = 0.44) were a significantly better predictor of personality than content variables, (M = 0.65, SD = 0.50), $p = 0.024$, and that SVM (M = 0.61, SD = 0.46) and RF (M = 0.62, SD = 0.46) were more accurate than XGB (M = 0.65, SD = 0.49), $p = 0.016$ and $p = 0.037$. No interaction effects were found.

2.3 Study 1 Short Discussion

The results from Study 1 showed that personality prediction from persuasive text can be done with accuracy levels comparable to general-purpose text. Agreeableness and Openness were the traits that can be predicted most accurately.

Surprisingly, personality did not predict the linguistic features of persuasive writing in our sample. One explanation is that our chosen features, which were selected in accordance with previous research on persuasion [46], may be important for persuasion as a whole, independently of personality. Instead, personality did predict the content of persuasive writing. These markers can be used to tweak the personality of persuasive agents; for example, based on these results, a more "open" persuasive agent may mention the heath benefits of sustainable behaviour more often. Crucially, our results left open questions as to whether these differences in persuasive text increase persuasion for different users: this will be the focus of our follow-up work.

3 Next Steps

3.1 Study 2 Provisional Research Questions

Building on results from Study 1, we plan to broaden the analysis to other characteristics beyond personality and to investigate how persuasive different statements are on different users. To compare the persuasiveness of different statements, we set out to build a taxonomy of "persuader types" in the wild, using a clustering approach. Then, we plan to test the persuasiveness of these persuader types on a sample of participants, considering the characteristics of both the persuaders and persuadees. This study explores the following research questions:

RQ1: *Which persuader types exist in the wild and what characteristics does their persuasive writing share?*

RQ2: *Do people rate text as persuasive if it was written by people who write like them?*

3.2 Study 2 Provisional Methodology

This study involves two groups of people: persuaders and persuadees. The data collected in Study 1 will serve as the persuaders group. More persuaders may be recruited to boost statistical power and generalisability. The dataset includes the persuaders' demographic characteristics as well as 100+ text-level features, both related to linguistics (LIWC dictionary) and content.

First we will pre-process the data by standardizing the text-level features. Principal component analysis may also be used to reduce the number of features used for clustering. We will then cluster persuaders based on the principal linguistic and content characteristics of their writing, to find 'persuader types' that write in similar ways. More than one clustering method may be compared for validation, such as K-Means, Nearest Neighbours, Hierarchical Clustering or Latent Profile Analysis. Once a number of clusters have emerged, they will need to be labelled as different *persuader types*; for example, if a cluster of writing samples contains a lot of logical reasons to engage in sustainability, it may be labelled as *'Type: logical thinkers'*; or if another cluster shows high certitude and assertiveness in their writing, it may be labelled as *'Type: assertive debaters'*. Different ways are available to conduct this labelling process, for example checking differences in text-level features across clusters, or conducting topic modelling to find dominant themes in each cluster. At this point we will have a number of labelled persuader types which are ready for evaluation by persuadees. The next step is to recruit a sample of participants, the designated persuadees, and assign them to the persuader type which is most similar to them. To enable similarity pairing, persuadees will be asked to provide a writing sample and then be assigned to the persuader type that matches their writing style the most, based on text-level features. Once persuadees have been assigned a persuader type, they will be exposed to persuasive statements extracted from all persuader types, to check if they tend to be more persuaded by text coming from the congruent persuader type. Successful persuasion in the persuadee sample will be measured using semantic differential scales, as previous research has shown they are effective at capturing subtle differences in change of stance [12]. For example, for each persuasive statement they are exposed to, participants would have to rate the statement on a 1–7 scale from bad-good, harmful-beneficial, worthless-valuable etc. We will then use ANOVA and post-hoc paired t-tests to explore differences in evaluation scores across categories, e.g., see if *'logical thinker'* persuadees prefer *'logical thinker'* persuaders, or if *'assertive debater'* persuadees prefer *'assertive debater'* persuaders. It could be the case that persuadees prefer persuasive statements congruent with their own type, or that they prefer statements from a different type, or even that some persuader types are generally more persuasive across the sample.

3.3 Study 3 Provisional Research Questions

Based on results from study 2, this study seeks to build and evaluate a personalised conversational agent for adopting sustainable behaviours that mimics different persuader types. A provisional research question for this study is:

RQ1: *Are users more likely to be persuaded by a conversational persuasive agent if it writes like them?*

3.4 Study 3 Provisional Methodology

If Study 2 finds a significant similarity-attraction effect between persuader and persuadees, this study will build a chatbot that is able to classify a persuadee into one of the pre-set persuadee types and then deliver personalised dialogue that reflects the appropriate persuader type. Generation of text in different persuader types will be achieved by training a Large Language Model over the types, and adding constraints to keep conversation within the realm of sustainable behaviours. Evaluation of such a system will involve a mixture of loss functions and judgements from participants. To tackle RQ1, different approaches to measuring successful persuasion can be considered, such as measuring attitudes towards a sustainable behaviour before and after interaction with the chatbot, or short-term behaviour change.

Eventually, we envision that this conversational agent should incorporate elements of personalised suggestions as well as personalised language. Personalising suggested behaviours is crucial in the context of sustainability, as personal circumstances determine which sustainable behaviours are easier to implement, or feasible at all. Such a system would build more complex user profiles which include the user's lifestyles and preferences, and employ ranking algorithms to suggest suitable sustainable behaviours.

Acknowledgments. This work was supported by the UKRI Centre for Doctoral Training in Socially Intelligent Artificial Agents, Grant Number EP/S02266X/1.

Disclosure of Interests. The author has no competing interests to declare.

References

1. Aafjes-Van Doorn, K. et al.: Language style matching in psychotherapy: an implicit aspect of alliance. J. Counseling Psychol. **67**, 509–522 (2020). https://doi.org/10.1037/cou0000433
2. Adams, M.A. et al.: An adaptive physical activity intervention for overweight adults: a randomized controlled trial. PLoS ONE. **8**(12), e82901 (2013). https://doi.org/10.1371/journal.pone.0082901
3. Ait Baha, T. et al.: The power of personalization: a systematic review of personality-Adaptive Chatbots. SN Comput. Sci. **4**(5), 661 (2023). https://doi.org/10.1007/s42979-023-02092-6
4. Ajzen, I.: Attitudes, Personality and Behaviour. McGraw-Hill Education (UK) (2005)
5. Al-Ansari, N. et al.: Testing tailored weekly feedback messages for behavioral change of people living with diabetes using a mHealth application. In: 2020 7th International Conference on Behavioural and Social Computing (BESC), pp. 1–4 IEEE, Bournemouth, United Kingdom (2020). https://doi.org/10.1109/BESC51023.2020.9348279
6. Alqahtani, F., et al.: Personality-based approach for tailoring persuasive mental health applications. User Model. User-Adap. Inter. **32**(3), 253–295 (2022). https://doi.org/10.1007/s11257-021-09289-5
7. Asbjørnsen, R.A. et al.: Combining persuasive system design principles and behavior change techniques in digital interventions supporting long-term weight loss maintenance: design and development of eCHANGE. JMIR Hum. Factors. **9**(2), e37372 (2022). https://doi.org/10.2196/37372
8. Baskerville, N.B. et al.: Crush the crave: development and formative evaluation of a smartphone app for smoking cessation. JMIR Mhealth Uhealth. **6**(3), e52 (2018). https://doi.org/10.2196/mhealth.9011
9. Beheshtian, N. et al.: GreenLife: A persuasive social robot to enhance the sustainable behavior in shared living spaces. In: Proceedings of the 11th Nordic Conference on Human-Computer Interaction: Shaping Experiences, Shaping Society, pp. 1–12 ACM, Tallinn Estonia (2020). https://doi.org/10.1145/3419249.3420143
10. Beun, R.J. et al.: Negotiation in automated e-coaching: an application in mobile insomnia treatment. In: Presented at the Proceedings of the 32nd International BCS Human Computer Interaction Conference July (2018). https://doi.org/10.14236/ewic/HCI2018.24
11. Boyd, R. et al.: The development and psychometric properties of LIWC-22 (2022). https://doi.org/10.13140/RG.2.2.23890.43205
12. Carter, R.F., et al.: The semantic differential in opinion measurement. Public Opin. Q. **32**(4), 666–674 (1968)
13. Celli, F. et al.: The Workshop on Computational Personality Recognition 2014. In: Proceedings of the 22nd ACM International Conference on Multimedia, pp. 1245–1246 ACM, Orlando Florida USA (2014). https://doi.org/10.1145/2647868.2647870
14. Cialdini, R.B., Sagarin, B.J.: Principles of interpersonal influence. In: Persuasion: Psychological Insights and Perspectives, 2nd edn, pp. 143–169 Sage Publications, Inc., Thousand Oaks, CA, US (2005)
15. Cohen, L., Kassis-Henderson, J.: Language use in establishing rapport and building relations: implications for international teams and management education. Manag. Avenir **55**(5), 185–207 (2012). https://doi.org/10.3917/mav.055.0185
16. Daskalova, N. et al.: Self-E: Smartphone-supported guidance for customizable self-experimentation. In: Proceedings of the 2021 CHI Conference on Human Factors in Computing Systems. Association for Computing Machinery, New York, NY, USA (2021). https://doi.org/10.1145/3411764.3445100
17. De Carolis, B. et al.: 'Keep the user in mind!' Persuasive effects of social robot as personalized nutritional coach (2019)

18. Dunlap, R.E.: The new environmental paradigm scale: from marginality to worldwide use. J. Environ. Educ. **40**(1), 3–18 (2008). https://doi.org/10.3200/JOEE.40.1.3-18

19. Figueroa, C.A., et al.: Ratings and experiences in using a mobile application to increase physical activity among university students: implications for future design. Univ. Access Inf. Soc. **23**(2), 821–830 (2024). https://doi.org/10.1007/s10209-022-00962-z

20. Fossati, A., et al.: The Big Five Inventory (BFI). Eur. J. Psychol. Assess. **27**(1), 50–58 (2011). https://doi.org/10.1027/1015-5759/a000043

21. Foulonneau, A. et al.: Stop procrastinating: TILT, time is life time, a persuasive application. In: Proceedings of the 28th Australian Conference on Computer-Human Interaction, pp. 508–516 Association for Computing Machinery, New York, NY, USA (2016). https://doi.org/10.1145/3010915.3010947

22. Graf, B. et al.: Nombot: Simplify food tracking. In: Proceedings of the 14th International Conference on Mobile and Ubiquitous Multimedia, pp. 360–363 Association for Computing Machinery, New York, NY, USA (2015). https://doi.org/10.1145/2836041.2841208

23. Halko, S., Kientz, J.: Personality and persuasive technology: an exploratory study on health-promoting mobile applications. In: Ploug, T., Hasle, P., Oinas-Kukkonen, H. (eds.), vol. 6137. Springer, Heidelberg (2010). https://doi.org/10.1007/978-3-642-13226-1_16

24. Hee, O.: Validity and reliability of the big five personality traits scale in Malaysia (2014)

25. Hirsh, J.B., et al.: Personalized persuasion: tailoring persuasive appeals to recipients' personality traits. Psychol. Sci. **23**(6), 578–581 (2012). https://doi.org/10.1177/0956797611436349

26. Jager, W., Amblard, F.: A dynamical perspective on attitude change

27. Jin, E., Eastin, M.S.: Birds of a feather flock together: matched personality effects of product recommendation Chatbots and users. J. Res. Interact. Mark. **17**(3), 416–433 (2022). https://doi.org/10.1108/JRIM-03-2022-0089

28. König, L., Jucks, R.: Influence of enthusiastic language on the credibility of health information and the trustworthiness of science communicators: insights from a between-subject web-based experiment. Interact. J. Med. Res. **8**(3), e13619 (2019). https://doi.org/10.2196/13619

29. Kubota, A. et al.: Get SMART: collaborative goal setting with cognitively assistive robots. In: Proceedings of the 2023 ACM/IEEE International Conference on Human-Robot Interaction, pp. 44–53 Association for Computing Machinery, New York, NY, USA (2023). https://doi.org/10.1145/3568162.3576993

30. Lindgren, H. et al.: Personalised persuasive coaching to increase older adults' physical and social activities: a motivational model. In: Demazeau, Y. et al. (eds.) Advances in Practical Applications of Cyber-Physical Multi-Agent Systems: The PAAMS Collection, pp. 170–182 Springer International Publishing, Cham (2017). https://doi.org/10.1007/978-3-319-59930-4_14

31. Liu, Z. et al.: CatGAN: category-aware generative adversarial networks with hierarchical evolutionary learning for category text generation. In: Proceedings of the AAAI Conference on Artificial Intelligence, vol. 34, no. 05, pp. 8425–8432 (2020). https://doi.org/10.1609/aaai.v34i05.6361

32. Minucci, E.: ElenaMinucci/Pers-pers-dataset (2024). https://github.com/ElenaMinucci/Pers-Pers-Dataset

33. Muir, K., et al.: Linguistic style accommodation shapes impression formation and rapport in computer-mediated communication. J. Lang. Soc. Psychol. **36**(5), 525–548 (2017). https://doi.org/10.1177/0261927X17701327

34. Oinas-Kukkonen, H., Harjumaa, M.: Persuasive systems design: key issues, process model, and system features. CAIS. **24** (2009). https://doi.org/10.17705/1CAIS.02428

35. Oyebode, O., Orji, R.: Persuasive strategy implementation choices and their effectiveness: towards personalised persuasive systems. Behav. Inf. Technol. **42**(13), 2176–2209 (2023). https://doi.org/10.1080/0144929X.2022.2112612
36. Paay, J. et al.: Promoting pro-environmental behaviour: a tale of two systems. In: Proceedings of the 25th Australian Computer-Human Interaction Conference: Augmentation, Application, Innovation, Collaboration, pp. 235–244 Association for Computing Machinery, New York, NY, USA (2013). https://doi.org/10.1145/2541016.2541045
37. Paay, J. et al.: Quitty: using technology to persuade smokers to quit. In: Proceedings of the 8th Nordic Conference on Human-Computer Interaction: Fun, Fast, Foundational, pp. 551–560 Association for Computing Machinery, New York, NY, USA (2014). https://doi.org/10.1145/2639189.2639195
38. Rajanna, V. et al.: Step up life: a context aware health assistant. In: Proceedings of the Third ACM SIGSPATIAL International Workshop on the Use of GIS in Public Health, pp. 21–30 Association for Computing Machinery, New York, NY, USA (2014). https://doi.org/10.1145/2676629.2676636
39. Richardson, B.H., et al.: Language style matching and police interrogation outcomes. Law & Hum. Behav. **38**(4), 357–366 (2014)
40. Santhanam, S., Shaikh, S.: A survey of natural language generation techniques with a focus on dialogue systems - Past, present and future directions. http://arxiv.org/abs/1906.00500 (2019)
41. Setiawan, I.M.A. et al.: An adaptive mobile health system to support self-management for persons with chronic conditions and disabilities: usability and feasibility studies. JMIR Form Res. **3**(2), e12982 (2019). https://doi.org/10.2196/12982
42. Starke, A. et al.: Effective user interface designs to increase energy-efficient behavior in a rasch-based energy recommender system. In: Proceedings of the Eleventh ACM Conference on Recommender Systems, pp. 65–73 Association for Computing Machinery, New York, NY, USA (2017). https://doi.org/10.1145/3109859.3109902
43. Stets, J.E., Burke, P.J.: Identity theory and social identity theory. Soc. Psychol. Q. **63**(3), 224–237 (2000). https://doi.org/10.2307/2695870
44. Tajfel, H.: Social psychology of intergroup relations. Ann. Rev. Psychol. **33**, 1–39 (1982). https://doi.org/10.1146/annurev.ps.33.020182.000245
45. Tajfel, H., Turner, J.C.: The social identity theory of intergroup behavior. In: Political Psychology. Psychology Press (2004)
46. Ta, V.P. et al.: An inclusive, real-world investigation of persuasion in language and verbal behavior. J. Comput. Soc. Sci. **5**(1), 883–903 (2022). https://doi.org/10.1007/s42001-021-00153-5
47. Taylor, P.J., Thomas, S.: Linguistic style matching and negotiation outcome. Negot. Confl. Manage. Res. **1**(3), 263–281 (2008). https://doi.org/10.1111/j.1750-4716.2008.00016.x
48. Van Baaren, R.B., et al.: Mimicry for money: behavioral consequences of imitation. J. Exp. Soc. Psychol. **39**(4), 393–398 (2003). https://doi.org/10.1016/S0022-1031(03)00014-3
49. Verberne, F.M.F., et al.: Trusting a virtual driver that looks, acts, and thinks like you. Hum. Factors **57**(5), 895–909 (2015). https://doi.org/10.1177/0018720815580749
50. Völkel, S.T. et al.: Manipulating and evaluating levels of personality perceptions of voice assistants through enactment-based dialogue design. In: Proceedings of the 3rd Conference on Conversational User Interfaces. Association for Computing Machinery, New York, NY, USA (2021). https://doi.org/10.1145/3469595.3469605
51. Wang, K., Wan, X.: SentiGAN: generating sentimental texts via mixture adversarial networks. In: Proceedings of the Twenty-Seventh International Joint Conference on Artificial Intelligence, pp. 4446–4452 International Joint Conferences on Artificial Intelligence Organization, Stockholm, Sweden (2018). https://doi.org/10.24963/ijcai.2018/618

52. Yang, Y., et al.: Mediating role of trust between leader communication style and subordinate's work outcomes in project teams. Eng. Manag. J.Manag. J. **32**(3), 152–165 (2020). https://doi.org/10.1080/10429247.2020.1733380
53. About Prolific. https://www.prolific.com/about. Accessed 25 Oct 2024
54. AR6 Synthesis report: Climate change 2023 — IPCC. https://www.ipcc.ch/report/sixth-assessment-report-cycle/. Accessed 17 Oct 2024

Family-Based Persuasion in Digital Parenting Tools: A Research Proposal

Shaima Moqbel[✉]

College of Science and Engineering, Hamad Bin Khalifa University, Doha, Qatar
shmo56828@hbku.edu.qa

Abstract. Parental control applications play a crucial role in digital parenting by helping parents manage children's online activities. However, most existing applications emphasize restrictive monitoring and surveillance, often at the expense of trust, transparency, and digital autonomy. This study evaluates current parental control tools through the lens of Social Learning Theory, Attachment Theory, and Persuasive Systems Design (PSD) to identify gaps in fostering collaborative digital parenting. Using a mixed-methods approach, the research involves qualitative interviews, focus groups, surveys, and usability testing with parents and adolescents (ages 10–15). The study examines how digital parenting strategies influence family relationships and child autonomy and explores the effectiveness of collaborative design features such as gamification, shared dashboards, and participatory goal-setting. Findings will contribute to the development of a guidance-based framework for parental control applications, shifting from a surveillance model to one that supports education, trust, and cooperative decision-making. The study's insights aim to inform developers, policymakers, and educators on best practices for designing ethically responsible and culturally adaptive digital parenting solutions.

Keywords: Digital Parenting · Parental Control Applications · Persuasive Systems Design · Social Learning Theory · Attachment Theory · Trust · Autonomy

1 Introduction

The increasing integration of digital technology into children's lives presents both opportunities and risks, requiring parents to navigate challenges such as cyberbullying, excessive screen time, and exposure to inappropriate content [1, 2]. Traditional parental control applications, including Google Family Link, Norton Family, and Qustodio, were developed to help parents manage their children's online experiences. These applications typically provide functionalities such as screen time monitoring, content filtering, and activity tracking, offering parents a sense of control over their child's digital environment [3, 4].

While these tools are effective in mitigating certain risks, their overemphasis on restrictive and surveillance-based features raises concerns about their impact on trust

© The Author(s), under exclusive license to Springer Nature Switzerland AG 2026
I. Wiafe et al. (Eds.): PERSUASIVE 2025, CCIS 2542, pp. 148–159, 2026.
https://doi.org/10.1007/978-3-031-97177-8_14

and autonomy [5, 6]. Studies suggest that excessive monitoring can lead to resistance, secrecy, and strained parent-child relationships [7, 8]. Adolescents, in particular, may perceive these tools as intrusive, undermining their sense of digital independence [9]. Research indicates that a more balanced approach—one that fosters open communication, transparency, and mutual decision-making—can improve digital literacy and encourage responsible online behavior [10, 11]. Additionally, studies show that excessive parental restrictions can lead to psychological distress, diminished digital resilience, and reduced self-regulation among children and adolescents [12, 13].

A shift in the design of parental control applications is necessary to move beyond a purely restrictive model. By integrating principles from behavioral theories, particularly Social Learning Theory and Attachment Theory, these tools can be redesigned to support collaborative digital parenting [14]. Social Learning Theory emphasizes that children learn behaviors by observing their parents [15], suggesting that parental modeling of responsible technology use is a key factor in shaping children's digital habits [16]. Attachment Theory highlights the importance of secure parent-child relationships in fostering resilience and emotional regulation, underscoring the need for digital parenting strategies that prioritize trust and communication [17, 18]. Research has demonstrated that secure attachments positively influence children's ability to navigate digital environments with autonomy and responsibility [19, 20].

Additionally, the Persuasive Systems Design (PSD) model provides a framework for designing technology that influences behavior positively [21]. The model categorizes persuasive system features into primary task support, dialogue support, system credibility, and social support [22]. Studies suggest that integrating PSD principles into parental control applications can enhance user engagement, foster digital resilience, and encourage cooperative decision-making within families [23]. Recent advancements in persuasive technology demonstrate that interactive parental control features—such as collaborative goal-setting, real-time feedback, and educational nudges—improve both parental and child satisfaction with digital parenting strategies [24, 25].

This study explores how parental control applications can be reimagined to balance safety with autonomy, fostering an environment where children and parents collaboratively navigate digital challenges. It aims to answer the following research questions:

RQ 1: What types of parenting styles and parental mediation strategies are utilized in managing children's digital behaviors?

RQ 2: Do existing and proposed features of parental control applications align with and support the creation of positive family environments?

RQ 3: How can parental control application features be redesigned based on role modeling principles to better support trust, collaboration, and empowerment within families?

RQ 4: What are the perceived benefits and challenges of integrating collaborative features into parental control applications from the perspective of both parents and children?

RQ 5: How do different parental control approaches impact children's digital autonomy, trust, and resilience over time?

By addressing these questions, this study seeks to provide a roadmap for the next generation of parental control applications, offering design recommendations that enhance digital parenting practices in a way that is both effective and family-centric.

2 Background and Related Work

This section introduces the theoretical background of digital parenting, focusing on how parental control applications influence parent-child relationships and digital literacy. It explores various mediation strategies, theoretical frameworks, and the limitations of existing parental control applications.

2.1 Parental Mediation Strategies

Parental mediation strategies have been widely studied in the context of digital parenting. As children's digital engagement continues to increase, understanding the interplay between parental control tools and family dynamics has become crucial. The literature on digital parenting strategies highlights various approaches, including restrictive, active, co-use, and technical mediation, each of which has distinct benefits and limitations [1, 2].

Restrictive mediation involves setting rules and limitations on digital device usage, such as restricting screen time or prohibiting access to certain websites or applications. While effective in maintaining immediate safety, excessive restrictions may reduce children's autonomy, leading to secrecy and potential conflicts between parents and adolescents [3, 4]. Research suggests that while restriction can mitigate certain online risks, it does not necessarily equip children with the skills needed for independent digital decision-making [5, 6].

Active mediation, on the other hand, promotes discussions between parents and children about digital use. This approach fosters critical thinking, enabling children to assess online risks and make informed choices [7]. Studies indicate that active mediation leads to better online behavior outcomes and stronger parent-child relationships [8, 9]. However, it requires time and engagement from parents, which may not always be feasible.

Co-use mediation is another strategy that involves parents and children engaging in digital activities together, such as watching videos, playing games, or browsing the internet as a shared experience. This approach strengthens family bonds and provides parents with opportunities to guide their children's digital experiences in real-time [10]. However, it is less effective in enforcing safety measures, as it relies on shared participation rather than structural restrictions [11].

Technical mediation employs parental control tools to monitor and regulate children's digital activities. These tools include features such as location tracking, app restrictions, and content filtering. While convenient, technical mediation has been criticized for being overly surveillance-oriented, potentially eroding trust between parents and children [12, 13]. Research indicates that while these tools provide immediate oversight, their long-term efficacy depends on transparency and whether they are used in conjunction with active discussions [14].

2.2 Theoretical Foundations

Several theoretical models help explain the effects of parental mediation strategies and inform the design of digital parenting tools. These frameworks provide insights into how children develop digital literacy and regulate their online behavior based on parental influence.

Social Learning Theory posits that children learn behaviors by observing and imitating their parents [15, 16]. In digital parenting, this suggests that children are more likely to adopt responsible online behaviors when parents model healthy technology use. Digital parenting tools should integrate role-modeling features, such as shared activity logs and notifications that encourage joint discussions about digital usage [17].

Attachment Theory emphasizes the importance of secure parent-child relationships in fostering trust, resilience, and emotional regulation [18, 19]. In digital contexts, strong parent-child bonds ensure that children feel comfortable discussing online experiences and challenges. Parental control tools should enhance, rather than undermine, these relationships by promoting transparency and facilitating open conversations [20]. Features such as collaborative rule-setting and shared reports on digital usage can support this approach [21].

The PSD model categorizes persuasive technology elements into four domains—primary task support, dialogue support, system credibility, and social support [22, 23]. Current parental control applications often excel in primary task support (e.g., monitoring and restriction) but lack dialogue and social support features, which are essential for fostering trust and collaboration. Integrating persuasive design elements, such as real-time feedback and gamification, can make these tools more engaging and effective for both parents and children [24, 25].

2.3 Gaps in Existing Parental Control Applications

Recent studies, including [28], indicate that parents' own digital habits significantly impact their children's internet addiction. Similarly, [31] emphasize the importance of distinguishing between digital engagement and digital dependence, highlighting that restrictive digital parenting without addressing parental behavior may be insufficient. These insights suggest that parental control applications should move beyond simple monitoring tools and instead incorporate educational strategies that foster balanced digital habits in both parents and children.

Prior research highlights the limitations of traditional parental control applications in addressing digital well-being concerns. [27] emphasized that inconsistent discipline and frequent parent-child conflicts significantly contribute to Internet Addiction (IA) in adolescents. This finding suggests that existing digital parenting tools, which primarily focus on monitoring and restrictions, may not effectively mitigate IA risks. Instead, research suggests that these tools should integrate family-centered approaches, promoting positive parenting practices, consistent discipline, and joint goal setting to foster healthier digital habits [27].

Additionally, [28] investigated the relationship between different types of internet use and Internet Addiction (IA) in adolescents. Their findings revealed that nonessential internet use significantly predicted IA, whereas essential use did not. This suggests that existing parental control strategies, which do not distinguish between essential and nonessential internet use, may be ineffective in addressing IA risks. They recommend that interventions should focus on guiding adolescents toward balanced internet use rather than imposing broad restrictions, highlighting the importance of context-specific, culturally sensitive approaches to digital well-being [28].

Furthermore, [31] examined how parental Internet behaviors influence adolescent digital addiction. Their research underscores the importance of distinguishing between digital engagement and digital dependence, reinforcing the argument that digital parenting strategies should focus on education and behavior modeling rather than mere restrictions. In line with this, [28] highlighted the need to differentiate between essential and nonessential internet use when addressing adolescent Internet Addiction (IA). Their findings suggest that broad restrictions on screen time may be ineffective if they do not account for the specific nature of digital engagement. Instead, interventions should guide adolescents toward balanced internet use, emphasizing culturally sensitive and developmentally appropriate approaches to digital well-being [28].

Furthermore, [29] explored how persuasive systems can influence online behaviors, particularly in adolescent internet use. Incorporating insights from persuasive systems design, our study will assess how gamification, shared dashboards, and participatory goal-setting can create a more balanced digital parenting approach that fosters trust rather than control [29].

Introduced the D-Crastinate method as a structured approach to reducing procrastination on social networking sites. Their study highlights the importance of self-awareness and personalized countermeasures, which align with our goal of fostering autonomy and collaborative decision-making in digital parenting applications [30].

Recent research highlights the significant role of social networking site (SNS) design in facilitating procrastination, leading to negative consequences such as reduced academic performance and increased stress. Studies emphasize that SNS features, including notifications, immersive design, and social interaction mechanisms, contribute to habitual procrastination by creating an environment of constant engagement. The D-Crastinate method was introduced to help users manage their digital procrastination by increasing self-awareness, identifying procrastination triggers, and applying tailored countermeasures such as goal-setting, task engagement tools, and self-regulation techniques. These findings suggest that digital parenting strategies should integrate educational and self-monitoring features that encourage responsible digital habits rather than relying solely on restrictive control mechanisms [31].

Research has explored how persuasive systems influence online behaviors, particularly in adolescent internet use. One study highlighted that incorporating gamification, shared dashboards, and participatory goal-setting can shift digital parenting strategies from control-based approaches to engagement-driven interventions. This aligns with the current study's focus on fostering trust and collaboration through persuasive system design in parental control applications. Additionally, the findings emphasize the importance of self-awareness and personalized countermeasures, supporting our goal of fostering autonomy and collaborative decision-making in digital parenting applications [29, 30].

Recent research by [31] explored the impact of parental Internet behaviors on adolescent digital addiction. The findings highlight the need to distinguish between digital engagement and digital dependence, emphasizing that digital parenting strategies should prioritize education and behavior modeling over restrictive measures.

These works collectively reinforce the need for redesigning parental control tools to move beyond restrictive monitoring and towards collaborative, trust-based approaches that consider user autonomy and behavioral patterns.

3 Research AIM

The widespread use of digital technologies in children's daily lives presents both opportunities and challenges for families. Parental control applications have emerged as tools to help parents manage their children's digital interactions; however, many of these tools rely heavily on restrictive and surveillance-based approaches. These methods, while effective in limiting access to inappropriate content, often lead to unintended consequences such as diminished trust, increased secrecy, and conflicts between parents and children [1, 2]. This study aims to rethink and redesign parental control applications to shift from a control-based approach to one that emphasizes collaboration, trust, and education in digital parenting.

A key goal of this research is to explore how digital parenting tools can be designed to empower children rather than simply monitor them. Many existing applications create an imbalance in digital authority, fostering a sense of restriction rather than mutual engagement [3, 4]. By integrating principles from Social Learning Theory, Attachment Theory, and Persuasive Systems Design, this study seeks to develop a framework that encourages parents and children to navigate digital challenges together, fostering open communication and shared decision-making [5, 6].

This research also aims to introduce and assess new interactive features that promote a balanced digital parenting model. This includes the development of tools such as collaborative dashboards, real-time feedback mechanisms, and gamification techniques that encourage children to develop self-regulation skills and digital literacy [7, 8]. Unlike traditional monitoring approaches, these features focus on empowering children with autonomy while ensuring parental guidance remains a supportive presence.

Moreover, this study will evaluate how redesigned parental control applications influence family dynamics, trust-building, and long-term behavioral outcomes [9, 10]. By focusing on educational and persuasive elements rather than punitive restrictions, the research aims to provide evidence-based recommendations for developers, and educators, to create more effective and ethically responsible parental control solutions [11, 12].

By achieving these aims, the study aspires to contribute to the evolution of parental control applications from surveillance tools to supportive digital parenting aids that promote healthy and responsible digital engagement in modern family environments [13, 14].

4 Research Objectives and Methods

This study employs a mixed-methods approach, integrating qualitative and quantitative research techniques to analyze parental control applications and user experiences.

The increasing integration of digital technologies into children's daily lives presents both opportunities and challenges for families. Parental control applications have become essential tools to help parents navigate their children's digital experiences, yet many of these tools focus primarily on restrictive monitoring and surveillance-based mechanisms. While such approaches can offer protection, they may also negatively impact trust and open communication between parents and children [15, 16]. This research aims to develop a collaborative, education-driven approach to parental control applications that fosters trust, digital literacy, and shared responsibility between parents and children.

4.1 Research Objectives

The overarching objective of this study is to redesign parental control applications to better support trust, collaboration, and digital autonomy in family environments. The study proposes shifting away from rigid, authoritarian monitoring models towards a role-modeling framework, integrating behavioral theories such as Social Learning Theory, Attachment Theory, and Persuasive Systems Design [17, 18].

Specific objectives include:

RO 1: Investigate the different parenting styles and parental mediation strategies utilized in managing children's digital behaviors.

RO 1.1: Identify common parenting styles (e.g., authoritative, authoritarian, permissive, neglectful) in digital parenting.

RO 1.2: Examine how different parenting styles influence children's digital behavior and online autonomy.

RO 2: Evaluate whether current parental control applications align with and support the creation of positive family environments.

RO 2.1: Analyze how commonly used features in parental control applications impact family communication.

RO 2.2: Identify gaps in existing parental control tools that may hinder trust and digital well-being.

RO 3: Propose a redesign of parental control applications incorporating role modeling principles.

RO 3.1: Define key role modeling principles relevant to digital parenting.

RO 3.2: Develop feature recommendations that support parental guidance while promoting children's digital autonomy.

RO 4: Explore the benefits and challenges of integrating collaborative features into parental control applications.

RO 4.1: Identify collaborative features that can enhance trust and mutual decision-making in digital parenting.

RO 4.2: Investigate challenges that may arise when integrating collaborative features into parental control apps.

RO 5: Assess the impact of parental control strategies on children's digital autonomy, trust, and resilience.

RO 5.1: Examine how different parental control approaches influence children's digital autonomy over time.

RO 5.2: Analyze the relationship between parental control strategies and children's trust in their parents regarding digital matters.

By addressing these objectives, this study aims to reimagine parental control applications as supportive tools that foster digital well-being, empower children with self-regulation skills, and strengthen family relationships in an increasingly digital world.

4.2 Research Methods

A well-structured research design is crucial for ensuring the accuracy and effectiveness of the study. The following diagram (Fig. 1) visually represents the step-by-step methodology used in this research. It outlines the logical sequence of data collection, analysis, and prototype development, allowing for a comprehensive evaluation of parental control applications and their redesign to foster collaboration, transparency, and trust.

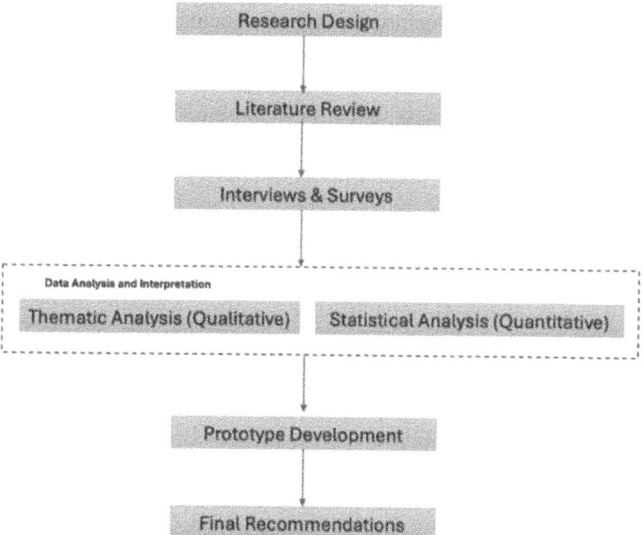

Fig. 1. Research Methodology Flowchart

Research Design
This study employs a mixed-methods research design, integrating both qualitative and quantitative methodologies to gain a comprehensive understanding of parental control applications and their effects on family dynamics.

Literature Review
A systematic review of parental control applications, digital parenting strategies, and behavioral theories will provide a foundational framework. Examining gaps in existing

research will highlight areas where improvements in design and implementation are needed.

Surveys and Interviews, and Participant Recruitment

Participants will be recruited using a combination of purposive and convenience sampling. The study will include 830 participants: 415 parents from the GCC and UK, and 400 adolescents from Qatar. Recruitment will take place through schools, online forums, and social media platforms.

Participants

The study will take place across multiple regions, with adolescent participants recruited exclusively from Qatar, while parents will be recruited from both the GCC and the UK. Schools and community organizations will play a key role in facilitating recruitment efforts.

This research will use a mixed-methods approach. The qualitative phase will involve semi-structured interviews and focus groups with parents and children (aged 10–15). Discussions will explore their experiences with parental control applications, concerns, expectations, and preferences for improved designs. Thematic analysis will be conducted to identify patterns related to trust, collaboration, transparency, and usability.

The quantitative phase will consist of structured surveys assessing perceptions of parental control tools' effectiveness, trust, and communication. Additionally, usability testing will evaluate prototype designs incorporating collaborative features such as shared dashboards, gamification, and participatory decision-making.

4.3 Data Analysis and Interpretation

Qualitative data will be analyzed using thematic analysis, focusing on identifying recurring patterns in parental mediation strategies, trust-building approaches, and digital engagement behaviors. Interview and focus group transcripts will be coded to extract key themes, which will then be compared across parent and adolescent responses to identify commonalities and differences.

Quantitative data will be analyzed using statistical techniques such as T-tests, ANOVA, and regression analysis to examine the relationships between parental mediation strategies, app features, and children's digital behaviors. The statistical findings will be triangulated with qualitative insights to provide a comprehensive understanding of how digital parenting strategies impact trust, autonomy, and digital well-being.

A comparative analysis will also be conducted to evaluate variations between Arab and UK participants, ensuring that the findings reflect cultural and contextual differences in digital parenting practices. These insights will be instrumental in refining the final framework for redesigning parental control applications to better support families in diverse settings.

4.4 Prototype Development and Evaluation

A prototype of a redesigned parental control application will be developed based on insights gathered from the qualitative and quantitative phases of the study. The prototype will incorporate features aimed at fostering collaboration, transparency, and trust, including shared dashboards, gamification elements, real-time feedback, and participatory decision-making tools.

Following the prototype development, an empirical evaluation phase will be conducted to assess its usability, effectiveness in fostering trust and collaboration, and overall user experience. This phase will involve structured usability testing sessions with parents and children, employing both qualitative and quantitative methods to measure engagement, satisfaction, and behavioral outcomes.

To ensure the prototype meets the intended objectives, the empirical evaluation will include:

- Usability Testing: Parents and adolescents will interact with the prototype and complete structured tasks designed to assess interface intuitiveness, ease of use, and perceived effectiveness.
- Post-Task Surveys: Participants will rate various aspects of the tool, including its transparency, trust-building potential, and ability to foster collaborative decision-making.
- Semi-Structured Interviews: Parents and children will provide feedback on their experiences using the tool, highlighting strengths and areas for improvement.
- Behavioral Impact Assessment: Changes in digital parenting behaviors and family communication patterns will be tracked to measure the real-world impact of the redesigned parental control features.

The insights gained from this empirical evaluation will inform the final design recommendations, ensuring that the proposed enhancements to parental control applications are both practical and effective in supporting digital parenting strategies in diverse family contexts.

5   Conclusion

This study highlights the limitations of traditional parental control applications and the need for a shift towards collaborative, trust-based digital parenting models. By integrating Social Learning Theory, Attachment Theory, and Persuasive Systems Design, the study addresses key research questions on parental mediation strategies, trust, and children's digital autonomy. The findings suggest that future parental control applications should prioritize engagement over surveillance by incorporating shared dashboards, real-time feedback, and gamified learning experiences. These features encourage self-regulation, digital literacy, and responsible online behavior while maintaining a balanced relationship between parental guidance and child autonomy. This research provides a roadmap for app developers, policymakers, and educators in designing the next generation of parental control applications that are ethically responsible, adaptable, and family-centric.

Acknowledgements. I gratefully acknowledge my supervisors, Prof. Raian Ali and Dr. Dena Al-Thani, for their valuable suggestions and guidance. This publication was supported by NPRP 14 Cluster grant # NPRP 14C-0916–210015 from the Qatar National Research Fund (a member of Qatar Foundation). The findings herein reflect the work and are solely the responsibility of the authors.

References

1. Livingstone, S., Helsper, E.J.: Parental mediation of children's internet use. J. Broadcast. Electron. Media **52**(4), 581–599 (2008)
2. Nikken, P., Opree, S.J.: Guiding young children's digital media use: Parental mediation in the context of children's media use. Media Psychol. **21**(1), 1–22 (2018)
3. Fu, M., Liu, Y., Wang, X.: Empowering digital parenting: features of effective parental control applications. J. Digital Parent. Stud. **12**(3), 45–58 (2020)
4. Byrne, J., Livingstone, S.: Risks and safety on the internet: The perspective of European children. LSE Research Online (2010)
5. Hamari, J., Koivisto, J., Sarsa, H.:. Does gamification work? a literature review of empirical studies on gamification. In: Proceedings of the 47th Hawaii International Conference on System Sciences, pp. 3025–3034 (2014)
6. Bandura, A.: Social learning theory. Prentice Hall (1977)
7. Bowlby, J.: A secure base: Parent-child attachment and healthy human development. Basic Books (1988)
8. Oinas-Kukkonen, H., Harjumaa, M.: Persuasive systems design:key issues, process model, and system features. Commun. Assoc. Inf. Syst. **24**(1), 485–500 (2009)
9. Cabello-Hutt, T., Cabello, P., Claro, M.: Online opportunities and risks for children and adolescents. New Media Soc. **20**(7), 2411–2431 (2018)
10. Dedkova, L., Smahel, D.: Digital parenting in the context of children's screen time. Cyberpsychol. Behav. Soc. Netw. **22**(8), 567–573 (2019)
11. Aiken, M., McMahon, C., Hegarty, J.: Developing trust in child-parent technology interventions. J. Fam. Psychol. **30**(4), 482–489 (2016)
12. Fogg, B.J.: Persuasive technology: Using computers to change what we think and do. Morgan Kaufmann (2003)
13. Brito, R., Francisco, R., Dias, P., Chaudron, S.: Family dynamics in digital homes: the role played by parental mediation in young children's digital practices. Contemp. Fam. Ther. **39**(4), 271–280 (2017)
14. Shin, W., Lwin, M.O.: How does "talking about the internet with parents" affect children's online risk-taking behaviors? Comput. Hum. Behav. **74**, 164–173 (2017)
15. Blum-Ross, A., Livingstone, S.: Families and screen time: Current advice and emerging research. Media Policy Brief 17, LSE Media Policy Project (2016)
16. Wartella, E., Rideout, V., Lauricella, A.: Educational media: the effects of screen time and learning. Children and Media **2**(1), 1–17 (2016)
17. Lwin, M.O., Stanaland, A.J.S., Miyazaki, A.D.: Protecting children's privacy online: how parental mediation strategies affect website safeguard effectiveness. J. Retail. **84**(4), 393–406 (2008)
18. Holloway, D., Green, L., Livingstone, S.: Zero to eight: Young children and their internet use. EU Kids Online (2013).
19. Wartella, E., Rideout, V., Lauricella, A., Connell, S.: Parenting in the age of digital technology. Northwestern University, Center on Media and Human Development (2014)
20. Clark, L.S.: Parental mediation theory for the digital age. Commun. Theory **21**(4), 323–343 (2011)
21. Kirwil, L.: Parental mediation of children's internet use in different European countries. J. Child. Media **3**(4), 394–409 (2009)

22. Zhang, W., Livingstone, S.: Inequalities in how parents support their children's development with digital technologies. J. Child. Media **13**(1), 29–47 (2019)
23. Mascheroni, G., Ólafsson, K.: Net children go mobile: Risks and opportunities. Europ. J. Commun. **29**(1), 5–26. (2014).*
24. Lau, W.W.F.: Effects of social media usage and social media multitasking on the academic performance of university students. Comput. Hum. Behav. **68**, 286–291 (2017)
25. Chemnad, K., Aziz, M.: Is it contagious? the impact of parents' internet addiction on their adolescents. J. Digital Well-being **9**(1), 77–89 (2022)
26. Al-Blwi, A.: Tools to reduce procrastination: the D-crastinate model. Healthcare **8**(4), 577–590 (2020)
27. Mousa, O., Alshakhsi, S., Yankouskaya, A., Panourgia, C., Ali, R.: Good technology requires a good environment: the role of parenting practices in adolescent internet addiction. In: Proceedings of the 2024 International Conference on Information Technology for Social Good, (pp. 143–150) (2024, September).
28. Chemnad, K., Aziz, M.: Internet addiction in adolescents: does it all start with their environment? Human Factors J. **2025**(1), e62955 (2025)
29. Hiniker, A., Schoenebeck, S.Y., Kientz, J.A.: Not at the dinner table: Parents' and children's perspectives on family technology rules. In: Proceedings of the 19th ACM Conference on Computer-Supported Cooperative Work & Social Computing, 1376–1389 (2016)
30. Valkenburg, P. M., & Piotrowski, J. T. (2017). Plugged in: How media attract and affect youth. Yale University Press
31. Alblwi, A., Al-Thani, D., McAlaney, J., Ali, R.: Managing procrastination on social networking sites: the D-crastinate method. Healthcare **8**(4), 577 (2020). https://doi.org/10.3390/healthcare8040577
32. Hargittai, E.: Digital na(t)ives? Variation in Internet skills and uses among members of the 'net generation'. Sociological Inquiry **80**(1), 92–113 (2010).
33. Aiken, M.: The cyber effect: A pioneering cyberpsychologist explains how human behavior changes online. Random House (2016).
34. Boyd, D.: It's complicated: The social lives of networked teens. Yale University Press (2014)
35. Wartella, E., Rideout, V., Lauricella, A.: Parenting in the digital age: A national survey. Media and Human Development Research Lab (2014)
36. Shin, W., Huh, J., Faber, R.J.: Tweens' online privacy risks and the role of parental mediation. J. Broadcast. Electron. Media **56**(4), 632–649 (2012)

Investigating Persuasive Software Features for Addiction Recovery

Hasan Selkan Taskan$^{(\boxtimes)}$ (iD) and Harri Oinas-Kukkonen$^{(\boxtimes)}$ (iD)

University of Oulu, 90570 Oulu, Finland
{hasan.taskan,harri.oinas-kukkonen}@oulu.fi

Abstract. This research investigates how and to what extent Persuasive Systems Design (PSD) in Behavior Change Support Systems (BCSS) influences recovery from digital and alcohol addiction. Although digital health interventions have shown promising results in behavioral change, there is still a gap in understanding how specific persuasive software features affect addiction treatment outcomes. Therefore, this research aims to expand our understanding of effective design elements and software features for addiction recovery. Interactions of persuasive software features with well-being, self-efficacy, addiction behavior change and user engagement outputs will be assessed in three stages. Stage 1 will lay the foundation of the application design, then in Stage 2 the application will be designed and developed, and a pilot study will be conducted. Following Stage 1 and Stage 2, two experimental research are planned to test the developed BCSS's effectiveness in Stage 3. The findings of the research will provide clear views on how a BCSS can be better designed and applied to real-world settings specifically for addictions.

Keywords: Persuasive Systems Design · Behavior Change Support Systems · Digital Addiction · Alcohol Addiction

1 Introduction

Addiction is one of the leading preventable diseases around the world [1]. It takes many forms such as alcohol, drugs, smoking, and more recently digital addictions. Drug-related disorders account for 1.5% of the total burden of disease worldwide, alcohol is a leading risk factor for death and disability among people aged 15–49, and smoking is a leading risk factor of death among men [2–4]. Also, digital addictions are increasing constantly around the world, which is particularly worsened by the COVID-19 pandemic. Studies estimate that its prevalence ranges from 6% to 27% within its subtypes such as game and smartphone addiction [5]. Thus, addiction, which comes in many forms, is devastating for societies in terms of its economic, psychological, and health consequences [1, 6, 7].

In recent years, the rapid advancement of digitalization has introduced new intervention strategies that address some of the challenges faced by traditional, in-person treatment approaches [8]. Studies indicate a growing body of evidence supporting the effectiveness of digital interventions for addiction, and their increasing adoption [9].

I. Wiafe et al. (Eds.): PERSUASIVE 2025, CCIS 2542, pp. 160–169, 2026.
https://doi.org/10.1007/978-3-031-97177-8_15

Multiple meta-analyses show that digital interventions are highly effective for different types of addictions [10–13]. Given the resource, accessibility, and scalability constraints of face-to-face addiction interventions, digital solutions emerge as viable alternatives offering new approaches to address these challenges [8]. However, in an area where even in-person treatments face challenges such as high relapse rates and low treatment adherence, a better understanding of information systems is needed in digital intervention approaches for addiction [14–17]. Therefore, the importance of information systems, particularly persuasive technologies in this case, comes into play when we are trying to build more effective digital solutions.

Persuasive technology allows us to shape the behavior, opinions, and habits of users through the medium they use. One of the foundational models of persuasive technologies is Persuasive Systems Design, which is a framework to guide the design and evaluation of information systems that aim to influence user attitudes and behavior without any coercion or deception [18]. Recent research shows that Persuasive Systems Design clearly helps maintain user interest and commitment to the intervention while increasing the likelihood of behavior change [10, 19, 20].

Since addiction is a biopsychosocial disease, it needs a multidisciplinary understanding which also makes it hard to develop effective interventions. One of the most widely used multidisciplinary treatment models for addiction recovery is the Minnesota Model [21]. It integrates different domains and professionals at the same time to reinforce behavioral management, social support, and structured recovery processes [22]. The emphasis on social support within the Minnesota Model is particularly important for this research, as the literature indicates that social support features are less implemented across different domains [20]. The understanding of addiction recovery makes the Minnesota Model a good fit to work together with Persuasive Systems Design and Behavior Change Support Systems. It addresses a critical gap by complementing both the implementation and exploration of social support features.

Therefore, this doctoral dissertation aims to investigate the software features that can be used in addiction treatment in depth by positioning itself in the intersection of information systems and psychology. To maintain a focused and rigorous research scope, the dissertation will focus on alcohol addiction and digital addictions. Alcohol addiction was selected because alcohol is still the most used substance around the world [23, 24]. In contrast, digital addictions will be investigated because it is an emerging topic and still there are a lot of gaps in the area [5, 25]. Having alcohol addiction and digital addictions also will let us to compare our findings in terms of substance-related and non-substance addictions, and their unique mechanisms.

2   Background

2.1   Persuasive Systems Design

Persuasive Systems Design (PSD) is a framework providing a structured approach for understanding when and how persuasion is effective while guiding persuasive strategies for behavior and attitude change. In terms of design principles, it has seven postulates explaining how designers see users, the persuasion strategies, and the actual system features. It also suggests three levels of persuasion context analysis: "the intent", "the event", and "the strategy". Postulates and persuasion context analysis together build up the design of system features. It outlines key principles as "primary task support", "dialogue support", "system credibility support", and "social support". Primary task support features make it easier for users to perform the target behavior effectively. Dialogue support features increase the interaction and keep users engaged with the system. System credibility support features ensure that users perceive the system as trustworthy as it increases the likeliness of engagement with the system. Lastly, social support features offer a social setting that motivates individuals through social interactions [18].

2.2 Behavior Change Support Systems

Behavior Change Support Systems (BCSS) is a socio-technical information system particularly designed to help individuals in making and maintaining positive behavioral changes. It foundationally uses behavior change theories to reach psychological and behavioral outcomes by forming, altering, and/or reinforcing attitudes, behaviors, or complying. It can be embedded into any digital medium such as web, mobile application, wearables, etc. Additionally, it must be non-coercive and non-deceptive and guide users through motivation, persuasion, and support mechanisms toward individuals' desired behavior change outcomes [26].

2.3 Minnesota Model

Minnesota Model is a widely used, established multidisciplinary approach to addiction. It has an established treatment setting mixing psychological, social, and medical knowledge. Unlike conventional treatment methods, which often focus on symptom management, the Minnesota Model explains addiction as a disease. Throughout the treatment, it emphasizes the "chronic disease" explanation and ensures that individuals do not see addiction as a personal weakness or moral failings. This approach builds up the need for ongoing management of disease just like in, for example, diabetes or heart disease. It also sees recovery as a learning process that transforms both the addicted individual and their "loved ones". Addiction affects the whole family and environment of the addicted person, so the recovery should happen together too. Therefore, peer support and family involvement are essential parts of the long-term treatment. It offers structured support systems for both individuals and their loved ones to help them heal and rebuild relationships. For these reasons, the emphasis on social support makes it an ideal choice for this dissertation [27].

3 Objectives of the Research

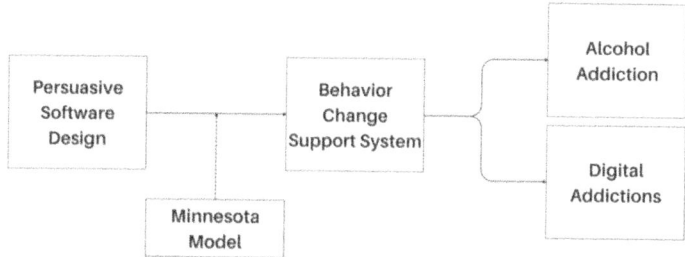

Fig. 1. Research Design Outlook

The fundamental premise of this research is to investigate how and to what extent persuasive software features can influence addiction recovery. By examining how the key principles of PSD affect individuals' well-being, self-efficacy, addiction behavior, and engagement, we aim to answer this main research question (Fig. 1):

"How and to what extent do PSD features impact engagement with BCSS, treatment adherence, and recovery outcomes for alcohol addiction and digital addictions?"

The hypotheses that are planned to be investigated in the research:
Primary hypothesis:

H1: Social support software features especially social learning, social facilitation, and cooperation will significantly improve recovery outcomes for individuals both with alcohol and digital addiction.
Secondary hypotheses:
H2: Primary task support software features specifically reduction, self-monitoring, simulation, and rehearsal will increase user engagement and awareness of their progress.
H3: Implementing the dialogue support strategy, especially praise, will positively affect adherence to the treatment program and well-being.
H4: System credibility support feature, trustworthiness, will enhance users' knowledge on addiction.
H5: Viewing peer progress and achievements will positively influence individuals' self-efficacy and well-being.

This dissertation will be structured around five publications and extend it to multiple studies. We divided the dissertation into three stages (see Fig. 3). The first stage is planned to include two studies: A scoping review and a second study that will explore the perception of persuasive software features and the secondary outcomes such as stress and strain based on the already existing data from Promo@Work project (funded by the Strategic Research Council, Academy of Finland) [28]. In stage two, we will conduct a pilot study that will describe the application, help us to fine-tune it. The third and the

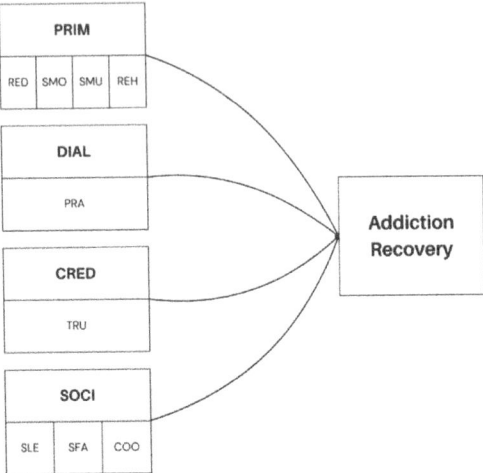

Note: PRIM: Primary Task Support; RED: Reduction; SMO: Self-monitoring; SMU: Simulation; REH: Rehearsal; DIAL: Dialogue Support; PRA: Praise; CRED: System Credibility Support; TRU: Trustworthiness; SOCI: Social Support; SLE: Social Learning; SFA: Social Facilitation; COO: Cooperation

Fig. 2. Persuasive Software Features Planned to Be Explored for Addiction Recovery

last stage will consist of two identical research with different target groups. One will investigate the effect of persuasive software features on alcohol addiction while the other one explores digital addictions.

4 Methodology

The primary objectives of the research are to investigate the effectiveness of PSD features in BCSS for alcohol addiction and digital addictions and to assess the impact of its principles on individuals' well-being, self-efficacy, addiction behavior change, and user engagement.

A software application will be developed to reach the objectives of this study. On a practical level, there will be two pathways within the application: one for alcohol addiction and one for digital addictions. The content of the two pathways will be tailored accordingly. Also, a persuasive software design analysis has been conducted to decide which features will be included in the application (see Fig. 2). The findings were carefully reviewed by both the supervisor and the researcher to make sure they aligned with the research goals. However, the selection process is kept flexible since the findings from Stage 1 and Stage 2 can shape the initial selections. The research methodology will rely on information system research methods, particularly design science and quantitative research. The mobile application will be the central artifact developed and tested, and numerical data will be collected to analyze usage patterns.

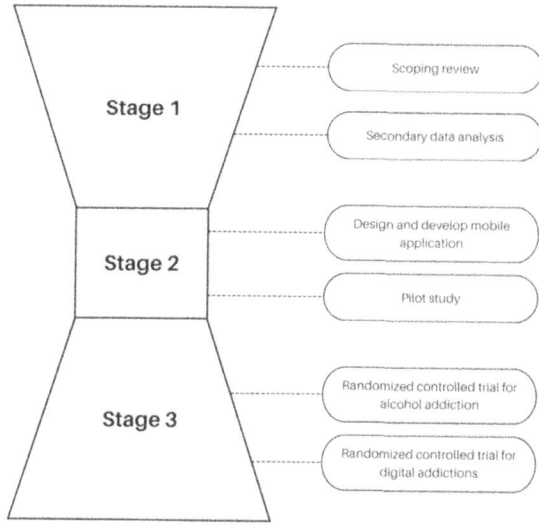

Fig. 3. Planned Stages of the Doctoral Dissertation

Stage 1: In the first stage, it is planned to conduct two different studies that do not require experimentation. They will lay a foundation for Stage 2 and Stage 3. In the first study, a scoping review assessing the levels of evidence associated with persuasive software features for alcohol addiction using the evidence-based medicine method is planned. In the second study, secondary data from Promo@Work project is planned to be used to analyze participants' perception of persuasive software features. It will provide empirical data on how users respond to persuasive elements in real-world settings, which will be a solid foundation for the pilot study.

Stage 2: In the second stage, it is aimed to design and develop a mobile application featuring persuasive elements such as reduction, praise, trustworthiness, and social learning. A pilot study with the developed application/platform will be conducted. This will be carried out with university students as they tend to be open to participating in scientific studies and are a good target group for digital addictions [29]. The intervention is planned to last for a fixed period with pre- and post-surveys. It aims to assess the perceived persuasiveness and usability of the system rather than its clinical effectiveness. This stage will serve as a critical step in refining the application for larger-scale studies in Stage 3.

Stage 3: In the third stage, two randomized controlled trials with different target groups (alcohol addiction and digital addictions) will be conducted. The sample size will be determined using power analysis based on the effect size of previous studies. Participants will be adults aged 18–65 with alcohol addiction or digital addictions. Participants will be randomly assigned to two groups:

1. Control Group: Group that will take BCSS with primary task support, dialogue support, system credibility support but not social support.

2. Intervention Group: Social support elements will be added back into the BCSS besides primary task support, dialogue support, and system credibility support.

Participants will use their assigned BCSS for a fixed period. Throughout the intervention period, they will provide survey and log data related to their well-being, sense of perceived self-efficacy, addiction behavior changes, and engagement with the intervention (engagement metrics such as time on task, error rate, task success rate and user experience). The Warwick-Edinburgh Mental Wellbeing Scale will be used to measure the well-being changes of participants since it covers both emotional and psychological well-being comprehensively. On the other hand, the General Self-Efficacy Scale will be used for the sense of perceived self-efficacy because it measures different domains of life. Moreover, the Alcohol Dependence Scale for alcohol and the Internet Addiction Test for digital addictions will be used for recovery outcomes and severity, since they are already standard tools to assess the severity of addiction. All the scales planned to be used in the research are widely used and well-validated scientific tools.

The study will ensure the participants' privacy, and voluntary participation. All the collected data will be anonymized or pseudonymized to protect participants' identities following the guidelines of the General Data Protection Regulation. We will also follow the ethical principles of the Declaration of Helsinki and obtain ethical approval from the institutional review board. Informed consent that is clearly informing the participants about the digital interventions and what the intended goals are will be obtained before their participation in the study. Also, even if the intervention is designed to promote recovery, we acknowledge the potential psychological risks such as emotional distress, anxiety, etc. To mitigate these risks, regular check-ins will be performed to monitor participants' well-being and address any concerns that may arise. Lastly, the study will be conducted in full compliance with national and international laws and regulations.

5 Preliminary Results / Future Work

In Stage 1, a scoping review exploring evidence levels of persuasive software features for alcohol addiction recovery has already been completed. The full manuscript will be submitted to a reputable information systems journal. The scoping review is particularly directed at alcohol addiction rather than digital addiction. The reason for this was the abundance of existing research on alcohol addiction that allows a comprehensive analysis of persuasive software features. Initial findings from the research indicate a strong need for research on social support features. This is also aligned well with the dissertation objectives and the design of Stage 3. Additionally, the distribution of persuasive features across different levels of evidence supports the feature selection for this study. As a result of the first research of Stage, the initial planning of the software features has been updated based on the findings, and the latest version is introduced in this manuscript. Also, the second deliverable of Stage 1, secondary data analysis using Promo@Work data, has been completed using structural equation modeling. The initial model derived from the analysis explores the relationship between persuasive software features and the perceived persuasiveness of micro-entrepreneurs. The manuscript for this study is currently in progress. In addition to these two studies planned for Stage 1, an additional manuscript exploring counseling strategies and their mappings to persuasive software features has been accepted for the 20th International Conference on Persuasive Technology 2025 (PERSUASIVE 2025). This study aligns with the objectives of Stage 1, which is laying a foundation for the latter stages of the doctoral dissertation. It explores five psychological approaches' counseling strategies (including the Minnesota Model) and their corresponding persuasive features.

Currently, the doctoral dissertation is in the early stages of Stage 2. The application design and development for the pilot study are in progress. The pilot study is planned to take place in Q2 2025, following the completion of the application design. Also, the experimental design of the pilot study is being planned. Following the pilot study, another manuscript is expected to be completed. The final adjustments and fine-tuning of the application according to the results of the pilot study are planned for Q3-Q4 2025. After that, the data collection for Stage 3 will begin in early 2026 and continue throughout the year. Additionally, two new manuscripts are planned for 2026, one is in early Q2, and another one by the end of the year. Lastly, the final phase of the dissertation is reserved for data analysis, dissertation writing, and dissemination of research findings.

The success of the project fundamentally depends on the successful collection, analysis, and evaluation of data. The potential risks in the research primarily revolve around data quality, analysis challenges, and most critically successful collaboration with partners in data collection. In the Stage 3 studies, we will rely on external partners for reaching the sample group. The data that will be collected may vary in quality and completeness, which could affect the reliability of the findings. To address the challenges, a data validation procedure and periodic quality checks will be applied in data anonymization to protect privacy and regular follow-up to prevent data loss. For the data collection, a clear communication protocol and regular meetings with partners will be established. Additionally, we will include at least an additional 10% reserve to the minimum required sample size for covering possible dropouts and problems arising from collaborations.

6 Conclusion

In conclusion, the research is expected to make a contribution to understanding the interplay between information systems and human behavior, particularly by explaining how and to what extent health behavior change support systems may help alcohol and digital addiction recovery and how to develop such systems. With the emphasis on the social support features, this study will also address a critical gap in existing digital health interventions. Understanding the evidence levels and user perceptions of persuasive features will provide practical and theoretical implications across multiple disciplines. It will guide stakeholders from various domains such as researchers, developers, and psychologists in designing more effective BCSS. Beyond academia, this research has the potential to influence real-world digital health applications for addiction. It will provide a foundation for designing effective applications by integrating persuasive technology with established psychological approaches, specifically the Minnesota Model.

References

1. World Health Organization: Global status report on alcohol and health and treatment of substance use disorders. Geneva: World Health Organization. License: CC BY-NC-SA 3.0 IGO (2024)
2. GBD 2016 Alcohol Collaborators: Alcohol use and burden for 195 countries and territories, 1990–2016: a systematic analysis for the global burden of disease study 2016. Lancet **392**(10152), 1015–1035 (2018). https://doi.org/10.1016/S0140-6736(18)31310-2
3. Reitsma, M.B., Marissa, B., Donald, S., John, T., Alex, P.: Spatial, temporal, and demographic patterns in prevalence of smoking tobacco use and attributable disease burden in 204 countries and territories, 1990–2019: a systematic analysis from the Global Burden of Disease Study 2019. Lancet **397**(10292), 2337–2360 (2021). https://doi.org/10.1016/S0140-6736(21)011 69-7
4. Connery, H.S., McHugh, R.K., Reilly, M., Shin, S., Greenfield, S.F.: Substance use disorders in global mental health delivery: epidemiology, treatment gap, and implementation of evidence-based treatments. Harvard Rev. Psychiatry **28**(5), 316–327 (2020). https://doi.org/10.1097/HRP.0000000000000271
5. Meng, S.Q., et al.: Global prevalence of digital addiction in general population: A systematic review and meta-analysis. Clin. Psychol. Rev. **92**, 102128 (2022). https://doi.org/10.1016/j.cpr.2022.102128
6. American Psychiatric Association: Diagnostic and Statistical Manual of Mental Disorders, 5th edn. (2022). https://doi.org/10.1176/appi.books.9780890425787
7. World Health Organization: International Classification of Diseases, Eleventh Revision (ICD-11) (2019/2021). https://icd.who.int/browse11
8. Marsch, L.A.: Digital health and addiction. Curr. Opin. Syst. Biol. **20**, 1–7 (2021). https://doi.org/10.1016/j.coisb.2020.07.004
9. Johansson, M., Romero, D., Jakobson, M., Heinemans, N., Lindner, P.: Digital interventions targeting excessive substance use and substance use disorders: a comprehensive and systematic scoping review and bibliometric analysis. Front. Psychiatry **15**, 1233888 (2024). https://doi.org/10.3389/fpsyt.2024.1233888
10. Theopilus, Y., Al Mahmud, A., Davis, H., Octavia, J.R.: Persuasive strategies in digital interventions to combat internet addiction: a systematic review. Int. J. Med. Inf. **195**, 105725 (2024). https://doi.org/10.1016/j.ijmedinf.2024.105725
11. Agulleiro, M.L., et al.: A systematic review of digital interventions for smoking cessation in patients with serious mental illness. Psychol. Med. **53**(11), 4856–4868 (2023). https://doi.org/10.1017/S003329172300123X
12. Bonfiglio, N.S., Mascia, M.L., Cataudella, S., Penna, M.P.: Digital help for substance users (SU): a systematic review. Int. J. Environ. Res. Public Health **19**(18), 11309 (2022). https://doi.org/10.3390/ijerph191811309
13. Boumparis, N., Schulte, M.H.J., Riper, H.: Digital mental health for alcohol and substance use disorders. Curr. Treat. Opt. Psychiatry **6**(4), 352–366 (2019). https://doi.org/10.1007/s40 501-019-00190-y
14. Daigre, C., et al.: Treatment retention and abstinence of patients with substance use disorders according to addiction severity and psychiatry comorbidity: a six-month follow-up study in an outpatient unit. Addict. Behav. **117**, 106832 (2021). https://doi.org/10.1016/j.addbeh.2021.106832
15. Kabisa, E., Biracyaza, E., Habagusenga, J.D.: Determinants and prevalence of relapse among patients with substance use disorders: case of Icyizere Psychotherapeutic Centre. Subst. Abuse Treat. Prev. Policy **16**, 13 (2021). https://doi.org/10.1186/s13011-021-00347-0

16. Kadam, M., Sinha, A., Nimkar, S., Matcheswalla, Y., De Sousa, A.: A comparative study of factors associated with relapse in alcohol dependence and opioid dependence. Indian J. Psychol. Med. **39**(5), 627–633 (2017). https://doi.org/10.4103/IJPSYM.IJPSYM_356_17

17. Brorson, H.H., Ajo Arnevik, E., Rand-Hendriksen, K., Duckert, F.: Drop-out from addiction treatment: a systematic review of risk factors. Clin. Psychol. Rev. **33**(8), 1010–1024 (2013). https://doi.org/10.1016/j.cpr.2013.07.007

18. Oinas-Kukkonen, H., Harjumaa, M.: Persuasive systems design: key issues, process model, and system features. Commun. Assoc. Inf. Syst. **24**, 28 (2009). https://doi.org/10.17705/1CAIS.02428

19. Lehto, T., Oinas-Kukkonen, H.: Persuasive features in web-based alcohol and smoking interventions: a systematic review of the literature. J. Med. Internet Res. **13**(3), e46 (2011). https://doi.org/10.2196/jmir.1559

20. Kelders, S.M., Kok, R.N., Ossebaard, H.C., Van Gemert-Pijnen, J.E.: Persuasive system design does matter: a systematic review of adherence to web-based interventions. J. Med. Internet Res. **14**(6), e152 (2012). https://doi.org/10.2196/jmir.2104

21. Gallagher, C., Radmall, Z., O'Gara, C., Burke, T.: Effectiveness of a national 'Minnesota model' based residential treatment programme for alcohol dependence in Ireland: outcomes and predictors of outcome. Irish J. Psychol. Med. **35**(1), 1–9 (2017). https://doi.org/10.1017/ipm.2017.26

22. Anderson, D.J., McGovern, J.P., Dupont, R.L.: The origins of the Minnesota model of addiction treatment–a first person account. J. Addict. Dis. **18**(1), 107–114 (1999). https://doi.org/10.1300/J069v18n01_10

23. Peacock, A., et al.: Global statistics on alcohol, tobacco and illicit drug use: 2017 status report. Addiction **113**(10), 1905–1926 (2018). https://doi.org/10.1111/add.14234

24. World Health Organization: Global status report on alcohol and health and treatment of substance use disorders. World Health Organization, Geneva, Switzerland (2024)

25. Karakose, T., Yıldırım, B., Tülübaş, T., Kardas, A.: A comprehensive review on emerging trends in the dynamic evolution of digital addiction and depression. Front. Psychol. **14**, 1126815 (2023). https://doi.org/10.3389/fpsyg.2023.1126815

26. Oinas-Kukkonen, H.: A foundation for the study of behavior change support systems. Pers. Ubiquit. Comput. **17**, 1223–1235 (2013). https://doi.org/10.1007/s00779-012-0591-5

27. Oinas-Kukkonen, H.: *Alkoholistin ja hänen läheisensä samanaikainen toipuminen vapauttavana oppimisprosessina Minnesota-hoidossa,* Doctoral dissertation, University of Oulu. Acta Universitatis Ouluensis. (2013). https://urn.fi/URN:ISBN:978-952-62-0296-9

28. Laitinen, J., Korkiakangas, E., Mäkiniemi, J.P., et al.: The effects of counseling via a smartphone application on microentrepreneurs' work ability and work recovery: a study protocol. BMC Public Health **20**, 438 (2020). https://doi.org/10.1186/s12889-020-8449-7

29. Han, S.J., Nagduar, S., Yu, H.J.: Digital addiction and related factors among college students. Healthc. Basel Switz. **11**(22), 2943 (2023). https://doi.org/10.3390/healthcare11222943

Author Index

I. Wiafe et al. (Eds.): PERSUASIVE 2025, CCIS 2542, p. 171, 2026.
https://doi.org/10.1007/978-3-031-97177-8

The manufacturer's authorised representative in the EU is Springer
Nature Customer Service Centre GmbH, Europaplatz 3, 69115 Heidelberg,
Germany. If you have any concerns regarding our products, please
contact ProductSafety@springernature.com

Printed and bound by CPI Group (UK) Ltd, Croydon, CR0 4YY
29/04/2026
02099768-0001